The Memory of Thought

The Memory of Thought

An Essay on Heidegger and Adorno

ALEXANDER GARCÍA DÜTTMANN

Translated by NICHOLAS WALKER

continuum
LONDON · NEW YORK

Continuum

The Tower Building, 11 York Road, London SE1 7NX
370 Lexington Avenue, New York, NY 10017-6503
www.continuumbooks.com

This English translation first published in 2002
English Translation © Continuum 2002

First published in German as
Das Gedächtnis des Denkens: Versuch über Heidegger und Adorno
© Suhrkamp Verlag 1991

Alexander García Düttmann has asserted his right under the Copyright,
Designs and Patents Act, 1988, to be identified as the author of this work

Die Herausgabe dieses Werkes wurde aus Mitteln von INTER NATIONES,
Bonn gefördert

British Library Cataloguing in Publication Data
A catalogue record for this book is available from the British Library

ISBN 0-8264-5900-5 HB
0-8264-5901-3 PB

Library of Congress Cataloging-in-Publication Data
García Düttmann, Alexander.
  [Gedachtnis des Denkens. English]
  The memory of thought : an essay on Heidegger and Adorno / Alexander
García Düttmann ; translated by Nicholas Walker.
     p. cm.
Includes bibliographical references and index.
  ISBN 0-8264-5900-5 - - ISBN 0-8264-5901-3 (pbk.)
  1. Heidegger, Martin, 1889–1976. 2. Adorno, Theodor W., 1903–1969.
  3. Holocaust, Jewish (1939–1945) 4. Philosophy, German- -20th century.
  I. Title.
    B3279.H49 G28513 2002
    193- -dc21   2001058296

Typeset by Acorn Bookwork, Salisbury, Wiltshire
Printed and bound in Great Britain by
MPG Books Ltd, Bodmin, Cornwall

For Silvia Bovenschen
and Philippe Lacoue-Labarthe

Contents

Contents

A proper name is without meaning. But there are many different ways of being without meaning.

Jacques Derrida

Abbreviations

The following abbreviations are employed in the text and the notes for frequently cited works:

GA : Martin Heidegger, *Gesamtausgabe*
GS : Theodor W. Adorno, *Gesammelte Schriften*

AT : Theodor W. Adorno, *Asthetische Theorie* (GS 7)
DdA : Theodor W. Adorno and Max Horkheimer, *Dialektik der Aufklärung* (GS 3)
GRh : Martin Heidegger, *Hölderlins Hymnen 'Germanien' und 'Der Rhein'* (GA 39)
MM : Theodor W. Adorno, *Minima Moralia* (GS 4)
ND : Theodor W. Adorno, *Negative Dialektik* (GS 6)

Translator's note

Whenever possible references have been supplied to English translations of cited texts (ET), although quotations in the text have generally been translated or adapted in the intetrest of terminological consistency throughout. Full details of existing translations of works cited are included in the bibliography

Introduction:
Of (From) Germania – after (to) Auschwitz

The *question* that motivates this essay on Heidegger and Adorno is the following: what happens when, as a consequence of the experience of a particular event, the name given to what has been experienced is referred to the totality of history itself, thus inaugurating and establishing this very totality – this historical unity, this unified history?

The *thought* that guides this essay can be formulated in this way: every name, insofar as it is the name of an event and is itself an event, tends to produce a totalising effect, even if the name – and even if the event – are not exhausted in that effect.

The *hypothesis* that this essay endeavours to substantiate – albeit without appealing to any methodological canons of verification – assumes the following form: in this century Heidegger and Adorno have experienced the force and power of the event in question, and consequently that of the name in question, as few other thinkers have done. And this most tellingly where the opposition between them seems to leap out at us most obviously: there where Heidegger – with explicit reference to Hölderlin – speaks of Germania and Adorno speaks after Auschwitz. In their own way and in their own language both thinkers have acknowledged the power of the name, and have inevitably fallen victim to that power themselves. Their thought can therefore teach us the impossibility of escaping the power of the name. And likewise the necessity of calling the event by its name, of perceiving the name as more than simply a conventional sign – more than an external linguistic mark of an event – and of recognising our subjection to the ineliminable blindness and opacity of the name.

The *approach* adopted in this essay is not that of a systematic investigation of the concept of the name, which degrades Adorno and Heidegger to the status of 'examples' of a philosophical position. Nor is it a comparative examination of the history of philosophy, one which would content itself with revealing the possible influence each thinker had upon the other, or perhaps with demonstrating an unbridgeable gulf between them. The approach taken here reflects a mode of argumentation at once static and dynamic, namely that of 'principled over-interpretation' which Adorno identified as characteristic of the essay: 'In comparison with other forms, in which a given content is indifferently communicated, the essay appears by virtue of the tension between presentation and presented subject-matter as more dynamic than traditional forms of thinking, but at the same time, by virtue of its constructed juxtaposition, it also appears as more static.'[1]

If this kind of 'principled over-interpretation', conditioning as it does a peculiar equalisation of static moments with dynamic moments, is to represent anything more than an arbitrary exercise, then it is solely because the essay as form 'responds to the blind spots in its objects', to that which strikes the concept itself with blindness. This blind spot, which stands in a relation of tension to the concept, and which can never be entirely dominated by the latter or brought into a symmetrical state of domesticated equilibrium with it – for it appears to conceptual knowledge as a case of blindness – is and has always been, if one follows the argument of *Negative Dialectics*, precisely the name. It is only of the name, and after a naming has occurred, that such over-interpretations are possible. And it is only over-interpretations that can do justice to the name in principle. The name itself dictates the form of the following essay precisely insofar as the name can never be entirely conceptually resolved or dissolved, although thought continually finds itself referred back to it – to the (be)-naming of the event and the event of (be)-naming. *Auschwitz* and *Germanien* are names of an event and mark a separation, a distance which cannot simply be reduced to a question of chronology (Heidegger continued to maintain the pre-eminence of the German language throughout his life, and Adorno did not explicitly develop a philosophy before Auschwitz – which naturally does not mean that he wrote no philosophical works before the 1940s[2]). They are names that represent, for all the essential differences involved here, for all the differences of perceptiveness and perspicacity, the blind spot in the thought of Heidegger and in the thought of Adorno. The following essay deciphers the instant of affirmation, of 'yea-saying', which Adorno like Nietzsche identified as the true measure of the essay, as the instant in which the name and the event are affirmed, as the instant that precedes all thought and without which there would be no thought, were the event the most terrible event and the name the most terrifying name.[3]

The dynamics involved here will reveal themselves all the more intensively, the more the statics of apparently unmediated and juxtaposed elements is emphasised. That is the *purpose* of the present essay on Adorno and Heidegger. The argument is not itself conducted from the perspective of one or other of these thinkers. The irreconcilable character of the names will not be softened, and their doubling – two names of a single event – will not be transformed or unified into a whole. Adorno's critique of the ontological need, of being and existence, of 'the jargon of authenticity' will remain largely undiscussed – though certainly not unread – since the task here is not to examine the justification or plausibility of this critique. It is, however, assumed that such an examination, whatever the eventual result, would make no essential or decisive difference to the hypothesis explored here. On the contrary, it is even possible that the hypothesis will, for the first time, shed light upon the critique in question.[4] The name marks the limit of 'negative dialectics' and of the 'destruction' or 'overcoming' of metaphysics, even if these approaches themselves first serve to reveal the limiting and limited character of the name. That is precisely what this essay – this over-interpretation – is intended to show.

Hermann Mörchen has described the relationship between Adorno and Heidegger as a 'refusal of philosophical communication'. The substantial volume which he dedicated to this 'refusal' – consisting of a 'prelude' and a 'more comprehensive treatment' – is consistently oriented towards 'the possibility of a *convergent* philosophising'.[5] If philosophy is intrinsically oriented towards communication and such communication is *refused* –

the choice of the word already reveals the priority accorded to discussion and communication – then the task must be precisely to seek out and to expose such convergence. The section of the book that is entitled 'Philosophy after Auschwitz' begins with a sentence that clearly reveals the difficulties which beset Mörchen's entire enterprise: 'It is more than superficially obvious that the *manner* in which the experience of the Third Reich entered into the motivation of Heidegger's thinking is utterly *different* from the way in which that experience also proved decisive for Adorno.'[6] Mörchen does not wish to reduce the character of this difference simply to a 'refusal of communication'. It is questionable whether one will be able to identify convergence if one can no longer appeal to 'the delusions of absolutised positions' and if one must consequently distance oneself from the danger of producing 'an all too levelling perspective': if there is thus no longer any first or immediate view of the matter which would fail to see through the 'absolutised positions'. Is not the idea of an 'all too levelling perspective', which quantitatively posits purely gradual distinctions, 'all too levelling'? It is precisely at this point – precisely 'here' as Mörchen himself emphasises – that the question concerning the possibility of 'philosophical communication' and 'convergent philosophising' reveals its full relevance. For if the distorted interpretations and absolutised perspectives are nothing but a symptom of a subjective refusal, of a certain incapacity on the part of the thinking subject, this certainly raises the problem of communication, but one that is basically without any specific philosophical relevance. If we are to speak meaningfully of a 'philosophical refusal of communication', then the reasons for the latter cannot be merely contingent empirical ones, or even reasons grounded in the conditions of intellectual or cultural history. It must be the object of thinking itself which 'motivates' the refusal in question. Mörchen's investigation in the section on 'Philosophy after Auschwitz' is more a collection of quotations than an example of rigorous argument. He calls 'Auschwitz' a 'defining code-word for everything that most inwardly motivates [Adorno's] intellectual labours,'[7] and refers to a passage from the *Notes to Literature* in which Adorno – allegedly – identifies this code-word as the name of a 'limit situation'. We are supposed to recognise Adorno's thinking as a thinking of extremity precisely in and through the word 'Auschwitz'. (Mörchen certainly mentions other possible interpretations, but he appears to appropriate this interpretation of the name as a 'defining code-word' for himself.) In fact, Adorno claims just the opposite, since the term 'limit situation' is itself an expression of the jargon of authenticity: 'Today everything is indeed objectively prescribed that would bestow meaningful sense upon existence, and even the denial of such sense, as with official nihilism, degenerated into a case of positivist assertion, an instance of delusion, that would if it could justify the despair of the world as its own essential content, in speaking of Auschwitz as a "limit situation".'[8] Auschwitz cannot be the defining code-word of Adorno's thought because the act which subsumes this name under the concept of a 'limit situation' is tantamount to a justification of what is being named. It is all the more astonishing that Mörchen overlooks this here since Adorno expressly introduces the text in question − 'On the Final Scene of Goethe's *Faust*' − by demanding an 'interpretative submersion into the texts which have been handed down to us': 'Shame resists the immediate expression of metaphysical intentions.' The misreading which violates this shame − this name − is a far from trivial one: it actually prevents Mörchen from relating the problem of the name which is meant to be a 'defining code-word' (does not a 'defining code-word' also and invariably function as a name?) to the problem of meaning itself, and therefore to that of a possible communication. It prevents him from creating a connection in which nothing would seem to be more difficult or more pressing than the prospect of 'convergent philosophising'. In his early 'Remarks on Karl Jaspers' "Psychology of World-Views"' (1919−21) Heidegger had already objected to the concept of the 'limit situation' which was itself coined by Jaspers. Heidegger argued that the 'antinomies' which are experienced in or as these situations at the limit (antinomies which destroy any unified totality insofar as they are oppositions conceived 'from the perspective of the absolute, from the perspective of value') cannot simply be 'rationally defined' or grasped as 'contradictions'. Any such 'distorting theoretical approach', designed as it is to grasp 'concrete cases as a series of consecutive contradictions', would already fail to identify the 'authentic significance' of the limit situation.[9] (One should not forget that, two years after the expression of this critique, Heidegger was attempting to form a philosophical 'common front' with Jaspers.[10]) Does 'convergent philosophising' (only) occur in limit situations?

While on the one hand Mörchen ascribes to the 'defining code-word' – the name 'Auschwitz' – a meaning that, according to Adorno, it cannot possess, on the other hand he reproaches Adorno for indulging in a certain excess of signification, for a certain shameless ostentation. Can anyone continue to live after Auschwitz? This question of Adorno's prompts Mörchen to the following reflection: 'Sympathy with the suffering and the oppressed is, very differently than with Heidegger, so *ostentatiously* presented as the motivating ground of Adorno's thought that certain doubts might arise as a result. This is not to deny the sincerity with which Adorno himself pondered upon such sympathy.'[11] What, then, are the doubts which might arise from the ostentation of the philosopher? It is precisely because he did not make 'sympathy with the suffering and the oppressed' into the 'motivating ground' of his thought, precisely because he did not subject his thought to the name 'Auschwitz', precisely because he refused ostentatiously to pursue the path from Germania to Auschwitz, to pursue the question of Germania after Auschwitz, that Heidegger's thought appears so 'crassly' different from that of Adorno. Mörchen thereby seems to be suggesting the following dilemma: the more one emphasises the fact that Heidegger – in contrast to Adorno – remained silent about 'Auschwitz' and cited the concentration camps merely as an example of the question concerning technology, the more succour one provides for those who regard this fact precisely as evidence of the truth of his thought; as evidence that 'sympathy with the suffering and the oppressed' is in truth a far more profound 'motivating ground' of Heidegger's thought than all ostentatious attention to the former would initially suggest. This dilemma, which could also be reversed (Heidegger remains ostentatiously silent and calls nothing by its real name, while Adorno utters the name itself), has its origin in the immeasurable and excessive character of the name. The name as name of an event and as event of language (the name of an event must be an event of language) cannot be exhausted by conceptual thought (otherwise the eventful character itself would be subsumable under the concept, would be nothing but a given fact). The name is therefore characterised both by an excess and a deficiency of meaning.[12] In other words: the name, in whose name one is arguing, always also escapes the domain of meaningful conceptual argumentation. Hence one constantly ascribes to the name a meaning which it cannot possess (one already does so by inserting it within a semantic context for whose necessity the name itself provides the ground: ... *to* Auschwitz ..., ... *after* Auschwitz ...). Neither the uttering of the name nor the refusal to utter it can function as an appropriate measure here: silent refusal and explicit utterance alike expose themselves to the suspicion of ostentation, and thus in the last analysis to the suspicion of avoidance. Yet these alternatives remain irreconcilable and present a challenge which itself cannot be evaded. Their incommensurability in the case of Heidegger and Adorno is all the greater because Heidegger did in fact once break his silence. That he seemed to content himself with mentioning the camps as an example of the question concerning technology, that he allowed himself to mention them simply as one example amongst a number of others, has struck Philippe Lacoue-Labarthe as 'scandalously inadequate'.[13] And the fact that Adorno also recognised the aporias of speaking out and remaining silent about the subject serves only to increase the incommensurability of the engagement with Heidegger. If 'all culture after Auschwitz, including its urgent critique, is garbage' (ND:359; ET:367),[14] then philosophy itself, which is necessary precisely because 'silence only promotes barbarism', also ineluctably falls victim to ostentation; through its mere existence, its own right to be, philosophy already pleads 'for the continued survival of a radically guilty and shabby culture'. Conversely, it is because of its essential – 'objective' – inappropriateness, that silence must be regarded as a 'subjective incapacity' that is just as ostentatious in its effects: 'Not even silence can escape the circle; it merely rationalises one's own subjective incapacity with the status of objective truth, and thus once again devalues the latter into a lie' (ND:360; ET:367). One will have to utter the name 'Auschwitz' and attempt to elucidate the event in conceptual terms without the prospect of protecting oneself from the force and blindness of the name. From this perspec-

tive, it is surely significant that Mörchen abandons all conceptual criteria with regard to the 'one-sidedness' of this name (and
thus once again with regard to the issue of ostentation or what
might prevent it):

> The usual criticism directed against Adorno's 'model of
> Auschwitz', and that of a 'negative' dialectics in general,
> complains not merely about its one-sidedness, but above all
> about its failure to draw positive consequences. Let us not
> endorse such (superficially valid) objections for our own part!
> They merely blunt the force of Adorno's urgent appeal and,
> insofar as they escape obscurity by recourse to a supposedly
> secure ethical and political doctrine behind them, actually
> reveal no solidarity with his own passionate errors. Adorno's
> truth is no more to be had without the latter than is Heideg-
> ger's; one must struggle through it with him.[15]

These remarks – they occur at the end of the section on 'Philosophy after Auschwitz' – may well be evaluated in opposing ways,
but they remain quite unintelligible unless they are brought into
relation to the immeasurable and excessive character of the name.
For what distinguishes this injunction 'one must struggle through
it with him' (an appeal which is supposed to apply to Adorno
and to Heidegger: to Germania and to Auschwitz) from a case of
simple exhortation? Mörchen does not grasp the possibility of
'convergent philosophising' radically enough. Which is to say
that he ignores the constraints of the name.

   The use of the name implies – if we wish to use the language
of Karl-Otto Apel in this connection – a 'performative self-
contradiction' in which thought (the thought of the name and
of the event) necessarily becomes entangled. But such a contradiction is not actually a 'performative self-contradiction' since
this term already asserts and establishes the essential primacy of
philosophical discourse. Apel leaves us in no doubt that it is a
reflexive criterion which is at issue here, a criterion which
governs argumentational reasoning and conceptual thought, the
discursive rationality which is supposed to ground all theory:

> The proscription concerning the performative self-contradic-
> tion is not introduced here like that concerning the proposi-

tional contradiction 'a and non-a' which functions as an axiom of logical theory. It results rather from an act of reflective insight: from the insight that the introduction of any conceivable theory, or of any conceivable axioms, already presupposes the performative self-consistency of discourse. The demand for self-consistency thus does not rest upon a particular assertion or decision, but constitutes rather the condition of the possibility of any potentially intelligible assertion or decision; as such it represents something that is irreducibly ultimate as far as thought or argumentation are concerned.[16]

The moment that the event is named in philosophical discourse one has already assumed reflexive or conceptual criteria of argumentative communication which are suspended by the uttering of the name. The name compels us to transcend the philosophical discourse that measures itself by such criteria, and in accordance with its own claims must so measure itself. That is why *inauguration* and *guilt* are inextricably entwined with one another in the essence of the name. The possibility of 'convergent philosophising', the anticipation of the ideal conditions of discourse which this involves, find themselves thwarted by the name. Does not the name then simply transform itself into an arbitrary name? Does not such discourse which transpires in the name of – another – name then resist all rational verification in principle? Is it not then impossible to justify why it is necessary to comprehend thinking precisely as thinking after Auschwitz?[17] One could answer these questions in accordance with Adorno by stating that the name demands the labour of the concept precisely because it transcends the concept and invites such transcendence. It is the irreducible indecidability itself which provokes a decision; the price which must be paid for the conceptually grounded decision (from/of Germania – to/after Auschwitz) is the undecidability conditioned by the name, by the blindness peculiar to it. Insofar as it thwarts the possibility of 'convergent philosophising', the name also enables intellectual engagement in the first place. Adorno does not isolate the name, but considers it rather in terms of its own profoundly tense relation to the concept. The name is therefore not to be regarded as some indivisible unity located in a site beyond the concept. And is not Heidegger too caught in an arbitrary attempt to prevent the coming of the name which is inscribed within originary and inaugural naming as the repetition of origination and inauguration? As a thinking after Auschwitz Adorno's philosophy is the thinking of *guilty debt*; but at the same time the name *inaugurates* thought. As a thinking of Germania Heidegger's philosophy is a thinking of *inauguration*; but at the same time the name which is to be repeated only increases the *guilty debt*. Where guilty debt and inauguration are intertwined in thought in such a way as this, thought must also be memory.

PART I
Guilts and Debts

One would gladly struggle free of the past: and rightly
so, because it is indeed impossible to live beneath its
shadow, because there can never be an end to terror if
guilt and violence must continue to be paid with
further guilt and violence; but wrongly so, because the
past from which one would escape very much lives on.

Theodor W. Adorno

1

Fate and Sacrifice

The average outlook tends initially to take the thought
of being 'guilty' in the sense of being 'indebted'.

Martin Heidegger

Adorno's comparison

How can thinking be indebted to something? What are the
consequences of thought remaining indebted and owing something? What does the debt of thought consist in? These are
questions one cannot help asking if one considers the following
passage from *Negative Dialectics* in which Adorno compares
Heidegger's philosophy to a 'highly developed system of
credit': 'According to a well-worn witticism it is the debtor
who has the advantage over the creditor since the latter after all
depends on whether the former ever pays up – it is much the
same with Heidegger who profits from all his unpaid debts . . .
Whatever critique identifies as its target, it can always be
disqualified as a misunderstanding' (ND:84; ET:76). If we
ignore the fact that misunderstandings perhaps arise only
through a critique which, in accordance with its own self-
understanding, attempts above all to identify and fix its object,
we could well ask whether Adorno's comparison does not
touch upon a problem at the very centre of his own thinking,
of the thought of the non-identical. 'Being' is neither a concept
nor a fact and, according to Adorno, is therefore 'exempt from
criticism' (a claim that surely unsettles this concept of critique
rather than it does the question concerning the meaning of
being); but so too the non-identical is neither a simple fact of
the matter nor something purely conceptual, and nor is it something else again that might in turn be identified in its own right.
Adorno's comparison remains ambivalent. For in the light of

the reflections of Adorno and Horkheimer in *Dialectic of Enlightenment* it is precisely the debt of thought, the fact that thought itself can remain indebted to something, which constitutes its guilt. That Heidegger always owes something, that his thought ultimately reveals itself as useless, precisely because one can never identifiably rely on it, is, from this perspective, a sign that it is not entirely dominated by a quantifiable debt, by the principle of equivalence, by the like-for-like of 'mythic ineluctability'. Could one not even claim that the ambivalence that attends any and every comparison is grounded in the fact that the latter always rests upon a process of bringing different meanings into line, upon a levelling down of meaning which represses or excludes other meanings, and thus perpetually exposes itself to their uncanny and unexpected return? Because of its indebtedness, the moment a comparison posits the principle of equivalence, it also exposes itself to the reversal of its own meaning: a reversal that threatens the principle of equivalence insofar as it springs from the possibility of perpetuating the indebtedness of thought. This perpetuated indebtedness at once sustains and destroys the system of like for like.

Guilt repeated

That thought is guilty, that self-reflection is simply a reflection upon 'its own guilt' (DdA:12; ET:xxii), is the principal idea behind *Dialectic of Enlightenment*. Self-reflection must therefore take the concept of guilt itself as its immediate theme. The work expressly examines the concept in connection with the mythical origin of law and right:

> Each of the mythic figures is programmed always to do the same thing. Each is a figure of repetition, and would come to an end should the repetition fail to occur. All bear traces of something which according to the punishment myths of the underworld – those of Tantalus, of Sisyphus, of the Danaans – is founded upon Olympian justice. They are figures of compulsion: the horrible crimes which they commit are the curse laid upon them. Mythic inevitability is defined by the equivalence between the curse, the crime which expiates it, and the guilt arising from the latter, a guilt which in turn reproduces the curse. All justice in history has

hitherto borne the mark of this pattern. In myth each moment of the cycle discharges the one before it, and thus helps to install the context of guilt as law'. (DdA:77; ET:58)

Fate – or 'mythical inevitability' – constitutes a context of guilt because judgement precedes guilt and thereby takes the form of a curse. Guilt is not, originally, a single case of guilt, but is essentially repeated guilt. This is what precipitates the *context* of such guilt. If the curse, in the primal history of exchange, represents the act of judgement which first installs the principle of equivalence and produces the context of guilt, then the 'ban', as Adorno writes in *Negative Dialectics*, is itself 'the equivalent of the fetish character of the commodity [in human experience]' (ND:339; ET:346). The schema which supposedly underlies the idea of the context of guilt is derived from a short essay published by Walter Benjamin in 1921 under the title 'Fate and Character'. Returning to this essay may help to clarify the reflections on guilt contained in the later *Dialectic of Enlightenment*.

Recourse to Benjamin

In his essay Benjamin leaves no doubt whatsoever that he is not discussing fate and character in a religious sense: 'An order whose only constitutive concepts are misfortune and guilt, and within which there is no conceivable path of liberation (since insofar as something is fate, it is misfortune and guilt) – such an order cannot be religious, however much the misunderstood concept of guilt may seem to suggest that it is.'[1] Fate is ineluctable because it can be read only through a single sign – one can never bring it entirely into view as it is 'in itself' – or because the equivalence of fortune and misery, of guilt and innocence, is incompatible with its essence. But if one can only read such fate in a *single* sign, do not then signifier and signified coincide with one another? If we attempt therefore to understand the concept of guilt from the perspective of that fate, then, according to Benjamin, we must not grasp the relationship of guilt and innocence as a symmetrical relation of opposed terms. The guilt which refers us back to fate and the context of fate has always already recuperated the moment of innocence, and at the same

time stands unrelated to it. Fortune and innocence are both
what frees mankind from 'the chain of fated events and the net
of one's own fate', and also 'the temptation to the greatest guilt
of all, to hubris'. There can only be temptation where fortune
and innocence are not 'constitutive categories' of fate, where the
downfall of the hero cannot be presupposed. Otherwise temptation would represent nothing but a transition within opposed
terms of equal value and significance. This is perhaps the only
way one can explain what Benjamin leaves unexplained in his
discussion of the significance of fate and guilt in the culture of
antiquity: why fortune amongst the ancients is related to fate
whereas innocence remains unconnected with it. Benjamin
considers the notion of fortune amongst the ancients in some
detail in another text written in 1916. There he is already
connecting fortune and hubris. The man of antiquity is blessed
with fortune because this fortune is assigned to him; when he
presents himself as a bearer of destiny, of what is assigned to
him, it proves to be disastrous.[2] Now the difficulty lies in determining the precise status of this definition of fortune. Benjamin
makes it quite clear that a definition is at stake here, that 'the
classical Greek articulation of the notion of fate' is for him
defined and understood as a temptation to guilt. On the one
hand, the absence of reflection[3] which is supposed to constitute
fortune in antiquity cannot itself be reflective in character – for
such reflection would already be an expression of hubris; on the
other hand, fortune of this kind finds its measure in the possibility of temptation, in the possibility of reflection – one is blessed
with fortune because one can be tempted to appropriate that
fortune for oneself, to procure the form of a fortunate human
being for oneself. Neither aspect here can be identified as one of
two alternatives. On the one hand, fortune and innocence have
always held reflection at bay; but then guilt and misery have
always transformed fortune and innocence into their opposites.
This reversal cannot be made good: fortune exists in antiquity
at the cost of its own loss. The loss of fortune has a preliminary
character: it has always already occurred. Fortune can entirely
elude fate, and the context of guilt, precisely because nothing
remains of fortune but the trace of an experience without
presence, precisely because it finds its measure in fate, precisely
because fortune and misery do not relate symmetrically to one

another at all. In the spirit of Benjamin's reflections, however, one would have to say this: it is not properly fortune, which is the more alien to fate the closer it stands to it, but rather freedom that leads us out of this entire context. The reason for the paradoxical structure of the argument lies in the asymmetry that dislodges the individual terms from any stable relationship with one another. Definition as reflection is already inscribed in this structure. Hence the movement which grasps and presents it as a paradox, cannot itself be merely a defining movement. But how does the asymmetry of misery and fortune, of guilt and innocence, arise? What is the origin of fate?

Bare life

The context of guilt, Benjamin tells us, is a context of law: the order of fate must therefore also be considered as an order of law. This order has survived because it has been confused with the order of justice: 'Law condemns us not to punishment, but to guilt. Fate is the guilt context of the living.'[4] And at this point Benjamin refers us to the origin of fate:

> [The context of guilt] corresponds to the natural condition of the living, that illusion not yet wholly dispelled from which man is so far removed that, under its rule, he was never wholly immersed in it, but only invisible in his best part. It is not therefore really man who has a fate; rather, the subject of fate is indeterminable. The judge can perceive fate wherever he pleases; with every judgement he must blindly dictate fate. It is never man but only the bare life in him that it strikes – the part involved in natural guilt and misfortune by virtue of illusion.

Fate has its origin therefore in the illusion or semblance of the natural. 'Myth' in Benjamin denotes the sphere of this semblance, this domain of 'bare life'. Thus when Adorno speaks of 'the context of illusion' he is simply providing a dialectical version of this thought from the perspective of the critique of ideology. In a section of *Negative Dialectics* dedicated to the elucidation of the concept of natural history in the Marxian sense he writes: 'Ideology is not spread over social being like some detachable layer, but dwells within it' (ND:348; ET:354). The illusion is an illusion, but it is never merely external: it belongs to the very essence of the order, that order whose own ineluctability is supposed to be the delusive semblance itself. If man were indeed wholly abandoned to this illusion, this fate, this 'guilt-context of the living', if guilt always remained his guilt and fate were laid upon upon him without remainder, then the latter would actually exercise no power over him at all. It is the essential indefinability of fate that at once releases him from it and entangles him all the more profoundly in the context of guilt. Fate is always a fate devoid of self, it remains always, in Hegel's words, 'a night devoid of consciousness, one which attains neither to any differentiation within itself nor to the clarity of self-knowledge'.[5] But this indefinability is not simply an indeterminacy: it is precisely because fate is not laid upon man as his destiny that it accomplishes itself with the greatest definiteness of all. If we follow Benjamin here then we can define fate as the definite ineluctability that springs from an essential indefinability.

We also encounter the idea of fate as 'the guilt-context of the living' in Benjamin's treatise on Goethe's *Elective Affinities* which was being written around the same time as the essay on 'Fate and Character'. In the essay the things through which life is introduced into the context of guilt are described as 'unchastely impregnated with certainty', as signs of fate which thus betray something about 'a natural life within man'. In the treatise, meanwhile, Benjamin more sharply articulates the thought of guilty significance in claiming that the life of 'apparently dead things' acquires a power at the level of natural life.[6] The order of guilt might well be called the order of apparent death: the things are not rescued, are not woken to their authentic life; man is not led from from his natural into his supernatural life. The context of guilt is a definite one because it is a context of significance. The blindness which attaches to 'the concatenation of guilt and expiation' – and this concatenation is precisely what forms a context here – afflicts everything with significance. From a structural perspective fate and allegory assume the same status: for the allegorical vision the thing only acquires the significance which the former has blindly bestowed upon it.[7] And the significance in question can only be the single significance of guilt. That blindness afflicts everything with significance is simply to say that everything constantly signifies guilt. If fate is 'the entelechy of events in the realm of guilt', in accordance with the definition provided by the *Origin of German Tragic Drama*, then the accent falls precisely on that guilt without which there could be no context of significance at all: for, as Benjamin notes, fate must be essentially distinguished from mere causality; the causal elements of all fatality are ineluctably themselves bound up with guilt as the decisive factor which unleashes fatality.[8] Guilt signifies, but the significance itself is guilty – it emerges from blindness and clings to natural life. In *Negative Dialectics* Adorno makes the claim that causality is marked by an aspect of 'archaic legal institutions of vengeance' (ND:264; ET:267). This suggests that one could trace causality back to the context of guilt as the origin of law, back to the vengeance which expiates guilt, even if a genealogical explanation of this kind would not be wholly sufficient.

Originary guilt of law

Why is it that one cannot escape the statutes of myth or the order of law? How are we to interpret the thought of a judgement that precedes guilt, the thought, that is, of an originary guilt, a guilt more ancient than any guilt? Why is it that one cannot avoid the transgression of the law? Benjamin begins from the thought of just such an unavoidable act in his essay 'The Critique of Violence':

> Laws and unmarked frontiers remain, at least in primeval times, unwritten laws. A man can unwittingly infringe upon them and thus incur retribution. For each intervention of the law that is provoked by an offence against the unwritten and unknown law is called, in contradistinction to punishment, retribution. But however unluckily it may befall its unsuspecting victim, its occurrence is, in the understanding of the law, not chance, but fate showing itself once again in its deliberate ambiguity. Hermann Cohen, in a brief reflection on the ancients' conception of fate, has spoken of the 'inescapable realisation' that it is 'fate's orders

themselves that seem to cause and bring about this infringement, this offence'. To this spirit of law even the modern
principle that ignorance of a law is no protection against
punishment, testifies, just as the struggle over written law in
the early period of the ancient Greek communities is to be
understood as a rebellion against the spirit of mythical statutes.[9]

Even if the law has been preserved in writing, the individual
who stands before it remains in ignorance and encounters
punishment. Because one comes to stand before the law,
because the statute has already defined its own limits, one can
do nothing to alleviate this absent knowledge, to extricate
oneself from guilt and the context that belongs to it. The
ineluctability of fate, which is ultimately what bestows inner
coherence upon the legal order itself and turns it into an order
closed upon itself, consists in the fact that the space in which
one moves has already been disclosed in advance. The law or
the statutes condemn us to a guilt before all guilt. That is why
the infringement of the order, the offence, the transgression, are
not simply caused or effected by the order of the law: on the
contrary, this order can only constitute itself because it already
presupposes guilt. One always steps forward *before* the law: 'it is
ontologically impossible to step into the realm of what is
already disclosed [*già aperto*]', as Massimo Cacciari points out in
his interpretation of Kafka.[10] The 'mythical power' which
Benjamin defines in opposition to 'divine power' must be
grasped as a positing of the law, as a delimitation: it is 'at one
and the same time the conviction and the expiation of guilt'.[11]
Guilt is already inscribed in this context as original guilt. Fate
therefore signifies the order of an irrecuperable pre-supposition.
The fact that particular laws within a legal system can change
leaves the immutability of that order inviolate. Man becomes
guilty because the future remains closed to him in the order
itself. It is only 'a law-destroying power' – and this is precisely
the character of the 'divine' power – which can breach the
context of guilt and open up the cycle of guilt and expiation.
Does not *every* transgression of the law come into contact with
this divine power, and is not this precisely the danger as far as
law is concerned?

Omens, presentiments, signals

The ineluctability in question reveals itself, according to Benjamin, in the phenomenon of prophecy and soothsaying. But the technique of prophecy depends upon the calculation of 'the most immediately calculable things'.[12] Fate, as a context of significance determined by guilt, allows us to read the signs. Whenever man abandons himself to 'the immediately calculable things' in this way, he has already fallen forfeit to the context of guilt. Benjamin counterposes the temporality of fate − or of guilt − to the temporality of rescue − which is also that of truth and of music.[13] The former remains an 'improper' form of time which is 'devoid of independence', which enjoys no present and knows only the past and the future in 'quite particular forms'. Thus fate reveals itself as inescapable, its course as ineluctable, precisely because it is grounded in a kind of time deprived of temporality. Benjamin explores this thought in his *One-Way Street*, in a short passage concerned with prophecy: 'It is more decisive to note precisely what transpires in a second than it is to know in advance the most remote of things. Warnings, presentments, signals course day and night through the human organism like crashing waves. The question is whether they should be interpreted or whether one should make use of them. But to do both is impossible.'[14] What is to happen communicates itself in signals which only subsequently reveal themselves as such, as something to be interpreted: namely when we have failed to act in accordance with the prophecy. Such a failure is the foundation for the reading of signs which takes the place of action. The communication of the future transpires accordingly in a double form: either as the seizing of what is to come in the very moment in which it communicates itself without communicating itself ('hardly do we know') or as the interpretation of its signs. It transpires immediately, as something directly communicated to the body, or in a mediated fashion through word or image. The concept of time, from the perspective of which we must grasp the context of guilt of the living, renders the future commensurable with the present insofar as it transforms what is to come into something past, into a sign. The present is not properly experienced as such. On the other hand, the incommensurability of the future, and thereby also that of the present, is itself inscribed within the seizing of what is to come in the moment, in the act which breaks through the context of guilt. The experience of the future is bound to the recognition of the present, to 'the bodily presence of spirit' which is capable of 'transforming the threat of the future into a fulfilled Now': it is the incommensurability of the future – which remains incommensurable with all knowledge – that constitutes the present, and not the present which provides the measure of the future. Peter Szondi rightly perceived that Benjamin's thought harbours an understanding of time which is determined with reference to the future; that is is why he would frequently cite the following remark from the section of *One-Way Street* under discussion here: 'Like ultraviolet rays memory shows to each man in the book of life a script that invisibly and prophetically glosses the text.'[15] It is only for memory that the future has become a kind of writing which calls now to be deciphered. Writing is the deciphering of the future which for its part requires this decipherment. For memory the context of guilt has already been formed. The time of memory is the fated time of a catastrophe declared as permanent: 'Hence, when you are taken unawares by an outbreak of fire or the news of a death, there is in the first mute shock a feeling of guilt, the indistinct reproach: did you really not know of this? Did the dead person's name, the last time you uttered it, not sound differently in your mouth? Do you not see in the flames a sign from yesterday evening, in a language you only now understand? And if an object dear to you has been lost, was there not, hours, days before, an aura of mockery or mourning about it that gave the secret away?' Memory produces the context of guilt which it presupposes – it must regard what is to come as something past, must forget it; at the same time, it seeks – in virtue of its own movement – to rescue the past and the forgotten as what is to come. Because the past has been a future it always continues to preserve a trace of the latter's power. 'It is true indeed that the path to the origin is a path that leads back, but back into the future', as Szondi notes.[16] It is not because everything that is to come reproduces the context of guilt that the future presents itself as threat – in that case what is to come would already be something past. Rather it is because we regard the future – in a fashion that is, perhaps,

unavoidable – from the perspective of a memory, of a forgetting, which the future itself discloses: for the possibility of interpretation, the possibility of transforming what is to come into
the past, belongs essentially to the future. The future is incommensurable precisely because we cannot identify it – for it is
that which first makes straight the path for memory and its
forgetting, as well as for all seizing of the future in the instant.
But it is only this seizing in the instant that experiences this
incommensurability, that alone possesses the experience of what
future means. The system of law marked by fate excludes the
possibility that a name should ever sound anew and differently.
For when one experiences the otherness of such a sound –
memory is not experience and yet it bears its trace – one has
already warded off what threatened to befall the bearer of the
name. The lot of fate itself has no sound – if it is true that one
can only hear what can also sound otherwise: music as the time
of salvation and rescue. That the one who is forfeit to the
context of guilt also knows of a future which does not become
fate is shown – above all else – by the interest in prophecy. The
time of fate is 'referred parasitically to the time of a higher and
less naturally entangled life'.[17]

The named head

Prophecy as the transformation of what is to come into the past
puts 'the natural life within man' – if we follow here the
thought of *Fate and Character* – in place of the 'named head'.[18] It
is the name therefore which cannot be accommodated within
the unchanging cycle of guilt and expiation. It is not, however,
the uttering of the name which breaks the order of the ever-
same, but rather the speechlessness of the tragic hero who holds
up his head because he recognises 'he is better than his gods'. In
tragedy – which Benjamin once defines as the 'action of expiation'[19] – it is this speechlessness which marks the separation of
the individual from fate: '*Fatum* [is turned to] freedom'.[20]
'Moral speechlessness' still belongs in the domain of 'natural
innocence', in the 'natural sphere' of character and the freedom
peculiar to it. This sphere is then separated from the moral: but
how then can speechlessness and character be united? How are
we to understand Benjamin's remark that the 'vision of charac-

ter' is connected with freedom 'on the basis of its affinity with
logic'? How does the freedom of character relate to that
freedom which 'will experience an essential transformation ...
with the attainment of a new concept of knowledge'?[21] In the
natural pre-moral sphere of freedom – which is alike the
freedom of character and character as freedom – there is
certainly no mention of the name. The name intends neither the
order of fate – the system of right and law – nor the order of
character – the order which should be 'liberating in every
form'. If Nietzsche, for example, connects the function of the
name with the fact that freedom itself once again becomes fate,
this idea cannot be reconciled with the way in which Benjamin
speaks of the name. At the beginning of the chapter from *Ecce
homo* which bears the title 'Why I Am a Destiny' Nietzsche
writes: ' I know my lot. One day the memory of something
monstrous will attach itself to my name – of a crisis such as was
never before seen on the earth, of a deepest collision of
conscience, of a decision invoked *against* everything which has
hitherto been believed, demanded and sanctified. I am no man,
I am dynamite.'[22] The decision which shall determine the
remembrance or the memory of the name here is that of the
will to power which posits its own values: '*Transformation of all
values*: that is my formula for an act of the highest self-reflection
on the part of mankind, an act that has become flesh and genius
in me.' Freedom and necessity coincide in this decision as an act
of highest self-reflection. The name here is not simply that of an
individual, it is also more than a mere metonymy which designates a nameless humanity: it is the name of the will to power
from which the individual and humanity will first receive their
meaning. That is why Nietzsche speaks of an 'incarnation', of 'a
fate *which becomes man*'. From Benjamin's perspective one could
interpret the decision which is at issue for Nietzsche as an
attempt to shape and define oneself, as a case of hubris which
finds its site in the context of guilt.

Gift and oblivion

With the 'gift of language', which makes naming into a human
task, God completes the act of creation, as Benjamin argues in
his essay 'On Language as Such and on the Language of Man'.[23]

It is the 'gift of language' which raises man above nature. And herein lies the 'peculiar revolution involved in the act of creation'. Man experiences his non-natural freedom in the act of naming. This act is not an attempt to shape and define oneself, since its possibility cannot be separated from the 'gift of language'. That the name of a human being is a matter of fate or destiny does not therefore imply that man, interpreted in accordance with the will to power, has formed or shaped himself to become his own fate, but rather that only so can the named individual be assured of his or her 'creation by God'.[24] But just as fateful misfortune befell the one who attempted to seize the fortune assigned to him, so too the human being that would want to know of good and evil, that would attempt the 'uncreative imitation of the creative word', is exiled from that 'blessed spirit' of the original language of names which indicates that the task of naming has been fulfilled. The guilt of hubris locates man in the context of guilt: he becomes a victim of the system of law and right. Analogously, the violation of the 'eternal purity of the name' which leads to the fall, provokes the 'stronger purity of the judging word, of the condemnation' to arise.[25] It is as if the fall of man were repeated within the sphere of nature, as if his fall posited yet another fall, even if it receives a different name. From this we may conclude that Benjamin always grasps guilt as the forgetting of something emphatically given – as the forgetting of language or of fortune. This forgetting is the origin of right and law within the order of which the gift can no longer be grasped. The gift is that which remains alien in essence to fate, yet without which there could be no fate.

Rationality of cunning

Why do we confuse, as Benjamin says, law and justice with one another (a confusion which is supposed to perpetuate the context of guilt)? If we now follow Adorno's and Horkheimer's attempted reconstruction of the transition from myth to enlightenment, a transition which at once ruptures and sustains the context of guilt, we can answer the question in this way: the confusion rests upon that mythical element which constitutes enlightenment itself.[26] Or otherwise expressed: it rests upon the fact that in the shape of right and law enlightenment also constantly restitutes the cycle of myth precisely in order to assert itself as enlightenment. It is the guilt of thought that thought shapes itself as the thought of indebtedness. The transition from myth to enlightenment transpires as cunning. Odysseus, who stands for the cunning protagonist here, sets himself against the mythic context of guilt:

> The self represents rational universality pitted against the ineluctability of fate. But because Odysseus finds that the universal and the ineluctable are so entwined with one another his rationality necessarily assumes a limiting form, that of the exception. He must withdraw himself from the all-enclosing and threatening structures of right and law which are inscribed at the heart of every and any mythical figure. He does satisfaction to the legal statutes in such a way that they lose their power over him – precisely insofar as he concedes this power to them. It is impossible to hear the sirens without falling victim to them: they cannot be denied. Defiance and delusion are one and the same, and he who defies them is thereby instantly lost to the myth which he opposes. But cunning is defiance become rational. (DdA:77; ET:58)

If the 'demanding mythical powers into whose realm Odysseus finds himself cast' represent 'petrified contracts and legal demands hailing from the pre-historical age', then 'rational universality' is inherent in myth itself: in its own universality, which is the universality of the statutes of law and right, myth has already programmed the self-extrication of the subject in the form of cunning. Precisely there, where the cunning protagonist hopes to release himself from myth by fulfilling the demands of its contract – and the self arises only in and through this movement – there he acts under the sway of mythical compulsion. 'Rational universality' is, according to its origin and in no way contingently, bound to the limitation of the exception: not only because it would assert itself against myth, and thus must except itself from it, but also – and above all – because the possibility of this assertion – the possibility of cunning – is harboured in myth itself. The ineluctability is precisely that of universality as the universality of law. It is represented by its bearer, by the self. To the degree in which the self is not identical with that universality and that its own identity is not based upon it, insofar therefore as it is an exception which cannot be defined in terms of the ineluctable, the self always experiences the law as a dead letter in which it cannot recognise itself. Or is it not rather the case that precisely the abstract dimension of law, which hinders all recognition, itself creates the domain where cunning moves and the duplicitous character of exception reveals itself? In the paragraph of *Negative Dialectics* entitled 'The Juridical Sphere' Adorno writes: 'Whereas a society without law, as in the Third Reich, became the prey of total arbitrariness, law in society preserves the moment of terror, and is always ready to use it with appeal to the existing statutes.' And he continues:

> Law is the primal phenomenon of irrational rationality. Here the formal principle of equivalence becomes the norm, the principle measures everyone by the same yardstick. Such equality, in which differences vanish, secretly colludes with inequality; it is the surviving myth of a spuriously demythologised humanity. For the sake of a seamless and total coherence the legal norms excise what cannot be accommodated, every experience of the specific that has not yet been homogenised in advance, and thus elevate instrumental rationality into a second reality *sui generis*. (ND:303ff.; ET:309)[27]

Myth triggers its own survival in enlightenment itself, which, as an exception that is no such thing, tolerates no exceptions: 'The rational system of law is regularly capable of destroying the appeal to fairness, which was once to represent a legal corrective against injustice, as a case of protectionism or unfair privilege' (ND:305; ET:311). The protection the law offers – as already in myth: for it is the universality of the statute, its repeatability in principle, which allows the cunning individual to oppose it – itself produces inequality which is essential to the realm of the ever-same. Law would only be able to dispense with its mythical features – which attach to it 'merely in form' and before all 'class-content and class-justice' – if it exposed itself to that which no longer falls under its own statutes: to that which is not equal and cannot be properly circumscribed within the existing system of law. But then it would also be exposed to the danger of becoming 'the prey of pure arbitrariness'.

Equality as inequality

The inequality that belongs to the essence of law, which is the reason why the latter continues to remain the law of the stronger, hinders the fulfilment of what the laws require: 'The right of mythical figures, as that of the stronger, merely lives off the unfulfillable character of their statutes. If these were ever to be satisfied, then it would spell the end of myth down to the very last generation' (DdA:78; ET:59). The persistence of statutes and laws before which all individuals are equal depends upon the fact that all individuals reveal themselves as equal before them, that is, that all individuals become victims of that inequality upon which the laws rest. The law cannot be satisfied; one always owes something. Cunning destroys, it is true, the mythical institution of law since it gives the lie to its unfulfillability. But cunning itself is the instrument of an indebted thinking, a thinking in terms of statutes and laws. The successful exercise of cunning stands for that process through which the law is not abolished but rather its indwelling inequality is extended. The cunning individual who stands before the law is stronger because his equality constitutes an accommodation which harbours inequality within itself. That is why whoever comes before the law can display cunning: with accommodation – and there is no accommodation without inequality – the possibility of manipulation is also given. In cunning, law exposes itself to its own self-constitutive inequality and thereby asserts itself with even greater force. Wherever cunning determines the relationship to others, these others have always already forfeited their otherness and thereby become disposable. The principle of law remains untouched by cunning, even if the cunning individual fulfils the mythic statutes and thus destroys them. If we define the universal as the inequality of what renders everything equal, then we can claim that cunning always remains the instrument of a universal that it never endangers. Even Hegel, whose concept of the universal is not that of an all-equalising process but rather that of a self-mediating and progressive movement of sublation, would seem to confirm this at the very moment in which he speaks of the 'cunning of reason': 'It is not the universal Idea which opposes itself to opposition and conflict, exposes itself to danger; it holds itself rather, untouched and undamaged, in the background. This can be called the cunning of reason: that it allows the passions to work for it, and that alone that through which it posits itself in existence is given over to loss and injury.'[28] The universal is the cunning which cannot itself be cunningly outwitted, whereas the individual, the cunning agent, can always be cunningly outwitted by others. Neither the cunning individual nor the individual outwitted by cunning is ultimately capable of the experience of otherness: they are capable only of the experience of universality.

Sacrifice and the principle of equivalence

Cunning presupposes the act of sacrifice. Adorno and Horkheimer interpret this act as the origin of exchange, of the principle of equivalence that is also the principle of law. In the first place they point to the function of the gift offered to the host:

> The Homeric gift is halfway between barter and offering. Like a sacrifice, it is intended to pay for forfeited blood (either the stranger's or that of the pirates' captive), and to seal a covenant of peace. But at the same time, the exchange of gifts stands for the principle of equivalence: actually or symbolically the host receives the equivalent value of his effort; the traveller obtains provision for the journey – the basic means of returning home. Even if the host receives no direct recompense for his service, he can count upon the same service for himself or his kin. As an offering to the elemental deities, the gift is also a rudimentary insurance against them. (DdA:67; ET:49)

The gift offered to the host represents the transition from the act of sacrifice to that of exchange. But this transition is possible only because the sacrificial offering was always already a form of exchange, 'a human means of prevailing over the gods, who are toppled precisely by the system in which they are honoured'. It is true, as Hegel emphasises in his early writings on religion, that only something heterogenous can be sacrificed in this regard. Yet exchange does not so much pervert the meaning of the sacrifice as unfold it. The principle of equivalence emerges from the sacrificial act as the primal form of exchange. If the self-relinquishment enacted in sacrifice always already serves self-preservation, one can understand why, 'under the persisting spell of magic, rationality as a mode of sacrificial behaviour becomes an exercise of cunning', why indeed nothing else is possible. Cunning, as defined by Horkheimer and Adorno, is an act of sacrifice. The fact that the cunning individual cannot extricate himself from the principle of equivalence involved in mythical law, from the binding rights and statutes of myth, means that he must substitute and therefore perpetuate the sacrificial offering with another: the hero 'evades the sacrificial offering by sacrificing himself. The history of civilisation is the history of the introversion of sacrifice. In other words: the history of renunciation. Everyone who practises renunciation gives away more of his life than he receives in return, more of the life which he represents' (DdA:73; ET:55). The inequality which is reproduced in the sacrificial act of renunciation belongs to the principle of equivalence. In the performance of the sacrificial act 'the priestly rationalisation of murder through the apotheosis of the chosen victim' has concealed the principle of equivalence and the inequality that attaches to it. But just as cunning must be different from that which the cunning individual opposes, thus marking an exception, so too the sacrifice must be more than an extension of itself:

All the innumerable and superfluous sacrifices are necessary – precisely against sacrifice itself. Odysseus, too, is the self who always restrains himself and forgets his life, who saves his life only to recall it as nothing but a wandering. But he also sacrifices his life for sacrifice to be abolished. His dominatory renunciation, as a struggle with myth, represents a society which no longer needs renunciation and domination, which acquires mastery over itself not in order to do violence to itself and others, but for the sake of reconciliation. (DdA:73f.; ET:55–6)[29]

How can we conceive of a reconciliation if its very concept involves sacrificial representation, a representation from which the 'deification of the sacrificial victim', which has a representative function, cannot be separated? On the one hand, a reconciliation which implicitly justifies the sacrifice is still bound to it: such a reconciliation continues to involve the possibility of a further additional sacrifice, even if the state of reconciliation would no longer conceivably require sacrifice at all. On the other hand, a reconciliation which shuns the danger of justifying the sacrifice – the danger, that is, of submitting to fate as the context of guilt – remains nothing but an empty assurance that could not be distinguished from an extorted reconciliation.

Reconciliation postponed

It is the double function of renunciation which reveals just how far the idea of reconciliation remains bound up with that of sacrifice. The 'rational law' of right, which sets itself against the statutes of myth, no longer produces the condition of equivalence immediately through the act of vengeance, but through the postponement and renunciation of the latter: the 'subjugation of everything that is natural' with which renunciation begins itself 'enthrones vengeance in mediated form, as vengeance exercised by the self upon itself' (DdA:74; ET:55).

> With its transference into the subject, with its emancipation from a mythically given content, this subjection becomes 'objective', objectively self-sufficient in comparison with all particular human aims, it becomes the universal rational law. Already in Odysseus' patience, and unmistakable after the slaughter of the suitors, revenge becomes legal procedure: the ultimate fulfilment of the mythic compulsion becomes the objective instrument of domination. Justice is restrained revenge. But since this legal 'patience' is formed on the basis of something outside itself, the longing for the homeland, it acquires human characteristics – even traces of confidence – that point beyond the specific revenge that has been refrained from. In fully developed bourgeois society, both are rescinded: together with the thought of revenge, the longing also becomes taboo. (DdA:97; ET:55)

This postponement points beyond vengeance because it can be accomplished only by the emergence or addition of something which stands outside the entire context of guilt: by the the emergence of a longing for home. If home is 'the fact of having escaped' (DdA:97; ET:78), then the longing for it must signify reconciliation: in a state of reconciliation man is precisely supposed to escape from the realm of myth – from sacrifice, from renunciation, from guilt. But since, through this movement of pointing beyond, this transcending of mythical immanence, the postponement causes what is postponed to disappear from sight, without sublating it, then that which sustains the postponement, the transcendence which was opposed to mythical immanence, ultimately disappears too. It disappears by virtue of the same movement which makes it possible and in which it reveals itself. The reconciliation without which no postponement could be conceived, is itself postponed: it creates a space for myth precisely where it interrupts the latter. Thus reconciliation reveals itself as mythical. At the same time, however, myth is never capable of producing a totally self-enclosed context of guilt. The possibility of postponement lies in myth: and this is exactly what the structure of sacrifice clearly exposes. That reconciliation cannot simply be opposed to myth, that the context of guilt cannot be absolute, is ultimately grounded in the fact that myth appears impotent in relation to its extension, in relation to the domination of nature, to cunning. This impotence harbours an experience of that other which Adorno and Horkheimer describe as nature, even though our experience of the latter always already forms part of an order shaped by the principle of equivalence. 'If belief in sacrificial representation implies a recollection of something that was not a primal component of the individual, but originated instead in the history of domination, it also becomes untruth in regard to the individual as it has developed. The individual – the self – is the human being no longer credited with the magical power of representation. The establishment of the self cuts through that fluctuating relation with nature that the sacrifice of the self claims to establish' (DdA:69; ET:51).

Space and time

The self owes its existence to the sacrifice made against sacrifice, to the experience of renunciation. Consequently it owes its existence to the 'sacrifice of the present moment to the future' and therefore involves a specific relationship to space and time:

> The opposition of enlightenment to myth is expressed in the opposition of the surviving individual ego to the multifarious vicissitudes of fate. The straying and wandering which lead from Troy to Ithaca describe the path which the self takes through the myths – always physically weak over against the powers of nature, and acquiring a consciousness of itself only in this journey. The prehistorical world is secularised as the space the self traverses; and the ancient demons inhabit the distant reaches and islands of the civilised Mediterranean, forced back into those forms of rock and cavern from which they once emerged in the dread remoteness of antiquity. But the epic adventures give each location a proper name and permit a rational overview of space itself. (DdA:64; ET:46)

And further: 'In the image of the journey historical time laboriously and conditionally separates itself off from space, the unconditional schema of all mythical time' (DdA:66; ET:48). When Adorno and Horkheimer call fate 'manifold', when they designate myth as 'the manifold, the distracting, the dissolving element', they are referring to the destructive power of myth, to that moment of otherness that is not exhausted in mythical ever-sameness, and whose subjugation renews the context of guilt. He who exposes himself to myth courts the mortal danger of the manifold that consumes identity. But since myth is the manifold precisely as the ever-same (a double definition of myth which enables Horkheimer and Adorno to pursue a double strategy of argument), it is also what makes the domination of nature possible through the self-identical subject. And here Adorno and Horkheimer cite a line of Hölderlin (which Heidegger also quotes in connection with the question concerning technology): 'Where danger grows, /There also grows the saving power'. Myth brings itself into opposition with an enlightenment that must also itself be more than myth. The task is to think the relationship of the self to space and time in accordance with this schema. For it is by no means the case that one could simply define myth in terms of space and enlightenment in terms of time. The space (of the Odyssey) is 'mythical time': a 'secularisation of the prehistorical world' and a site of errance through which the power of myth asserts itself. Between 'mythical time' and 'historical time' stands the name. At the moment in which space is named, and thereby becomes identifiable and recognisable, the identifying self is no longer subjected to it: the erring journey becomes history. This transformation is what is known as adventure. Horkheimer and Adorno observe that the unified self cannot be conceived simply in 'rigid opposition to adventure', but rather forms itself 'in its rigidity' only 'through this opposition. The self is a unity merely in the manifold which that unity denies' (DdA:65; ET:47). Within purely 'historical time' there can be no adventure. It is only the entwinement of the latter with 'mythical time', with space, which makes the idea of adventure possible. Adventure is chanced, its risk overcome, where history can suddenly reveal itself as errance and errance as history. It is through adventure, in which cunning knows how to preserve itself, that wandering becomes journeying. In this process the self learns how to name space. If the constitution of the self is accomplished as 'the sacrifice of the present moment to the future', this also involves the possibility of naming. For every name sacrifices the present moment: otherwise it would never be able to fulfil its task. If the name were to hold only in the moment of naming, it would destroy itself before it could name anything at all. In other words: the name is mythic to the extent that, after death and disappearance, it vouchsafes the recognition of what has died and disappeared, to the extent therefore that it has always assumed the guilt of the ever-same. Every name is guilty. And: one is convicted of guilt in every name.

A rational overview

Naming inevitably transpires in the spirit which Nietzsche describes as 'the spirit of vengeance' and Heidegger analyses as follows:

> Vengeance is the will's unwilling response to time, and that means: against the phenomenon of transience and the pastness which belongs to it. For the will this is something which it can no longer do anything to counter, something against

which its willing constantly stumbles. Time and its 'It was' is
the stumbling block which the will is powerless to remove.
Time as transience is a rebuff the will is forced to suffer. This
suffering will becomes itself a suffering of transience, a suffering which wills its own transience, and thereby wills that
everything that is deserves to pass away. The unwilling
response to time debases the transient.[30]

There is no name which would not require this debasement of
time: the name, without which no 'rational perspective' would
be successfully accomplished, sets the ever-sameness of what is
exempted from time against the ever-sameness of the transience
which belongs to fate. Name and law alike presuppose the
'sacrifice of the present moment to the future': since it permits
all the achievements of identifying thought, the name is the
unity which guarantees the functioning of the principle of
equivalence. But that in turn means that myth as fate, as the
context of guilt which rests upon this same principle, structurally presupposes the name. The sacrifice offered up against
sacrifice, the renunciation that postpones vengeance, reveals
itself as vengeance.

Nietzsche's 'spirit of vengeance'

If we attempt therefore to grasp that state of reconciliation,
which according to Horkheimer and Adorno no longer
requires renunciation, as the liberation from the 'spirit of
vengeance', we should not begin from the model of the
contract based as it is upon the principle of equivalence. In
Zarathustra Nietzsche gives a voice to a madness in whose
ravings the captive will that cannot break the hold of time
redeems itself: 'Can there be any redemption if there is an
eternal law? Ah!, the stone "It was" cannot be moved: all
punishments must remain eternal punishments! ... No deed can
ever be destroyed: how could a deed be made undone through
punishment! This, this is the eternal burden of the punishment
that is "existence" that the latter must always and eternally
return as deed and guilt!' The 'creative will' turns against that
will whose willing becomes a failure to will – and here
Nietzsche alludes to Schopenhauer. But the creative will must

also will something 'higher than all reconciliation', it may not rest content with a 'reconciliation with time'. As 'will to power' it must itself will to 'will back'. Consequently it is the unity of will to power and the eternal return of the same, of the 'what' and the 'that', that must be regarded as that which is higher than reconciliation.[31] Heidegger, who in a 'dialogue on thinking' entitled *Releasement* speaks of a 'non-willing' that 'remains utterly beyond any kind of willing', and that has nothing to do with 'the denial of the will to life',[32] refers to the 'redemption from the spirit of vengeance' in Nietzsche by emphasising the irreconcilability of such redemption with all contractual thought:

> Nietzsche's thought is directed towards a spirit which, being the freedom from vengeance, precedes all mere fraternisation, but also any desire to mete out punishment. It precedes all efforts for peace and every prosecution of war. It precedes the spirit which would ground and secure peace, *pax*, through pacts. The domain of this freedom from vengeance also lies before all feeble withdrawal from events and the shirking of sacrifice, just as it lies before all blind action pursued at any price.[33]

The fact that Horkheimer and Adorno do not conceive of reconciliation as the unity of will to power and eternal return should not obscure their agreement with the Nietzschean thought here mediated through Heidegger's interpretation. One cannot escape 'the spirit of vengeance' there where myth, where 'eternal law', guilt and punishment prevail and where the overcoming of the same remains subject to their sway – as a mere denial of will or as a 'lawful' guarantee.

Sacrifice as appropriation

Heidegger mentions sacrifice. But why does he do so? The passage quoted derives from *What Is Called Thinking?*, the series of lectures which Heidegger delivered in the winter semester of 1959. Ten years earlier Heidegger also mentions sacrifice in his lecture on Hölderlin's hymn 'Der Ister'. The significance of the date in question hardly needs to be underlined.

We only stand at the beginning of historicality proper, that is, of action which lies within the essential and which stems from an ability to wait for the sending of what is one's own. Yet being able to wait is not an actionless or thoughtless readiness to let events take their course, it is not a closing of one's eyes in the face of some dark foreboding. Being able to wait is a standing that has already leapt ahead, a standing within what is indestructible, in whose neighbourhood devastation belongs as the valley belongs to the mountain. Yet could such a waiting ever occur without a kind of historical humanity which belongs to the beginning, and which, growing through the pain of sacrifice, proves to be prepared for this beginning, for that which is its own?'[34]

The 'thoughtless readiness to let events take their course' corresponds to the 'feeble withdrawal from events' in the passage from Heidegger's later lecture, while the 'closing of one's eyes in the face of some dark foreboding' corresponds to the 'shirking of sacrifice'. In both cases the sacrifice in question is one that allows an appropriation of what belongs most properly to oneself, and indeed there where the latter is threatened by war and devastation. It is true that Heidegger interprets this 'own' as the 'beginning' that is destined to a certain kind of 'historical humanity', but also as an act which discloses the realm of the more than human, since the first part of the lecture series *What Is Called Thinking?* is itself a discussion of Nietzsche. However, the distinctive description of 'the freedom from vengeance', in which the reference to sacrifice occurs, allows one to wonder whether in fact Heidegger is merely presenting Nietzsche's train of thought here. Especially since, according to Heidegger, the epoch of completed nihilism, essentially characterised as it is by the overman as 'the will of the eternal return of the same',[35] permits, and indeed demands, a double interpretation. If we refer here to the language of Heidegger's lecture on Hölderlin, we could express this double interpretation as follows: indestructibility is only what it is because at every moment it is also threatened by devastation. The objection that even in the lecture on Hölderlin's hymn the reference to sacrifice is contextually determined, that it forms part of the discussion concerning the poet's idea of the relationship between the German and

the Greek heritage, loses its force when we see how Heidegger
transfers the question concerning what is properly one's own to
the historical present: 'We know today', Heidegger writes in
the section of the lecture under discussion here,

> that the Anglo-Saxon world of Americanism is determined
> to destroy Europe, that means the homeland, and that means
> the beginning of the West. The beginning is indestructible.
> The entry of America into this planetary war is not an entry
> into history, but is already the last American act of ahistori-
> cality and self-devastation. For this act is the repudiation of
> the beginning and a decision in favour of that which knows
> no beginning. The hidden spirit of the beginning in the
> West will not even spare an expression of scorn for this
> process of self-devastation practised by that which knows no
> beginning.[36]

It is because this 'Americanism' is bereft of beginning and
history, because it practises devastation as self-devastation and
cannot even be recognised by 'the spirit of the beginning', by
history – the spirit scorns even to scorn it – that it also knows
nothing of sacrifice. Only the spirit which has access to what is
properly its own, to the beginning, can make a sacrifice. Of
course self-devastation cannot be entirely separated from the
devastation which threatens those who hold fast to the indestructible and the experience of what is properly their own. For
the 'Americanism' which is incapable of entering history and
consequently does not participate in historical devastation
derives for its part from a historical forgetting, or indeed from
forgetting as history.

We can therefore see that for Heidegger sacrifice stands in the
service of an appropriation of one's own.[37] And just as, according to such a view, one's own cannot exist without sacrifice, so
too the reconciliation, which Horkheimer and Adorno describe
as a condition no longer requiring sacrifice, is inconceivable
without sacrifice, without that sacrifice against sacrifice which
can be understood as being effected by the name. It must of
course be conceded that Heidegger does not speak of a sacrifice
against sacrifice, that one's own is *not* simply to be identified
with reconciliation, but perhaps one cannot avoid speaking in

the name of sacrifice at the moment in which one turns self-sacrificially against sacrifice. The question as to whether sacrifice liberates from 'the spirit of vengeance' or does not rather perpetuate it remains open. Is it necessary to oppose two different forms of sacrifice here? To put the question in another way: is there a sacrifice which would remove the guilt without renewing it?

The commanding name

It is striking that in repudiating all contractual thought Heidegger should interpret peace in Latin terms as *pax*. So interpreted, peace represents a fundamental feature of 'the imperial', defined by Heidegger as an essential domain in which subjugation as 'bringing-down', the *falsum* which derives from the Greek *pseudos*, holds sway:

> 'Bringing-down' here is the act of 'going-behind', the 'trick', a word which has not coincidentally been taken from 'English'. To trick and betray someone, externally regarded, is a complicated and therefore indirect way of bringing them down in contrast to a direct and immediate form of subjugation. In this way the one brought down is not destroyed, but also in a certain sense raised up again within the limits defined by the prevailing power. This defining is expressed in Latin as *pango*, hence the word *pax* – peace. In terms of the imperial this is now the established condition of the one brought down ... It is not in war but in the *fallere* of deceitful conduct and the exploitation for the purposes of the ruling power that the authentic and 'impressive' aspect of the imperial reveals itself.[38]

Warning against the identification of freedom from the spirit of vengeance with peace as *pax*, Heidegger brings Nietzsche's remarks on 'eternal law' from *Zarathustra* into direct relationship with the Roman interpretation of law (an imperial interpretation which is ultimately rooted in 'peace' and not, like the originally Greek interpretation, in 'war') in struggle and contestation: 'The common way of looking at the matter thinks as follows: right or law is intrinsically inscribed somewhere or other, and with its help and in its application conflict is precisely decided and eliminated. No! Originally speaking, and in accordance with its essence, law first presents itself, shapes and preserves itself, reveals its truth only in struggle and conflict. It is the struggle that defines the struggling sides; the one side is what it is through the other, in mutual self-recognition'.[39] From this perspective, the transition from myth to enlightenment, accomplished in terms of the name as Adorno and Horkheimer clearly show, presents itself as the transition to the imperial in a generalised sense: for it is precisely the name which is supposed to guarantee the 'rational overview' which subjects nature. Heidegger, as we shall see, does not restrict the imperial to the Roman Empire: but the latter does reveal the essence of dominion and of command. Law, as a form of equivalent exchange, rests upon the name as the selfsame unity of identification exempted from time, and is essentially imperial in character to the extent that the name remains bound to territorial dominion, as Adorno and Horkheimer both assume. The fact that the name procures a 'rational overview' there where it specifies the limits and frontiers of space can also be formulated in the following fashion: the name occupies, identifies and governs a domain, places everything that falls within the latter at its own disposal and excludes everything it cannot grasp and integrate: what is thus excluded remains at the frontier, at the 'distant margin'. (In Adorno's and Horkheimer's eyes too, the myth that has been brought down is not simply destroyed; its statutes forfeit their power, but the song of the sirens survives within 'artistic music'.)

Imperium is the domain grounded upon the commandment in which others are commanded. *Imperium* is an order in the sense of commandment. Understood in this fashion, the order is the essential ground of dominion and not something like its effect, and certainly not merely a form of its exercise. The God of the Old Testament is also a 'commanding God': 'Thou shalt not', 'Thou shalt' is his word. This 'Shalt' is inscribed upon the tables of the law. No Greek god is a commanding god, but rather one that shows something forth, that points the way. The Roman '*numen*', which is what typically marks the gods of Rome, on the other hand sig-

nifies 'summons' and 'will' and reveals a commanding character . . . It is in the essential domain of the 'command' that
Roman 'law', *ius*, belongs. The latter word is connected
with *jubeo*: to call upon someone by command to do something, to determine what is done or left undone.[40]

(Two genealogies touch upon one another, intersect, and yet do
not coincide here: on the one hand the Judaeo-Roman-English
one and on the other the Graeco-German one if we wished to
insert the name as the guarantee of a 'rational overview' in this
context, we should have to relegate it to the former.)

The name, the unit of identification, is the 'essential ground
of dominion'. The debasement of time, the dependence upon
the 'spirit of vengeance', and also the commanding character all
reveal themselves as features of the name. In truth the 'spirit of
vengeance' is one with the essence of the imperial: the latter
accomplishes in respect to space what the former accomplishes
in respect to time. In the series of lectures *What Is Called Thinking?* Heidegger writes: 'In any case, all naming and being named
is the familiar idea of "calling" only because naming itself
consists according to its essence in calling in the proper sense, in
the call to come, in a calling and commanding.'[41] It is true that
Heidegger speaks of 'calling in the proper sense' and carefully
distinguishes 'commanding' from 'giving orders and organising'. It is therefore unlikely that he is intending to refer here to
the imperial. And yet the use of the word 'commanding'
perhaps betrays that the imperial function of naming is already
harboured within calling itself and not merely an external
contamination. It is only because calling is a commanding
("calling" signifies in short: "commanding" ') that the name
can exercise an imperial effect, even if the 'deep-rooted
meaning' of commanding cannot be reduced to the imperial.
But in that case one could, with all due caution, generalise what
Heidegger says about commanding in his remarks on Nietzsche.
These remarks confirm that the name stands in the service of the
domination of nature and self-preservation insofar as it fulfils
the function of calling and of commanding: 'As a representing
of what is, of what is constant, as a confirming and a securing,
recognition is a necessary part of the essential constitution of
life. Thus life possesses within itself in its vital character – the

essential characteristic of commanding. The securing of human life transpires, accordingly, in terms of a decision which concerns what is to count as existing, and what is to be called being.'[42] If calling is a commanding, if the name can assume a commanding character, then every naming opens up the realm of representation, of a 'rational overview', quite irrespective of whether it can be reduced to the latter.

Purifying rage

That Horkheimer and Adorno connect the transition from myth to enlightenment, the transition from space to time, with the name signifies that it is not the concept which first subsumes the manifold but already the name which makes over otherness into the same. The ever-sameness of the principle of equivalence that is supposed to inhere in the (enlightened) legal order results exclusively from the act of identification: from the ever-sameness of the commanding name in which the spirit of vengeance prevails. The equality of equivalence is a result.

Around 1919 Benjamin wrote a short piece concerned with time and the moral world. His reflections are very instructive in connection with the problem of space, time and law. Benjamin distinguishes the realm of law from that of the moral world by recourse to the concept of retribution. Even if we should not underestimate the fact that in modern law retribution possesses a specific temporal measure of its own – 'almost as if it hesitated to reach out beyond the domain of a single human life' – this circumstance does nothing to change the structural indifference of retribution to the dimension of time. Benjamin limits himself to justifying this claim by reference to the observation that retribution 'can remain in undiminished force through centuries': it is said to be 'known from ancient forms of law that this power of retribution is capable of extending its reach down even to the furthest generation'.[43] But the contrast drawn between 'more ancient forms of law' and the realm of 'modern law' is not sufficient to demonstrate that indifference to time must be sought for in the structure of retribution as such. This indifference could reveal such a determining character only if it could be derived from the principle of equivalence itself. The like-for-like can be bound to time: in the first place through fulfilment of the statutes. But such a fulfilment already presupposes indifference with regard to time: the principle of equivalence, which alone bestows sense on retribution, can only affirm itself as such if equality can in principle – that is: irrespective of all transformation – be re-established, if, that is, an innocent must atone for guilt. In the realm of guilt retribution always and inevitably falls on the innocent, whether in a given case this is actually so or not. The temporal measure (the idea of the lapsing of law) should not be allowed to obscure the fact that one must relate indifferently to time if there is to be talk of guilt and retribution at all. The 'power of retribution' reaches down 'even to the furthest generation' because it has always already selected an innocent for its victim. But the self which according to Horkheimer and Adorno constitutes itself through 'sacrifice of the present moment to the future' is not innocent of guilt. The indifference to time, without which the self could never be formed – without which myth could never pass over into enlightenment, or space into time – makes this sacrificing, naming self, into a victim. Benjamin provides an example that is supposed to demonstrate retribution's indifference to time: the 'pagan conception' of the Last Judgement. The latter is meant to represent a 'settlement' since it is essentially determined by the thought of retribution – and not that of forgiveness. According to this conception the Last Judgement is 'the point at which an end to all postponement, a stop to all retribution, is presented'. The interpretation of the Last Judgement in terms of retribution could be understood with Horkheimer and Adorno in the following way: the vengeance whose postponement grounds the law finally catches up with the law. The ultimate authority of the law is drawn from this possibility, constantly present within it as the 'spurious infinity' of its 'empty tarrying' and postponing permanence. Benjamin appeals to forgiveness as against retribution:

> And yet this thought, which scorns postponement as an empty tarrying, cannot grasp the immeasurable significance of the Day of Judgement, constantly deferred and ceaselessly fleeing into the future as it is. This significance is closed to the world of law, where retribution holds sway, but reveals itself only there where, in the moral world, it encounters for-

giveness. But this latter, in order to contend with retribution, finds its mightiest configuration in time itself. For time, in which *Ate* pursues the transgressor, is not the lonely lull and calm of terror, but rather the roaring storm of forgiveness before the ever-approaching judgement, and against which it is powerless. This storm is not merely the voice in which the terrified cry of the transgressor is drowned, it is also the hand which wipes away the traces of his offence, even though it devastate the earth in order to do so. Like the purifying hurricane which precedes the tempest, so too the wrath of God roars through history in the storm of forgiveness in order to sweep away what would otherwise be consumed in the lightning flash of the divine tempest.[44]

The indifference to time announces itself as much in the temporality of 'empty tarrying' as it does in the retribution that has come to pass. The postponement of the retribution does not signify the disappearance of indifference. If retribution is constantly postponed because the principle of like-for-like already harbours inequality – can there be a different kind of retribution, is the idea of the Last Judgement as the final act of retribution not itself an effect of its inevitable postponement? – then this permanence is precisely the evidence of indifference to time. But it is precisely because time also inscribes itself in the principle of like-for-like, it is precisely because the permanent postponement is nothing but such an inscription, that time can acquire power over the principle of equivalence. That the world of law assumes the form of indifference to time, that its temporality is indifferent in character, can do nothing to prevent the conflict between retribution and forgiveness. Permanence as the distance which separates guilt and expiation, which stretches between the terrible deed and its retribution, can transform itself, any time, into the time of forgiveness. Time itself is indeed nothing but forgiveness, and it only needs to be experienced as such in order to escape from the context of guilt. The context of guilt consumes itself, as it were, simply because it is a context. The conflict of retribution and forgiveness transpires within the same temporality to which the world of law is bound. It is time which struggles with itself, with 'empty tarrying', with guilt. For where there is guilt, there is also the demand both for retribution and for forgiveness. A guilt that calls for no retribution is no guilt; a guilt that does not ask forgiveness cannot be recognised. Benjamin suggests just how closely retribution and forgiveness are bound up with one another when he claims that the 'storm of forgiveness' can devastate the earth in order to contest the permanence of retribution. Forgiveness therefore also harbours a peculiar abstention from time (as permanence), an indifference that constitutes the essence of time itself. Forgiveness is the time that wipes away the traces of guilt which have been left behind at a particular moment of time: it does not first arise from the effects of time. But what then is the sense of the Last Judgement if the 'storm of forgiveness' — time as purifying rage, as cathartic blinding, as the wrath of God — sweeps away everything that should stand before it? Forgiveness and retribution are incommensurable, and no negotiation can put an end to their conflict. The more they resemble one another, the more incomparable they are. Time, Benjamin remarks at the end of his text, does not merely eliminate 'the traces of the terrible deed'. Beyond 'all remembering and all forgetting' it is time 'in its very permanence, and in a truly mysterious fashion, that promotes forgiveness'. It is of course true, as the author adds, that it does not promote reconciliation. The permanence in whose emptiness the world of law stands is disproportionately long: that retribution and forgiveness are caught in conflict means that retribution always comes too late, that it always comes as belated retribution. Permanence as such threatens to annul the retribution that in turn requires that permanence, whether it brings about the oblivion of guilt or not. Retribution is the time which, on account of guilt, has tarried and missed its own opportunity.

Dialectic of sacrifice, promise of happiness

The mythical time of the ever-same, as understood by Horkheimer and Adorno, is not merely the time of the ever-renewed context of guilt but also that of the promise of happiness. In this connection historical time appears as the time of labour: adventure therefore represents the transition to labour and naming represents its possibility. Happiness is simultaneously acquired through labour and through its opposite. In the *Odyssey* those who have sought happiness at the cost of total forgetfulness and loss of will are called the Lotus-eaters. They represent an 'original state devoid of labour':

> This kind of idyll, which recalls the happiness of narcotic drug addicts reduced to the lowest level in a hardened social order, who use their drugs to enable them endure the unendurable, is impermissible for the adherents of rational self-preservation. It is actually the mere illusion of happiness, a dull vegetating state, as meagre as an animal's bare existence, and at best merely the absence of the awareness of unhappiness. But happiness harbours truth, and is essentially a result, revealing itself along with the overcoming of pain and suffering. Therefore the patient sufferer who proves too impatient to stay with the Lotus-eaters is justified. He represents their own concern, the realisation of utopia, and he does so through historical labour; whereas mere lingering in the shade of the image of bliss removes all vigour from the dream. (DdA:81f.; ET:62–3)

Labour, and thereby dialectics itself, is therefore a sacrifice; that dialectics is at issue here is indicated by the definition of happiness as the result of a movement whose negativity unfolds and reveals truth. But this sacrifice is not a sacrifice against sacrifice; rather, it is a sacrifice against the sacrificing of sacrifice. Not the sacrifice of sacrifice, which no longer is a sacrifice, but only the sacrifice as a sacrifice against sacrifice is supposed to be capable of bringing about the reconciled condition, the condition without renunciation. Innocence in its immediacy is guilty because it lacks the 'consciousness of unhappiness', which in this context means: because it does not know of guilt. The context of guilt is formed both through the abstractly mediating principle of like for like and through the immediacy of the unmediated, of abstraction. Dialectics as sacrifice presupposes a dialectical interpretation of sacrifice. It is just such an interpretation which is intended to put an end to the fatality of all sacrifice. Rationality represents, as renunciation and as sacrifice, what 'the original state without labour' is incapable of accomplishing. But insofar as rationality perceives its rights 'it enters compulsively into the context of doing wrong'. The action of

Odysseus arises 'as something immediate' for the sake of dominion (DdA:82; ET:63). Dialectic reflects the sacrifice as a means
of mere domination and sublates what has been sacrificed. But
Horkheimer and Adorno do not subscribe to this dialectics as a
historically closed process: 'Whatever abundant anguish men
suffered in their primal history, they are still incapable of
imagining a happiness which does not live off the image of that
history' (DdA:82f.; ET:64).

Similarity to the animal

It is only against the background of this dialectical interpretation
that the happiness connected with an immediacy of an 'original
condition without labour' can appear as an illusion. In *Minima
Moralia* Adorno discusses the relationship between utopia and
dialectics; just as in the passage from *Dialectic of Enlightenment*
the animal figures here too: '*Rien faire comme une bête*, lying on
water and gazing peacefully at the sky, "being, nothing else,
without any further definition and fulfilment", might take the
place of process, act, satisfaction, and so truly keep the promise
of dialectical logic that it would culminate in its origin'
(MM:179; ET:157). Although it is dialectics and its result that
are at issue, happiness – which Adorno does not mention explicitly but certainly alludes to – is compared with indeterminate
immediacy, indeed identified with it, without any attempt to
devalue the latter. What *Dialectic of Enlightenment* rejects as
insufficient from the dialectical perspective and what triggers
the dialectical process, appears in *Minima Moralia* (and, from the
chronological point of view, at almost the same time) as the
result, accomplished through substitution, of this process itself.
However, the fact that Adorno introduces indeterminate immediacy as a result shows just how little he is actually concerned at
this point with a dialectic of happiness. Whether happiness is
defined as determinate immediacy, or as indeterminate immediacy: it is the relationship of happiness to language that proves to
be decisive in both cases. Thus again in *Minima Moralia* we
discover a fragment which deals with language as a medium
which abandons happiness. We know that we have been happy
because we entertain 'a consciousness of unhappiness', rather
than one of happiness:

To happiness the same applies as to truth: one does not have
it, but is within it. Indeed happiness is nothing other than
being encompassed, an after-image of the original shelter
within the mother. But for this reason no one who is happy
can know that he is so. To see happiness, he would have to
pass out of it: to be as if already born. He who says he is
happy lies, and in invoking happiness, sins against it. He
alone keeps faith who says: I was happy. The only relation
of consciousness to happiness is gratitude: in which lies its
incomparable dignity. (MM:124; ET:112)

In *Dialectic of Enlightenment*, by contrast, the possibility of happiness is bound to the possibility of language – and thus to truth
as result: only one who can speak, only one who is capable of
emerging from happiness, in order as it were to contemplate
the latter from outside, first experiences happiness. Happiness
must be conscious of itself – must be capable of evoking itself –
and it is precisely this self-reflection which the animal is incapable of attaining, thereby revealing itself to be indistinguishable
from the Lotus-eater:

An animal answers to its name and has no self; it is shut up
in itself and yet at the same time utterly exposed. Every
moment brings some new compulsion beyond which no idea
can reach. Deprivation of comfort does not secure for the
animal any alleviation of fear, or unconsciousness of happiness any respite from pain and sorrow. If real happiness is to
materialise, bestowing death upon existence, there must be
an identifying memory, a mitigating knowledge, the religious or philosophical idea – in short, a concept. (DdA:284;
ET:246)

If on the other hand we wished to find passages which endorse
the identification of happiness with animal existence, we could
always cite the following text from *Aesthetic Theory*: 'The
human species has not so totally succeeded in repressing its similarity to the animal that it would be incapable of suddenly
recognising the latter and being thereby overcome with happiness' (AT:182; ET:119). This 'sudden recognition' is not so
much the 'identifying recollection', to which in *Dialectic of*

Enlightenment the experience of happiness clings, as rather the recognition which Horkheimer and Adorno regarded as a lack because it does not represent the possibility of identifications which transcend the 'identification of what is vitally prescribed'. If we choose the perspective opened up by *Dialectic of Enlightenment* then the human being who suddenly recognises its similarity to the animal and thereby experiences happiness is behaving precisely in accordance with this similarity. Thus animal existence reveals itself on the one hand as happiness in its indeterminate, that is to say, its pre-linguistic immediacy – as the happiness of 'sense certainty' in the Hegelian sense. From a dialectical point of view such happiness is of course condemned by the verdict that while there are indeed happy animals their happiness is a 'short-lived' one (DdA:284; ET:246). On the other hand, animal existence reveals itself as a fated condition precisely because it lacks language and can therefore never break out of this condition.

In *Negative Dialectics* the existence of the animal is not only expressly excluded from the context of guilt but is even stylised as an exemplary image of a life without guilt: 'The only social morality that remains would be to finish with the bad infinity, the vicious exchange of retribution. As it is the individual is simply left with that morality for which Kantian ethical theory – conceding affection but no respect to animals – has no respect but only scorn: to try and live in such a way that one can at least believe oneself to have been a good animal' (ND:294; ET:299). The exemplary character of animal existence here is the precise opposite of the exemplary character which is ascribed to human existence in *Dialectic of Enlightenment*. Here the latter is opposed to the bad infinity of the 'intensively empty existence of the animal'. The lack which is supposed to mark the animal – which is the lack of all unmediated happiness – is referred back to an 'inscrutable and terrible misfortune' which occured almost before time began: the 'dumb wildness' in the animal's eyes, the idea of our being transformed into animals as a consequence of punishment or damnation, both remind us of this misfortune or catastrophe (DdA:285; ET:246). The hypothesis of such a catastrophe, such an original guilt, can only express the thought that in the beginning the animal too was capable of language, and thus once formed a kind of community with the human being. Perhaps Horkheimer and Adorno call the misfortune or catastrophe an 'inscrutable and terrible' one because the animal, unlike the creatures of fable, cannot speak and by doing so beg for redemption. 'In the song of birds', Adorno writes in his *Aesthetic Theory*, 'there lurks something terrifying, because it is not song, and because it remains under the spell which binds the birds' (AT:105; ET:66). Perhaps this 'past', which supposedly renders man one with the animal and obliges him to seek for the 'language of redemption' to which 'the stony heart of infinitude will finally yield at the very end of time' (DdA:285; ET:247), represents not merely the ancient animality of man but the lost community of a language. Does not man himself baptise the animal, does he not give the animal the name to which it answers precisely because he seeks the 'redemptive word'? In *Aesthetic Theory* Adorno says that 'nothing is so expressive' as the eyes of animals which 'seem objectively to grieve for the fact that they are not human beings' (AT:172; ET:113). The 'dumb wildness' and the grief both suggest a lack and a privation. If Circe − like the Lotus-eaters − dissolves the self and consigns it to forgetfulness, if her sorcery seizes upon the 'rigid order of time' and 'the rigid will of the subject which steadies itself with reference to that order', if she confers an animal form upon the men she has seduced, then their happiness must be denounced as the mere 'semblance of reconciliation' (DdA:89; ET:70). Circe and the Lotus-eaters both bestow death upon existence, but they do so not like human beings who are capable of happiness, but like the animals which, according to Horkheimer in his notes to *Dialectic of Enlightenment*, possess 'no consciousness that might protect them from the fear of death'.[45] The happy human being bestows death upon existence because he has a concept of death.

Image

Happiness without language, at once innocent and guilty, is an image: an 'image of bliss', an 'image of primal history'. Adorno and Horkheimer oppose the image to language: the image appears there where there is no language. Thus Odysseus in Hades encounters his mother in the form of an image: 'But the mother's image is impotent, blind and speechless. It results from a delusion and is as delusive as those moments in epic narrative when language is relinquished for the image. Sacrificial blood is required as a pledge of living memory before the image can speak, can struggle free of mythic muteness, in however abortive and ephemeral a fashion' (DdA:95; ET:75–6). The image will speak only at the cost of sacrifice: 'living memory' is therefore based upon a 'fungibility that is hostile to memory',[46] at least if exchange arises from the act of sacrifice. If language owes itself to sacrifice, it remains caught up in myth. But in sacrifice myth itself vouchsafes life as well as death. Thus the sacrifice, which the image demands and which itself signifies the forfeit to death – to semblance, and that also means to the 'bare and meagre existence of animals' – must be distinguished from life-giving sacrifice:

> Only when subjectivity acquires mastery over itself by acknowledging the nullity of the images of the shades can it participate in that hope of which these images are only an ineffectual promise. The celebrated land of Odysseus is not the realm of archaic imagery. All the images eventually show Odysseus their real natures as shades in the world of the dead; and their real nature is semblance – illusion. He becomes free of them once he has recognised them as dead, once he has excluded them from the sacrifice with the imperious gesture of self-preservation; he will reserve sacrifice for those who can afford him some knowledge useful to his own life, in which, having been transposed into the realm of spirit, the power of myth asserts itself only as imagination. The kingdom of the dead, where these emasculated powers assemble, is the remotest point of all from the homeland, and communicates with it only at the furthest possible remove. (DdA:95; ET:76)

In the section on the Lotus-eaters Horkheimer and Adorno interpret the 'imperious spirit of self-preservation' as the immediacy of action which places Odysseus – 'rationality' – in the wrong insofar as it is directed against the image of happiness. Yet at the very moment when the 'uttermost station of the actual journey' is reached no wrong would seem done to those images from which sacrifice has been withheld: transference into the realm of spirit or imagination does justice to them. The theme which both authors are intent on emphasising is the 'abolition of death' as the 'innermost cell of any and every anti-mythological thought': one is all the more forfeited to death the less one possesses language, the less one possesses a concept of death, the less one has a mediated experience of happiness. The opposition of two sacrifices, the opposition of image and language, corresponds to the relegation of the animal. In *Negative Dialectics* Adorno still maintains that the thought of 'death as the utterly ultimate' is 'unimaginable' (ND:364; ET:371). In *The Jargon of Authenticity* he even conceives of an 'abolition of death' through the progress of science and 'in view of the potential for manipulating and disposing over organic processes'. It is only from this perspective that one can understand the kind of 'anthropological speculation' which asks 'whether the turn in his developmental history which bestowed upon the human species its overt consciousness and with it the consciousness of death does not contradict an equally persistent animal constitution that will not permit us to endure that consciousness' (ND:388; ET:395). One who thinks by virtue of possessing consciousness, and thus the consciousness of death, one whose thought is ultimately directed upon the abolition of death, cannot avoid reflecting upon the false abolition of death – upon that unconscious being which is incapable of thought, the animal: 'But what is an animal if man does not reflect upon it?'[47] The double abolition of death does not contradict the double bestowing of death upon existence. Rather, the false abolition of death coincides with the false bestowing of death upon existence; and the bestowing of death upon existence of which the human being is capable, the being which has a consciousness and a concept of death, can lead to a happy existence, to an existence which is free of the fear of death because death has been abolished.

The opposition between two sacrifices also remains problematic. For is it not the case, as Horkheimer and Adorno constantly emphasise, that the life-giving sacrifice, which first allows subjectivity to take possession of itself and constantly assumes the function of a sacrifice against sacrifice, itself confirms the mythic power which it breaks? Does not every sacrifice mark the irreducible character of the context of guilt, however 'utterly remote' a sacrifice may be with regard to another, relating to it only through such distance? Can one bring image and language into the kind of oppositional relationship suggested by the interpretation in *Dialectic of Enlightenment*? If, despite all the necessary distinctions and oppositions, sacrifice is life-giving only to the extent that it preserves the mythical and guilty character of life, its determination by fate, then an image can be discovered within language. It is always already an image that speaks. The 'living memory' which is supposed to be produced through language arises out of the 'fungibility that is hostile to memory', arises out of the principle of equivalence.

The 'minimal meaninglessness' of language

That the opposition between language and image cannot be sustained, not even if the 'uttermost remoteness' between image and language, that is: the slightest resistance of the one to the other, creates a certain proximity, is revealed by Adorno himself in a text which is not in *Dialectic of Enlightenment* but certainly belongs, according to the author, to studies associated with it. This text, which was not included in the main work, and was entitled 'On Epic Naivety', develops the thought that the image not merely embodies guilt but simultaneously expiates the guilt of language. Adorno investigates the function of a 'co-ordinating particle' with reference to a verse from the *Odyssey*:

> In the minimal meaninglessness of this co-ordinating particle the spirit of logical-intentional narrative language collides with the spirit of the wordless representation that the former is preoccupied with, and the logical form of co-ordination itself threatens to banish the idea, which is not co-ordinated with anything and is really not an idea any more, to the place where the relationship of syntax and material discourse dissolves and the material affirms its superiority by belying the syntactic form that attempts to encompass it ... While in these enclitic expressions language, in order to remain language at all, still claims to be a propositional synthesis of relations between things, it renounces judgement in the words whose use dissolves those relations.[48]

If Adorno ascribes a certain priority to 'wordless representation', which is determined here as a linguistically opaque and therefore blind image, over against what he calls 'logical-intentional language' – for the latter depends upon the former – then language can never succeed in dissolving this 'minimal meaninglessness'. The dependence in question is the essence of its spirit and already programmes its conflict with the 'spirit of wordless representation', its conflict with the image. Or otherwise expressed: the image testifies to a 'minimal meaninglessness' without which language could not be what it is, and it can only be what it is by consuming itself. Adorno correlates law and sacrifice with image and language:

> The epic form of linkage, in which the train of thought finally goes slack, is the mercy which in language tempers the justice of judgement, even if the judgement remains constitutive of language. The flight of ideas, discourse in its sacrificial form, is language's flight from its prison ... The image developed in language becomes forgetful of its own meaning and draws language itself into the image rather than making the image transparent and revealing the logical sense of the relationship.[49]

The sacrifice language makes to the image is constitutive of itself: this is no external arrangement if indeed a 'minimal meaninglessness' belongs to the conditions of its possibility. But Adorno does not simply evaluate this essential sacrifice as a tribute to the nothingness of images, to their semblance or illusion, to death. For the sacrifice opens up the context of guilt which every judgement renews – and it is as judgement that language is distinguished from the image. The idea of mercy corresponds here to the language of fairness in *Negative Dialectics*. In the originally mythic image sacrificed language relinquishes its own mythic features. But language is not simply and purely directed against myth. Image and language do not stand in an unambiguous relationship of mutual opposition. That is why there is always more at stake than merely one single form of sacrifice. One can also understand the sacrifice of language as vengeance, which is 'the mythical prototype of exchange',[50] as vengeance through which the image reproduces guilt.

In his essay on Hölderlin, Adorno returns to the motif of a caesura involved in the 'logical form of syntactic continuity'. Parataxis is the form which produces this caesura. The repudiation of 'predicative assertion', of a 'fixed form of logical judgement' as a unity which levels out the internal variety of the words, draws our attention to the 'narrative moment of language' in which language 'escapes the subsumptive activity of thought'. Adorno no longer simply identifies this narrative character with 'logical-intentional language'. On the contrary, he formulates a principle of presentation which privileges the narrative moment and thereby withdraws itself from the sphere of 'logical-intentional language'. 'The more truly epic the presentation, the looser the synthesis of elements which it no longer rigidly governs'.[51] Adorno's reference to the 'texture' of Hegel's thought reveals that such a hiatus, which deprives linguistic-conceptual synthesis of its force, is to be found in philosophy as well as in poetry and literature. In the last of the *Three Studies on Hegel* Adorno writes: 'The ideal is a non argumentational form of thinking ... The one is always virtually the other: the argument is the predication of what belongs to the matter at issue, is therefore thesis; the thesis is judging synthesis, is therefore argument.'[52] In his essay on Hölderlin's later poems, Adorno emphasises that the 'continuous particles in this poetry no longer serve the continuous progression of thought'. The investigation of the function of a 'co-ordinating particle' in Homer resulted in the claim that the image, as a 'representation that is remote from meaning', is a 'figure of objective meaning which arises out of the negation of subjectively rational meaning'.[53] This movement is repeated in the 'drift towards the formless' which characterises Hölderlin's poetry: a process through which 'the form-giving, detached and, in the double sense, absolute subject becomes aware of its negativity'.[54] This 'drift towards the formless' reveals that the 'objective meaning' does not coincide with that of the subject as absolute subject. Thus the 'idea of sacrifice' – Hölderlin sacrifices the spirit 'which always sacrifices what is not identical to itself'[55] – shows itself to be 'irreconcilable with that repressive sacrifice which otherwise can never make too many sacrifices'.[56] Once again a second sacrifice is discovered within the first, a sacrifice against sacrifice.

In a discussion with Adorno, Horkheimer expresses the
thought that the 'inhibition provoked by the idea of speaking'
is perhaps connected with the 'inhibition provoked by the idea
of predicative thought itself'.[57] If so, then the image (always
dumb in the first instance), happiness in its indeterminate immediacy, and the animal bereft of concepts suddenly appear in a
new light. They would all represent that 'minimal meaninglessness' which incapacitates the judgement in the very moment it
claims its right – even if it is only with the animal that one
could properly speak of inhibition.

Art and philosophy

Where there is guilt, one can always become entangled in it: it
is only at the cost of this perpetually possible entanglement that
one is capable of extricating oneself from the context of guilt.
That is the reason why animal and happiness, image and
language cannot be forced under any simple conceptuality.
Guilt demands vengeance or sacrifice: if vengeance is exacted or
the sacrifice is made, then they are themselves perpetuated
through subjection to the principle of equivalence. If one
refrains from vengeance or refuses sacrifice, then one inevitably
becomes guilty of unexpiated guilt and thus prolongs it once
again. We have seen that image and language do not stand in
any pure relation of opposition because they are not conceptual
oppositions in the sense of a speculative dialectic. Language is
sustained by a 'minimal meaninglessness' which relinquishes it
for the image, although we can never decide in advance exactly
how this relinquishment is to be described. Similarly we cannot
bind art and philosophy, either in their distinctive and respective
character or in their mutual relationship with one another, to a
single definite meaning. The refusal of sacrifice which the image
demands leads both to philosophy – thus to an imageless
language – and to art – thus consigning the image to the realm
of the imagination. In *Negative Dialectics* we read: 'The enlight-
ening intention of thought, demythologisation, eliminates the
image-character of consciousness. That which clings to the
image remains entangled in myth, in idolatry' (ND:205;
ET:205). That the dependence of consciousness upon the image
is described here as 'idolatry' refers us to the convergence

between imagelessness and the ban on images (ND: 207; ET:207). In *Aesthetic Theory* the argument directed against the image is based precisely upon the ban: 'The Old Testament ban on images has an aesthetic as well as a theological dimension. That one shall make no image, namely no image of anything, also says that no such image is possible' (AT:106; ET:67). The imagination does not stand in the service of imitation or reproduction. But since the imageless language belongs pre-eminently to philosophy, since the artistic duplication of what appears as nature does not present it as something merely negative – and that such presentation bears the 'index of the momentary' makes no difference here – it is philosophy which accords better with the ban than art does, thus enjoying a certain primacy. On the other hand, it is precisely the essential image–character of art which comes to assistance when the imageless language of philosophy remains impotent – and guilty: 'Art corrects conceptual knowledge because it accomplishes, separated off as it is, what that knowledge vainly expects of the imageless relation between subject and object: that a subjective achievement should reveal something objective' (AT:173; ET:113). A certain primacy must therefore be accorded to art inasmuch as it is art which first fulfils the expectations of philosophy. Can this fulfilment consist in the advent of an 'imageless condition' in which art disappears?[58] This imagelessness could be interpreted as a condition into which philosophy has already vanished when the disappearance of art occurs. Or else it could be interpreted as the imagelessness of the 'objectivity' which only the essential image–like essence of art, and not the imageless language of philosophy, is capable of approaching. Certainly, the lifting of the ban on images, to which the 'imageless condition' points, is not conceived as the manifestation of the true image. Does this not itself establish the priority of philosophy, even if the latter necessarily continues to need art as well? Has not philosophy already revealed what can come to expression in art? Or is there an art which is more imageless even than philosophy?

According to Adorno, music is permeated by intentions and meanings which save it from falling back into that mythic ambiguity which lies upon it like a curse and which, from the point of view of *Dialectic of Enlightenment*, reveals its similarity with the dumb image. However, it is also an 'attempt to name

the name itself rather than to communicate meaning', no matter
how futile this attempt turns out to be. Music aims at an 'intentionless language'.[59] It is not that music is an interrupted intentional language, but rather that the intentional moments are
interruptions of its continuum. This interpretation could be
understood as a philosophical determination of art: one respects
the ban on naming the name and thus the ban on images, the
ban which forbids us to absolutise myth, because one hopes to
approach the name, from a distance and at the cost of interruption. But at the same time it is an interpretation which arises
from the essence of art, from its original ambiguity. Only
where something like an image still remains, something which
may well have undergone many transformations, can the claim
to name the name be raised, whether because art in its ambiguity constantly recalls myth and the delusive images of idolatry,
or because the name must be understood as the 'minimal meaninglessness' of language.

Philosophy lies closer to the name than art, and its imageless
language remains more faithful to it than the art which profanes
it. On the other hand, art approaches most closely to the name
insofar as meanings and intentions cannot foreclose art's access
to it in advance. The image, withdrawn as it is from the
meaning of intentional language, respects the ban on images
and thus comes close to the name. Or: the image's remoteness
from meaning brings it immediately into the nearness of the
name that no meaning can identify.

Progress in the realm of spirit

In the context of guilt every element can mean at once guilt and
mercy, and it is only in the course of such duplication or division that it can reveal itself as what it is. Mercy itself, which in
contrast to vengeance and sacrifice would seem to resist the
renewal of the guilt context, cannot remain untouched by guilt.
Horkheimer and Adorno regard the emphasis upon mercy or
grace as a specific characteristic of Christianity:

> The God of Judaism demands his due and calls to reckoning
> those who do not pay it. He entangles his creatures in the
> net of guilt and merit. Christianity, on the other hand, has

emphasised the concept of grace, which is already present in Judaism as the covenant between God and man and in the messianic promise. It has lessened the horror of the absolute by allowing the creature to find his own reflection in the deity: the representative of God is called by a human name and dies a human death. His message is: Fear not; the Law loses its power before faith; love, the only commandment, is greater than all majesty. But, through the same factors by which Christianity lifts the interdiction on natural religion, it once again produces idolatry itself, although now in a spiritualised form. (DdA:201f.; ET:197)

To the extent that the Jewish God is spiritual in essence, he already raises the context of guilt out of its radication in nature. But his power – 'the iron word I am that suffers no other beside itself' – replaces and even outdoes the power of 'the more ambiguous oracle of anonymous fate'. The Jewish God, spirit opposed to everything unspiritual, sustains the context of guilt at the moment in which it breaks the power of fate that rules the natural course of things. The avenging of any and every transgression can leave only debtors. Through its spiritualisation of the unspiritual – of the human name and of death – Christianity breaks the power of spirit that perpetuates guilty entanglement. But in return for the forgiveness of guilt, for the donation of divine grace which is not so alien to Judaism either, and which the Christian interprets as the significance of the cross, Christianity pays the price of idolatry. Both Judaism and Christianity represent – at least from this angle – a spiritualisation of the guilt context. If it were only philosophy that respected the ban on images, the ban on naming the name – and every naming amounts to an illustration – one should have to see in every philosopher a Jew, and in every artist a Christian.

In *Moses and the Religion of Monotheism*, Freud analyses the 'genealogical myths' which belong to the history of religion and tries to detect the Egyptian origin of the name of the Jewish God. Horkheimer and Adorno do not refer the dialectic of enlightenment perpetrated by the fatality of guilt to an original act of parricide. But just like them, Freud cannot imagine any progress, any 'progress in the realm of spirit', that does not involve an even deeper entanglement in guilt. Sacrifice and vengeance appear as constants in a history which ceaselessly perpetuates guilt:

> The guilt-consciousness of the time had long since ceased to be limited to the Jewish people, and had taken hold of all the peoples of the Mediterranean area as a vague sense of general dissatisfaction, as a presentiment of disaster, the reasons for which no one could precisely identify. ... The clarification of this oppressive situation first arose within Judaism. Irrespective of all other similar approaches and anticipations existing at the time it was nonetheless through the spirit of a Jewish man, Saul of Tarsus, who as a Roman citizen called himself Paul, that this knowledge first emerged: 'We are so wretched because we have killed God the Father'. And it is entirely understandable that he could only grasp this piece of truth in the delirious garb of the good news: 'We are released from all guilt since one of us has sacrificed his life in order to expiate for us' ... Once the Christian doctrine had shattered the framework of Judaism, it also absorbed elements from many other sources, renounced many aspects of pure monotheism, accommodated itself in many particular respects to the ritual practices of the other Mediterranean peoples. It was as if Egypt were now avenging itself once more upon the descendants of Akehnaton. It is worth remarking the precise manner in which the new religion contended with the ancient ambivalence of the patriarchal relationship. Its principal content was indeed the reconciliation with God the Father, the expiation of the offence committed against the latter, but the other side of the affective relation showed itself in the fact that the Son, who had taken the task of expiation upon himself, now became God himself alongside the Father, and indeed in place of the Father. Having first arisen from a religion of the father, Christianity became a religion of the son. It could not escape the fate of having to displace the father ... Why it proved impossible for the Jews to participate in the progress which the confession of murdering God, for all its distortions, represented, would have to constitute the object of a special investigation in its own right. They have certainly assumed a

tragic guilt thereby, and one for which they have had to pay most dearly.[60]

Those who satisfy what guilt extorts from them, those who make the sacrifice, become guilty in turn: in the like-for-like the sacrifice expiates the guilt and demands the recognition that already procures the next victim. But he who refuses to recognise the sacrifice, and thus all previous guilt, leaves it unexpiated and fails to participate in the 'progress which takes place in the realm of spirit'. He is denied the possibility of ever liberating himself from guilt: blinded as he is – this is how we should have to express it from the perspective of those who do recognise the guilt – he rebels – and that is precisely the tragic predicament of which Freud speaks. Of course, if liberation harbours new guilt within itself, the refusal in turn appears as liberation. Freud defines the difference between Judaism and Christianity – as do Horkheimer and Adorno – as inherent to the context of guilt and definable only in terms of this economy.

The caesura of remembrance

Contract/cunning, space/time, animal/human, feminine ambiguity/patriarchal order, happiness/labour, semblance/language: these conceptual pairs, which neither designate simple opposites nor lend themselves unconditionally to assimilation by a process of speculative dialectics, permeate the entire interpretation of the *Odyssey* as testimony to a dialectic of enlightenment. Horkheimer and Adorno bring these themes together in their reading of Ulysses' encounter with the Sirens. This episode clearly reveals the schema of guilt as unfolded in *Dialectic of Enlightenment*. And it is the concept of time which governs the interpretation. Time is articulated in terms of the way space is divided into individual elements: 'The realms of time are divided [for the hero] just like water, earth and sky' (DdA:49; ET:32). Time must therefore be grasped as the paradigmatic form in which the emergent subject asserts itself in its process of separation from myth. But the subject can only accomplish this insofar as it makes the present serviceable to the future and denies the past any power over this present: the past is 'irrevocable' and thus stands at the disposal of the present as 'practical knowledge'. Self-relinquishment to the present, to the moment, corresponds to a self-relinquishment to the past. The forfeiture to the past is a forfeiture to the space which contradicts the articulation in which temporal consciousness is constituted. Consequently the abstract articulation of time in terms of its 'three realms' is quite incapable of adequately capturing the concept of time. Time, as the consciousness in which the self experiences itself as present and identical to itself, only functions as such insofar as it rests upon a relegation of the past and a privileging of the future. The past becomes the 'material of progress' (DdA:50; ET:32), an expression which indicates that past and future here constitute a system that transforms what is to come into something irrevocable and thereby establishes its power all the more firmly. Any distinction from the mythical past can only occur within an already developed consciousness of time which must both privilege the future and limit this privilege if it is to consolidate itself. The future is virtually already the irretrievable past, the 'material of progress', so that the limit, through which the consciousness of time both sepa-rates itself from myth and integrates myth into itself, can never definitively secure its course. Irretrievable, the past is always the past of the myth, too. Time reproduces that to which it opposes itself.

The Sirens are waiting at this insecure and insecurable limit. They promise pleasure:

> While they directly evoke the recent past, with the irresisti-ble promise of pleasure as which their song is heard, they threaten the patriarchal order which renders to each man his life only in return for his full measure of time. Whoever falls for their trickery must perish, since only a perpetual presence of mind wrests an existence from nature. The Sirens who know all that has happened demand the future as the price of that knowledge, and the promise of the happy return is the deception with which the past ensnares the one who longs for it. (DdA:50; ET:33)

The reference to Circe and the animals, contained in the follow-ing sentence, cannot be separated from the reference to the effect of the 'narcotic intoxication which pays for the euphoria in which the self is suspended with a death-like sleep': one thinks of the Lotus-eaters whose life is supposedly as meagre and bare as that of the animals, death-like because bereft of the consciousness of death. The patriarchal order, the order of the 'identical, purposefully directed, masculine character' which raises a claim to the 'full measure of time', is indeed the order of time itself and as such excludes the − feminine − 'promise of pleasure' or neutralises that promise. It is the totality to which, according to *Minima Moralia*, homosexuality belongs: 'While the subject disintegrates it negates everything which is not of its own kind ... Insofar as [the masculine principle of dominion] turns all without exception, including all supposed subjects, into its objects it reverts to total passivity, reverts virtually to the feminine' (MM:51f.; ET:46). The subject disintegrates because, as the embodiment of 'the masculine principle of dominion' − but not of the principle of masculine dominion − it is the bearer of the totality which duplicates the closure of myth in order to survive against it. It thereby only reveals passivity as its essence. Passivity is the state of exposure supposedly characteristic of the feminine: it is the Sirens who lead the travellers into such expo-sure. The character of (male) homosexuality clings incessantly to self-preservation; (male) homosexuality is regarded as self-preservatory and, like all self-preservation, as consequently self-destructive. Adorno, of course, assumes that homosexuality is equivalent to the negation of otherness.

'Narcotic intoxication' suspends 'the limit between the self and all other life'. The suspension of this limit where names stand guard − they are the guarantee of a 'rational overview' − is the suspension of the limit that separates time from mythic space, given that the genesis of the concept of time is supposed to depend upon self-preservation. It is noteworthy that 'narcotic intoxication' is conceptualised on the one hand as an 'attempt of the self to survive itself', as a 'social arrangement that mediates between self-preservation and self-destruction', and on the other hand as a 'promise of happiness' which represents 'at every moment' a threat to civilisation. For 'obedience' and 'labour', which ensure the survival of civilisation, have repudiated happi-ness and given it the form of semblance. This contradicts the dialectical interpretation of happiness which governed the section on the Lotus-eaters and the 'bliss of narcotic drugs', yet simultaneously confirms it, just as the idea of a happiness sustained by the image of primal history contradicts and confirms such an interpretation. Semblance, 'beauty disempowered', testifies to the impotence of happiness and the renunciation of cognition which produces the disempowerment of art. The essence of art lies, in the last analysis, in this disempowerment: 'The urge to rescue what is gone as what is living instead of using it as the material of progress was appeased only in art, to which history itself appertains as a presentation of past life. So long as art renounces any claim to cognition and is thus separated from praxis, social practice tolerates it as it tolerates pleasure. But the Sirens' song has not yet been rendered powerless by its reduction to the condition of art' (DdA:50; ET:32).[61] The recognition that art already owes itself to disempowerment, even as it also opens up the way to cognition and knowledge, stands in a symmetrical relationship to the emphasis placed upon those passages from the *Odyssey* which can be read as a transition from 'mythic song' to the language of the novel: 'the transposition of myths to the realm of the novel effected by narratives of adventure' drags myth into the sphere of time and directs our gaze to both the 'abyss separating myth from homeland and reconciliation', and the vengeance which civilisation wreaks upon myth and the primal world (DdA:97; ET:78).

The rescuing of the past which transpires in or as art marks the difference of speech. Speech or eloquent discourse is a form of language which stands in opposition to 'mythic song' – which is also the song of the Sirens – and to self-preserving and nature-dominating rationality. Memory, which does not reveal itself in speech or through its contents as such since speech *is* memory, expiates the guilt of vengeance. Vengeance must therefore be regarded as a memory – of the deed – bereft of language, in the sense that the song essentially hostile to memory is bereft of language. Homer's account of the 'mutilation of the goatherd Melanthios' is said to represent the 'cruellest document' of vengeance. The account allows the violence to be suspended: 'Speech itself, eloquent discourse, language in contradistinction to mythic song, the possibility of retaining in the memory the disaster that has occurred, is the law of Homeric escape, and the reason why the escaping hero is repeatedly introduced as the narrator. The cold distancing of narration which represents the most horrifying events as if they were merely a subject of diversion, also allows the horror to appear, the horror which in the song is solemnly confused with fate' (DdA:98; ET:78–9). Speech and eloquent discourse are a caesura which holds confusion at bay. But the distance which memory and the act of remembrance require is created by a caesura which affects speech itself, a caesura that speech makes possible because it itself is already a caesura. This caesura lets the essence or the 'true remainder' of speech come to the fore – that 'cold distancing', that petrifying silence without which speech would be powerless. At the same time, the silence which interrupts speech transforms what speech accounts for into something which is 'long past', thereby making it the object of remembrance: 'In the narration of atrocity, however, hope clings to the fact that it all happened a long time ago. Homer offers consolation for the entanglement of prehistory, savagery and culture by recourse to the remembrance that is captured in the expression "once upon a time". It is only as novel that the epic passes over into fairy-tale' (DdA:99; ET:80). Horkheimer and Adorno refer to Novalis's saying that philosophy is a kind of homesickness; but the authors of *Dialectic of Enlightenment* are careful to add that such longing should not exhaust itself in a delusive semblance, in 'the phantasm of something immemorially lost' (DdA:97; ET:78). The fairy-tale, as Adorno notes in *Minima Moralia*, expresses melancholy, expresses 'the idea that salvation might emerge once more, without semblance, from the figures of semblance'; it allows us to perceive the voice which tells us, even as we hope for salvation, that salvation is not to be had: 'and yet it is this powerless voice alone which permits us even to draw breath' (MM:138; ET:121). It is not in vain that this striking parallel can be drawn here. For to the extent that *Dialectic of Enlightenment* is to be grasped as the primal history of history itself, the work is an attempt to rescue 'the past as living'. And this is not merely the task of art in the narrower sense, but one which, as the authors claim, falls to the presentation of history as well. Theory or critical theory, which is properly no such thing ('If we say theory, this is already false, for theory is a deduction from fixed principles'[62]), resembles art in that it must transform what takes place, and that means the past and the present which perpetuates the past, into the semblance of a happening precisely in order to divest it of its semblance. That is why the famous metaphor of theory as a message in the bottle has a structural justification. If representation inevitably transforms its object into 'something past' – the only way in which the object can be rescued – then this representation can only be directed, in a condition in which what it represents is not yet past and in which the necessity of theory is revealed, to those for whom it will have become a matter of the past. Of course, the caesura which permits remembrance through the transformation in question, also turns what has been transformed into disposable material. For the time which belongs to the domination of nature and to self-preservation results precisely from the transformation of present and future into an irrevocable past. *Dialectic of Enlightenment* struggles with this aporia no less than does art. It is the aporia that first produces that uncertainty which is the fate of the message in the bottle. Perhaps Adorno explicitly recognised the difficulty of memory and remembrance in the tension between gesture and concept. In a letter to Horkheimer of 1941 he wrote: 'Our texts will increasingly have to become gestures drawn from concepts and therefore be less and less theory in the traditional sense. But this still requires the relentless labour of the concept.'63

Holding course

The schema of guilt can be exemplified in the choice and decision Odysseus makes when he refuses to follow the mythic song of the Sirens. The hero

> knows only two possibilities of escape. One of them he prescribes for his men. He plugs their ears with wax, and they must row with all their strength. Whoever would survive must not hear the temptation of that which is irretrievable, and he is able to survive only by virtue of being unable to hear it ... Odysseus, the feudal lord who makes others labour for him, chooses the other possibility. He listens, but only while bound impotently to the mast; the greater the temptation the more he has the bonds tightened around him. (DdA:51; ET:34).

In order to escape from the context of guilt one must first perceive a possibility as such. In the context of guilt every possibility is *a priori* a possibility of escape. But to perceive a possibility means: to make a decision, to choose between two possibilities. In the context of guilt the possibility – that of escape – is always the possibility of cunning. Cunning at once fulfils and violates the contract, is the decision which cannot choose the one possibility without choosing the other, which only enjoys the possibility of choosing at all because it also chooses the other. But it is not a question here of the particular contingent conditions of an existing situation, as if under other conditions one might be able to choose otherwise. Cunning – and with it guilt – is harboured in every decision. For a decision which was not inevitably compelled in choosing one possibility also to choose the other, would be an absolute decision and would simply destroy itself in the act of deciding.

> Odysseus does not attempt to find another route which would enable him to avoid sailing past the Sirens. And he does not attempt, say, to presume upon the superiority of his knowledge and to listen freely to the temptresses, imagining that his freedom will be ample protection enough. He abases himself; the ship takes its predestined, fatal course; and he realises that, however consciously alienated from nature he may be, he remains subject to it if he listens to the sirens. He keeps to the contract of his thralldom and struggles in his bonds at the mast, trying to cast himself into the destroyers' arms. But he has found an escape clause in the contract, one which enables him to fulfil the statutes even while eluding them. The primeval contract does not provide for the possibility of the seafarer listening bound or unbound to the bewitching voices. Bonds belong to the stage when the prisoner is not immediately put to death on the spot. (DdA:77f.; ET:59)

Perception of the saving possibility coincides therefore, in the light of what has already been said, with the genesis of the consciousness of time. Odysseus' guilt, however, does not simply result from the fact that he hears the song and is responsible for the 'meaninglessness of song in civilisation', a meaninglessness which indicates both the guilt of civilisation and the guilt of song itself. The guilt results rather from the fact that the hero reproduces the like-for-like, and precisely by virtue of the inequality which is constitutive of the principle of equivalence. (Is it not this inequality – the inequality of all levelling – which renders the genesis of the concept of time possible?) The necessity of choosing the path which was not chosen, if one is to be in a position to make any choice at all, is the necessity of participating in the like-for-like. Of course, it is crucial that there is no mediation between accommodation to the conditions of the contract, which distinguishes cunning from simple violation, and the violation which destroys the contract. The companions of Odysseus cannot hear the 'mythic song': they 'know only of the danger of the song but not its beauty, and leave Odysseus at the mast in order to save him and themselves' (DdA:51; ET:34). The like-for-like depends precisely upon this lack of mediation: cunning produces the like-for-like through the inequality which essentially belongs to cunning itself, does not permit the unequal to remain – as something mediated – in its difference: the unequal is not acknowledged in its difference and, as such, related to what is other than it. But nor is it sublated dialectically. The cunning which merely simulates acknowledgement or recognition and which opposes what is supposedly recognised to the other in abstract immediacy, immediately secures the escape which the movement of mediation always puts at risk. Cunning and mediation can be distinguished from one another only if the failure of mediation is not merely external to it, that is, if mediation fails because its outcome necessarily remains uncertain and undecided. Its success is bound to this failure. Cunning is grounded in the principle of equivalence and does not fail; or at least its failure is irrelevant if it is placed in relation to mediation. Escape thus emerges as cunning: thought is always already guilty, *Dialectic of Enlightenment* can only be written after the catastrophe. That mediation is not already secured in advance is precisely what imperils mediation itself. It is under constant threat of turning into cunning. On the other hand, the recognition, however simulated, of what it opposes signifies an unavoidable danger for cunning. The ship must hold a fatal course; there alone lies the opportunity. And this is the reason why a final separation of cunning and mediation remains inconceivable.

Odysseus represents his companions and allows his companions to represent him. Capacity for representation is the 'measure of domination' (DdA:52; ET:34) that governs the division of labour; this division also involves, as complement to labour, the exceptionality which indicates the lack of means and the condition of unemployment just as much as it indicates the independent state of the powerful. Odysseus' experience of happiness is marked by the division of labour. Representability is already inscribed in the structure of cunning, in the guilty escape from the context of guilt which depends upon a doubling. Domination thus reveals itself as a category of guilt, if representability implies that the most powerful of all is the one 'who is capable of being represented in the greatest number of tasks'.

2

Dialectics and the Ban on Images

Selfhood

If thought is guilty because rationality derives from the principle of equivalence and because the concept subsumes the non-identical, the unequal, the non-conceptual, then we must ask how it is possible to think otherwise. In *Negative Dialectics* Adorno replies to this as follows: 'The answer to the question how one should think finds its vague and remote model or archetype within language when it orients itself towards the names which, at the cost of their cognitive function no doubt, refrain from enveloping the thing or the object in categories. Undiminished cognition desires ... what the names that are too close serve to obscure' (ND:61; ET:52). The concept relates to the name as does labour to happiness, language to image, time to space, human to animal, man to woman ... The resistance to the dialectic of happiness is the resistance offered by the name to the concept, the resistance which makes the name into a model or an archetype, into an 'original image'. Whereas the name without the concept is 'blind' – like intuition in Kant – the concept that has cut itself off from the linguistic experience of the name lacks a relationship to thinking. Music, by its very essence close to the name, is capable of binding and enslaving the listener, the hearer who hearkens to the 'mythic song' from which it derives. The name must literally be regarded as 'original image': it functions like every image and disrupts intentional and communicative language. No thought without name: the name, not itself thought, is the interruption, the intermittence, the disturbance which distinguishes thinking from the logically correct progress of a chain of thought: 'To think philosophically amounts to thinking the intermittences, to being disturbed by what is not identical to thought itself.'[64] When considered in relation to the concept, the name appears to stand for the self-hood which, as art reveals, constitutes the essence of language, provided language is more than the communication of a content alien to it. This selfhood – the selfhood of the thought not identical with itself – should not be confused with the results of identificatory mental processes. It is rather the non-identical, and as such is the 'absolute ... which would only emerge once the compulsion to identity were broken' (ND:398; ET:406). It is in the expressive character of art that Adorno perceives the non-signifying moment of language in terms of which he defines the selfhood in question:

> The true language of art is without language, it is silent or non-linguistic; art's non-linguistic moment takes precedence over the signifying moment of poetry and literature, which is not wholly absent from music either. The Etruscan vases seem to be akin to language in that they suggest something like 'here I am' or 'this is me', something like a selfhood not simply extracted by identificatory thought from the interdependence of existing things. In the same way, a rhinoceros, the mute animal, seems to say: 'I am a rhinoceros'. (AT:171f.; ET:112)

Does the rhinoceros that names its name while remaining mute name a proper name or the name of a species? The naming which precedes identification indicates a point of indifference at which genus, species and individual cannot be distinguished, a point at which the generic name and the name of the species do no longer or do not yet represent cases of subsumption. Prior to all identifying operations something reveals itself, offers itself up, which can only subsequently be identified.

Determinate negation

But if the name is literally to be taken as an 'original image' and if the image is also always 'impotent, blind, bereft of language', then the concept must maintain a certain distance from the name. Only by virtue of this distance does the name appear as the 'original image' to which thought must look. The closeness of the name to the thing, to what is named, is historically speaking a remoteness which, for the sake of nearness, enjoins the remoteness of the name. History separates the concept from the mythic image as much as it separates intentional language from a fully recognising language, from the divine language which Benjamin describes as the unity of creation and cognition in the act of naming. Both these themes can be traced in *Dialectic of Enlightenment*, although the connection between them is not explicitly discussed. But does not myth presuppose a certain (non-magical) unity of the name, a unity which preserves the 'link between name and being'? Such a unity is recognised 'in Jewish religion, where the idea of the patriarchate culminates in the destruction of myth'; it is recognised by 'the ban placed upon pronouncing the name of God' (DdA:40; ET:23). A certain unity of the name must precede myth if the ban directed against it is to make sense in the first place. But then myth would represent the withdrawal of the name: the one who fails to respect this withdrawal, who seeks to name the name, and who renounces the concept, who produces an image of the world and falls victim to the power of images, betrays the name and abandons it to magic: 'The disenchanted world of Judaism conciliates magic by negating it in the idea of God. Jewish religion allows no word that would alleviate the despair of all that is mortal. It associates hope only with the prohibition against calling on what is false as God, against invoking the finite as the infinite, lies as truth. The pledge of salvation lies in the rejection of any belief that would permeate it, just as knowledge lies in the denunciation of delusion and madness' (DdA:40; ET:23). The origin of critical thought itself is clearly revealed here: critique – and that includes the critique of ideology – is essentially bound to the relationship between the concept that renders cognition possible and the name that vouchsafes it. For it is not a question here of 'opposing everything positive, regardless of what it is', but of what Horkheimer and Adorno describe with Hegel as 'determinate negation'. A determinate negation is directed against both the 'complacency of already knowing the truth in advance' and the 'transfiguration of negativity into redemption': 'The right of the image is preserved in the faithful pursuit of its prohibition. This pursuit, "determinate negativity", does not receive from the sovereignty of the abstract concept any immunity against corrupting intuition, as does scepticism, for which both true and false are equally vain. Determinate negation rejects the defective conceptions of the absolute, the idols, differently than does rigorism, insofar as it confronts them with the Idea they can never live up to' (DdA:40f.; ET:24). The ban on pronouncing the name passes over immediately into the ban on images. Is it not the case that 'determinate negation' only escapes 'the sovereignty of the abstract concept' because the concept only ever acquires its cognitive function in relation to the name, to the image? How does dialectic respect the ban on pronouncing the name, on harbouring images of the truth? It transforms the image into writing. Through this transformation, the image admits to its falsity: 'Dialectic reveals every image as writing. It shows how the admission of its falsity, which deprives it of its power and leads it towards truth, is to be read in the lines of its features. Language thereby proves to be more than simply a system of signs' (DdA:41; ET:24). Hence writing is the supplement of the withdrawing name. In its withdrawal the name marks itself as writing. No concept that reduces language to a system of signs representing the signified is capable of acknowledging this marking. Horkheimer and Adorno do not regard the image as the opposite of language: it is itself linguistic in character, has a share in language through its transformation into writing. This share is not insignificant since it is only in the experience of the transformation into writing that the essence of language – that a surplus which distinguishes language from 'a mere system of signs' – is disclosed to the speaker. The experience of language here is in the last analysis – and that means: through writing – the experience of the name.

But the 'determinate negation' which Hegel opposes to scepticism – for the sceptic is incapable of grasping negation as a result – cannot initially be separated from speculative dialectics, from the thinking of just such a result. How can the idea of a 'determinate negation' be reconciled with a definition of dialectics that arises from the withdrawal of the name and the ensuing necessity of writing, from the relationship of the concept to the name? There is no doubt that the authors of *Dialectic of Enlightenment* hardly adhere unconditionally to a speculative dialectics whose movement culminates in an absolutely necessary knowledge, and therefore in a final result.

Could they be accused of transgressing the prohibition themselves, of not respecting the ban? 'With the concept of determinate negativity Hegel emphasised an element that distinguishes
the Enlightenment from the positivist degeneration to which he
attributes it. By ultimately turning the totality of the system
and of history – the conscious result of the whole process of
negation – into an absolute, he contravened the prohibition and
himself fell back into mythology' (DdA:41; ET:24). The image
requires writing if it is to be read. As such it indeed partakes of
language, at least to the extent that language reveals its essence
through the transformation of the image into writing; but the
image remains illegible if it is not revealed as writing. It inflicts
blindness on others because it is always itself blind. If we follow
the argument which Horkheimer and Adorno direct against
speculative dialectics, it appears that, in the end, Hegel was
unable to read the image and failed to recognise language
insofar as it is harboured in the image. The name communicates
itself in its very illegibility to the one who reads the image and
who alone is capable of preserving the 'pledge of redemption'.

Particularity of Judaism

In his *Lectures on the Philosophy of Religion* Hegel turns to discuss
the 'exclusive Lord and God of the Jewish people'[65]. If God
essentially 'has a relationship to self-consciousness, inasmuch as
finite spirit is the ground on which his purpose appears', this
relationship presents itself amongst the Jews as purely external:
one secured merely through a pact, an alliance, a contract, a
covenant – through the external existence of stone: 'Jehovah
himself, according to the story, has engraved the laws in stone'.
It is not 'God's love to man' that establishes unity in the relationship between the infinite power and self-conscious subjectivity. Of course, we are no longer merely concerned here with
the 'original and indissoluble unity with the essential being' that
was characteristic of the religions of nature. The 'standpoint' of
the 'religious attitude' which Hegel is investigating is 'absolute
reflection-into-itself as abstract being-for-itself'. Hegel shows
that the religious relationship in Judaism possesses a certain
particularity 'which considered from the human point of view
could be called contingent, since everything finite is external to

the absolute power and finds no positive determination within the latter'. The particular character of this particularity is crucial: it is not merely 'one particularity alongside others, but rather a select and infinite advantage'. Only the Jews stand in a particular and special relationship to God. The particularity that stems from the absoluteness of divine power becomes a particularity in relation to every other relationship – of particularity – that might obtain between God and human self-consciousness. This in turn is possible only because God will suffer no other god to stand alongside of him. The particularity itself is particular: hence the reduction of the universal to the particular or the universalisation of particularity. The more contingent and indeterminate the existence of the Jews, the more determinately this existence testifies to the absolute power of God. The deeds which God demands from the Jews, privileged as they are in their contingency and finitude, are determined arbitrarily, they are not characteristic of the free, spiritual and ethical human being and can therefore only assume the form of serving and cultivating the possessions which God has bestowed upon self-consciousness. 'Precisely because man exists here in the absolute negativity of self-relinquishment to the utterly positive and thus once again in immediacy, his concern as already relinquished finite interest reverts to the relinquishment of relinquishment, and thus into the realised finite individual, his happiness and his possessions.'[66] The 'realised finite individual' is not a personality, is not recognised as an owner of property. According to Hegel the Jewish people, the Jewish religion of sublimity, is condemned to slavery, blindness, externality, abstractness and sensuousness. Yet precisely in its irrationality – characteristically manifest in the indifference to property and the blind obedience of service – it knows itself to be privileged and can suffer no other people to stand alongside it. As far as the relationship of self-consciousness to its absolute essence is concerned Judaism is not simply a 'standpoint', but rather the over-determination of this standpoint. That is why the slavish self-consciousness of the Jews is uncommonly striking: 'This exclusiveness is naturally conspicuous in connection with the Jewish people, for such attachment to nationality totally contradicts the idea that God be conceived in terms of universal thought rather than according to any particular determination.'[67] That God exists only for thought, not for sensuous apprehension, means that his unity must be conceived without reference to images. The spirit of Judaism consists in that limitation of imageless universality which is supposed to vouchsafe access to it in the first place – it is an image without image, as it were. Does this not create a difficulty for the dialectical transition to the next level where God appears as 'the God of free human beings'?

In his early sketches concerning the 'spirit of Judaism' Hegel had already assembled certain essential elements of his later treatment of the subject. The Jews who are incapable of showing or inspiring love are left with nothing but the testifying revelation of their own 'willingness to serve' and the 'pure, empty need of preserving physical nature'. The contrast between the Jews and the Greeks, so often emphasised in the lectures, is drawn in the early writings in this way: 'The mighty tragedy of the Jewish people is no Greek tragedy, it can arouse neither fear nor pity, for these arise only from the fate of a necessary error on the part of a beautiful existence; their tragedy can only arouse disgust.'[68] Is this not the same disgust as that provoked by the 'bodily peculiarity' which Abraham laid upon himself and his descendants in insisting upon their 'separateness'? Is it not the same disgust as that provoked by the body through which Abraham rendered his people 'strikingly conspicuous'? If we read the lectures and the early text on the spirit of Judaism simultaneously, we can say that the conspicuous over-determination of the particular which marks the relationship of Jewish self-consciousness to the absolute power of God corresponds to the conspicuousness of a 'bodily peculiarity'. The over-determination of the particular renders both the Jewish spirit and the body of the Jews conspicuous. The Jew is all the more visible, obtrudes himself all the more obviously, the more invisible, the more spiritual – God's – universality proves to be. The abstractness of the particular corresponds to the abstractness of this universality. But without preference, without privilege, without visibility, invisibility itself would be quite inconceivable according to the religious conviction of the Jews, and thought itself would be inaccessible. There would be no access to the – divine – universality of thought. The Jews are not merely visible, they are too visible: perhaps it is this excess of visibility which expresses resistance to the dialectical movement and thus provokes disgust. Negativity is always already transformed into something positive even before it can be determined as such – as a limitation. That sublimity – even a certain Greek sublimity – is connected with a 'bodily peculiarity' is something Hegel suggests in his remarks on 'the spirit of Judaism'.

> These antitheses (the Jewish people on one side, the rest of the human race and the world on the other) are the true, pure objects, something over against what is outside of themselves and infinite, something without content and empty, without life, not even dead – a nothing, and only something insofar as the infinite object makes them into something, something made, not a being, that has no life, no right, no love with respect to itself. The priests of Cybele, that sublime divinity who is everything that is, or was, or shall be, and whose veil no mortal has ever lifted – her priests were emasculated, unmanned in body and soul.[69]

In the religion of sublimity the 'bodily peculiarity' points to a spiritual one. The Jew is neither dead nor alive. He is not actually dead because his existence is strikingly conspicuous, is a kind of self-exhibition. But because he displays himself as something made – and making here means exhibiting – he is not actually living either. The visibility of the Jew no more reveals life than it reveals death. The distance from visibility, from the image, from matter, is all the greater the greater the dependency upon them. Consequently the Jew is always too alive to be dead, and thus not even dead. Nor does he know what a feeling is – the feeling of love:

> The infinite subject had to remain invisible; for everything visible is something limited; even before Moses had his tent, he showed the Israelites only fire and clouds which held their gaze in a constantly various and indeterminate play without fixing it in a rigid form. An image of the divine to them was just stone or wood – it sees not, neither does it hear, etc., with this litany they think themselves miraculously wise and despise what does not relate to them, they suspect nothing of what an image can be if it is deified in the intuition of love or the enjoyment of beauty.[70]

Jacques Derrida writes in relation to this passage:

> It is always the same law: the Jews deal only with stone, and
> they have only a negative relation with stone. They do not
> even think death as such, since they relate only to it. They
> are preoccupied only with the invisible (the infinite subject is
> necessarily invisible, insensible), but since they do not see the
> invisible, they remain at the same time riveted to the visible,
> to the stone that is only stone. They deal only with what is
> invisible and what is visible, with what is insensible and what
> is sensible, but they are incapable of seeing the invisible, of
> feeling the insensible. They are incapable of feeling the invisi-
> ble in the visible, the insensible in the sensible (feeling has a
> mediatising, agglutinating function). They are incapable of
> letting themselves be affected by the unity of the sensible and
> the insensible, of the finite and the infinite, a unity which is
> disclosed by love, beauty and the love of beauty.[71]

Christian love

In a deleted paragraph of his fragments on the 'Spirit of Christianity', Hegel claims that Jesus could not simply 'oppose love
to the lovelessness of the Jews'. Why not? Because Jewish lovelessness is not simply negative, but something that reveals itself
in the positive, in a form, in 'law and right'. Love as such,
however, recognises no oppositions. It does not set itself in
opposition to the objectivity posited in or as law: 'Only love
knows no limit; what love has not unified is not objective to it
at all, it has overlooked or not yet developed it, it does not
stand in opposition to it.'[72] Of course love alone is not yet religion. This can be seen, according to Hegel, in the love-feast, in
the Last Supper, when Jesus took farewell of 'his friends'. It is
precisely because the feast expresses love so purely, precisely
because the imagination does not objectify the 'union of love',
that the meal is incapable of representing an 'authentic religious
act'. Thus love as such, in its purity, cannot be opposed to the
'lovelessness of the Jews' because over against the objectivity of
Jewish religion – itself an external religion with arbitrary regulations – it reveals itself as powerless, powerless indeed by virtue
of its power to transcend all limits. 'In the feast of love', as

Hegel observes, 'there is also something objective to which sensibility can be connected, but which is not united into an image, and that is why the eating wavers somewhere between a common meal of friendship and a religious act, and this wavering makes it difficult to identify its spirit precisely.'[73] The sensation is objective, is bound to an object, to the bread. An external observer therefore could always interpret the meal as a mere sign and thus fail to grasp its significance, 'just as when, if parting friends break a ring and each retains one half, an observer sees nothing but the breaking of a useful thing and its division into two useless and worthless pieces'. The onlooker cannot grasp 'the mystical dimension of the pieces'. But who is this third person, this onlooker who produces the unspiritual – not living but dead – connection between the sign and the signified here, who is incapable of drawing any mystical significance from the latter? Who is the alien onlooker who sees in the 'giving of the body' and the 'shedding of blood' nothing but use, advantage and benefit, for whom the bread and wine are merely objects of the detached understanding? For reasons of structural necessity, this other party can only be the Jew, or, to be more precise, this other party must always also be a Jew. His lovelessness prevents him indeed from understanding the difference between a symbolic connection and a subjectively felt unification – and thus, in the last analysis, from understanding the significance of the act at all.

The Jew does not understand the return of writing – of the stone – to the spirit:

> The spirit of Jesus, in which his disciples are united, has become a present object, a reality, for external feeling. Yet the love made objective, this subjective element become a thing, reverts once again to its nature, becomes subjective once more in the act of eating. This return may perhaps in this respect be compared with the thought which becomes a thing in the written word and which receives back its subjectivity out of an object, out of something dead, when we read. The comparison would be more striking if the written word were gathered and absorbed in the act of reading, if by being understood it actually vanished as a thing, just as in the enjoyment of bread and wine not only is a feeling for these

mystical objects aroused, not only is the spirit given life, but the objects themselves vanish as objects. Thus the action seems purer and more appropriate to its end insofar as it bestows spirit alone, feeling alone, and robs the limited understanding of its own, that is, destroys the soulless element of matter. When lovers sacrifice before the altar of the goddess of love and the adoring expression of their feeling intensifies the latter into an incandescent fire, the goddess herself has entered into their hearts, even though the marble statue remains standing before them. In the love-feast, on the other hand, the corporeal element vanishes and only a living feeling is present.[74]

If the power of love derives from its limitlessness, love also dissolves, by virtue of its own power, the objectification which it requires if it is not to fall back behind its own achievements to a lower level, to the stage where sign and signified, writing and spirit, feeling and intuition, faith and thing, corpse and living power remain separated one from another. The 'wavering' that makes it difficult to determine the spirit of the Last Supper is ultimately the wavering between Judaism and Christianity, between one spirit and another, between spirit in its Jewish shape and spirit in its Christian shape. The Jew who cannot read – or who reads uninterruptedly, and all the more so the less the reading affects the writing – will never produce the image that unites objectivity and subjectivity within itself, the image which, according to Hegel, first constitutes religion itself and distinguishes it from friendship. The Christian who partakes of the communion meal, who feels himself one with the absolute in the sacrament, remains a Jew: the imagination fails to present him with the true image, the unity of religion. The farewell for him is an everlasting farewell: he cannot succeed in liberating the corpse from its abstract materiality, from its soullessness, the corpse that cannot be reconciled with the idea of living forces. The Christian retains only death, an indissoluble residue, and cannot enter into life, into spirit, just as if he resembled the Jew because of his inability truly to acknowledge immortality and truly to resist the abstraction of a God who binds by a covenant alone: 'After the supper the disciples began to grieve for the impending loss of their Master.

After a genuinely religious act, however, the whole soul is at peace. And, after partaking of the supper, Christians today feel a reverent wonder which is either devoid of serenity or is marked by a melancholy kind of serenity, because the intensity of the shared feeling and the understanding both remained one-sided, and because worship was incomplete inasmuch as something divine was promised, and it merely melted away in the mouth.'[75]

Negative dialectics

Hegel would doubtless have his own response to the objection that speculative dialectics had transgressed the ban on images and rendered itself culpable by relapsing into 'mythology'. Arguing from the perspective of the lectures as well as that of the early writings on Christianity and Judaism, he would probably claim that Horkheimer and Adorno are, objectively speaking, in the same position as those Jews who, as the interpretation of the Jewish standpoint in terms of a dialectical movement reveals, are torn both ways between extremes. Horkheimer and Adorno would thus be torn between a condition of imagelessness and the infinite variety of arbitrarily produced images which cannot conceal their contingency and lack of unity. They would be torn between what they call the 'abstractness and remoteness' of the Jewish God and what they call the 'idolatry' of the Christians. Both the abstraction from the image and its adoration are entangled in the context of guilt. Adorno and Horkheimer would thus appear as mere onlookers presented with the external manifestation of the covenant, the contract, the pact; they would appear as such onlookers because, in accordance with their very standpoint, they remain quite unable to read the name. They cling to the sensuous certainty – precisely through respect for the name; they are the real positivists – whether out of secret contempt for the object or out of insufficient insight into the unlimited and illimitable character of true speculation.

The objection raised against speculative dialectics thus presupposes a transformed conception of what dialectic is. Adorno calls the dialectical approach that has renounced the claim to totality a negative dialectics. Negative dialectics is defined essentially in terms of the illegibility of the name. Without the concept – without the inherent claim to identity which animates the concept – one cannot read the name: but the illegibility of the name – which does not serve subsumption – is always already posited along with the concept. Name and concept are 'antitheses' if one interprets this term in Adorno's sense – in the sense of a negative dialectic: 'If anything might still claim the name of philosophy, then it is precisely such antitheses. Insofar as they continue to stand unreconciled, thought expresses its own limit: the non-identity of the object and its concept. The concept must both demand the identity with its object and grasp the impossibility of such an identity.'[76] The terms of the antithesis cannot be brought into a stable relationship – as if the limit in question represented a self-limitation or a restraint of the concept or the name. The concept always demands more than can be fulfilled, and it is only to the degree that it demands this surplus that it encounters its limit. But the 'grasping' of its impossibility does not cancel the demand to which its own possibility is bound; for in that case the concept would simply relinquish itself and the antithesis – with all its tension – would be dissolved. In its antithetical relationship to the name – or to the object whose singularity is the singularity of the name – the concept experiences its internal disproportionality, the imbalance which constantly obstructs the self-identification of the concept. The concept cannot re-cognise itself as concept. It does not grasp itself. If it is the name which, within language, presents the 'vague and distant' model or archetype of thought – of the concept – then this constitutive inability to grasp itself must be seen as the mark of language: marking precisely that in language which is not simply a means of expressing meaning – of expressing that which can be grasped and understood by means of concepts. Adorno accuses Hegel's dialectic of being 'bereft of language' (ND:165; ET:163). The unity of the concept is a unity postponed through language. The identity with the object claimed by the concept also implies an identity of the concept with itself. The concept necessarily presupposes a claim to be identical and identifiable. But it cannot recuperate what it thus presupposes. In the act of conceptual grasping the concept must lay claim to an identity which lies beyond all grasping.

The origin of performative contradiction

Jürgen Habermas has opposed the overall argument of *Dialectic of Enlightenment* by arguing that enlightenment must use 'its own means' to denounce its 'tendency to develop in a totalitarian manner'. He certainly admits that Adorno was fully conscious of this 'performative contradiction involved in the act of critique', but claims that such a 'position' is untenable. After citing the section on determinate negation and the ban on images, Habermas argues that the 'escape from an aporetic situation' has not properly been accomplished. At the end of his essay on 'The Entanglement of Myth and Enlightenment' in Horkheimer and Adorno, he writes: 'In the process of argumentation critique and theory, enlightenment and justification, are always *implicated* in one another, even if the participants in the discourse *must assume* that under the unavoidable communicative presuppositions of argumentative speech only the unforced force of the better argument is effective.'[77] The 'performative contradiction' which Habermas locates at the level of critical argumentation is already prefigured, if we follow Adorno's argument, in the structure of the concept itself. Enlightenment 'denounces' enlightenment: it must lay claim to enlightenment, must presuppose itself as enlightenment, in order to 'denounce' itself. This contradiction can be formulated in another way: the concept criticises the concept; it must lay claim to itself as concept, must presuppose its own unity, in order to criticise itself, in order to 'grasp' its own 'limitation' or 'limitedness'. Now to the degree in which thought is conceptual thought and essentially identifies and subsumes the non-identical, a 'performative contradiction' cannot be avoided in principle. This does not mean that thought wholly exhausts itself in the concept and is simply identical with conceptual cognition; it means that the argumentative figure which is identified as a 'performative contradiction' has only a conditional and limited validity as a possible counter-argument. When we object to an argument by claiming that it has entangled itself in a 'performative contradiction', we must also recognise that thought 'unavoidably' finds itself in such a contradiction. The 'assumptions' of argumentative speech – which necessarily involve the 'unity of the concept', at least if thought can never be separated from conceptual cognition – are not pure assumptions at all. They are 'idealisations' that cannot be isolated from the 'performative contradiction' of thought.

Such an isolation, such a reduction of the experience of singularity and alterity, proves to be unavoidable when one treats 'the radical sceptical refusal to argue' as an 'empty demonstration' because it too remains bound to the 'presuppositions of everyday communicative praxis'.[78] For all the differences with regard to the possibility of an 'ultimate justification or foundation', and despite all the 'pro-sceptical arguments' which Apel accuses Habermas of introducing, the argumentation of these two theorists of communicative discourse is basically very much the same. Apel argues as follows: 'The possibility of refusing to participate in discourse can only be presented as an *argument* by someone who does not refuse discourse.'[79] Habermas stresses that the presuppositions, to which according to Habermas the radical sceptic or the 'drop-out who wishes to be consistent' remain bound, are 'at least in part identical with the presuppositions of argumentation in general'. This is the reason why the argument of one who refuses argumentation is no argument at all but simply an 'empty demonstration'. For Habermas 'suicide or serious mental illness' are the price to be paid by any subject that refuses discourse and thus relinquishes its 'soundness of mind', its 'accountability', its capacity for argumentation. It is clear that Habermas cannot avoid stigmatising suicide here. Apel describes a refusal of discourse which cannot be traced back to strategic motives or accidental reasons as a 'serious existential-pathological case that might be alleviated by therapy (including therapeutic discourse)'. Obviously it is not necessary to impugn the justification of clinical discourse in general, or the significance of argumentation, in order to show that discourse itself becomes a symptom whenever the recourse to therapy indicates a failure to account for the 'performative contradiction' of thought and simply ignores it.

It is the irreducible 'performative contradiction' of thought which first makes both thought and action possible. And since thought and action are possible only because or on the grounds of a 'performative contradiction', this contradiction is one without which there would be no 'performative contradictions'. What is at stake here is an original performative contradiction, an indissoluble intrication of myth and enlightenment, one in which the possibility of enlightenment is to be sought.

Dialectics without dialectic: the vertiginous

Negative dialectics is not a dialectics, unless dialectics can be thought independently of the 'thesis of identity' – independently of the totality: 'Without the thesis of identity dialectics is not the whole; but nor is it then a cardinal sin to leave dialectics behind in a dialectical step. It is inherent in the idea of negative dialectics that it does not rest content with itself alone, as if it were indeed the whole. This is the shape hope assumes in negative dialectics' (ND:398; ET:406). It is not through any lack of insight into the dialectical movement that negative dialectics is no longer a dialectics: it is precisely in the accomplishment of dialectics itself, as Adorno says, that thought leaves dialectics. Adorno clarifies this further in his 'critique of positive negation' where he legitimates the use of the dialectical concept of determinate negation by measuring the determinacy of negation against its unruly refusal to restitute positivity:

> The negation of the negation does not simply take this negation back, but reveals that it was not negative enough ... To restitute identity by smoothing out the dialectical contradiction, a contradiction which is an expression of the indissolubly non-identical, would be to ignore what it tells us, and to return to a pure thinking in terms of coercive logical conclusions and concatenations. Only someone who already presupposes positivity, that is, something capable of being conceptualised as a whole, can defend the claim that the negation of the negation is equivalent to positivity ... To object that this critique of positive negation severs the vital nerve of Hegel's logic and no longer permits any dialectical movement at all, is surely tantamount to deferring to his authority and to reducing dialectics to Hegel's own understanding of it. While it is unquestionably true that the construction of his system would collapse without that principle, dialectics finds its experiential content not in the principle but in the contradiction between otherness and identity. (ND:162f.; ET:160)

The negation is all the more determinate the less it tends to remain one with itself. This unrest, this disquieting negativity, does not, however, revert to positivity. Negating even itself, it rather plunges into an 'openness' that prevents it from constituting itself as the unity of the negative, as the identifying and identifiable concept of negativity. Adorno's own train of thought forces us towards this conclusion, even if Adorno continues to speak of 'negativity' throughout *Negative Dialectics*.[80] The movement of negative dialectics, the experience it harbours, is a 'vertiginous' one which disempowers the principle of equivalence: 'The equivalence of guilt and expiation has transferred itself to the concatenation of thoughts ... The process of cognition, if it is to be fruitful, differs from such a concatenation in that it abandons itself to its objects, and does so *à fonds perdu*. The vertigo which this provokes is an *index veri*; the shock of openness and its negativity – the form in which it necessarily presents itself to what is secured and eversame – appear as something untrue only to what actually is untrue' (ND:43; ET:33). The mark or the trace of language which thwarts the unity of the concept and reveals the vertiginous effect at the heart of the concept itself – does not the antithetical and logically indissoluble relationship to the name exercise a vertiginous effect? – is the writing into which – negative – dialectics transforms the image. Writing marks the negative-dialectical antithesis of concept and name as the vertiginous moment of language. To read such writing means to acknowledge this antithesis. The experience of language is the experience of the openness that separates concept and name and also allows them to strive towards one another. Concept and name are not identical terms of an antithesis. Just as the concept can never wholly secure its identity, so the name harbours no legible unity within its illegibility. The name can only be read to the extent that it remains illegible for the concept and triggers its conceptual labour. As such, the name is 'all too close'. Conversely and analogously, one could claim that the concept is 'all too remote'. Concept and name, regarded in and for themselves, are blind: what is 'all too near' reveals itself as 'all too remote', and what is 'all too remote' reveals itself as 'all too near'. If reading – legibility and illegibility – cannot be thought independently of the antithesis in which name and concept are

caught, neither of these is legible or illegible, if they are considered in their inconceivable isolation. The concept is the illegible
moment in the name, the name the legible moment in the
concept. Name and concept are elements in an economy of
reading which does not close itself off as an organised whole.
Hence the non-identical is not simply the name − or the named
singularity with which the name is supposed to coincide. The
non-identical is not just one term of an antithesis which constitutes the original performative contradiction of thought; it is
the antithesis itself in its disproportionality, in its vertiginous
openness, in its character as language.

3

Constellation and De-constitution

The non-identical speaks

The name is non-identical only for the concept which claims identity; it is only for the concept that the non-identical is unreadable and bereft of language. There is no reading in the realm of purely conceptual thought. Such thought is indeed, as Adorno recognises, 'bereft of language': 'In the emphatic sense Hegel did not require language because with him everything, even that which is opaque and lacking language, is supposed to be spirit and spirit the sustaining context' (ND:165; ET:163). But a dialectics which relinquishes this 'supposition' does not, as one might assume, require language in order to make the non-spiritual speak and let that which is 'opaque and bereft of language' find its way to language. What appears to be 'opaque' is such 'only with regard to the totalising claims of identity'. As something non-identical, however, it already seeks 'after a voice' and has thus always already begun to speak. That which is 'opaque and bereft of language' has become what it is, emerging 'in a polar relationship with the concept at which it now stares and to which it is now rigidly beholden'. It has fallen mute and withdrawn back into itself, into its 'singular and isolated existence': it has petrified. The 'singular and isolated existence', the 'pure selfhood', is itself the product of petrification and rigidification. But because the polarity of identity and non-identity is ruptured, because the concept stumbles against the name and loses its own identity before it has secured it, the claim to identity, and thus the polarisation, remains indeed in force – thought can become guilty; yet 'the non-identical which cannot be dissolved in any preconceived context' transcends 'its own taciturnity, its own impenetrability'. The 'impenetrability', the 'singular and isolated existence', the 'ban of selfhood' which

only 'language can lift', are effects of the concept. It is necessary
to distinguish selfhood as a conceptual fabrication and preparation, as something which cannot simply be inserted into a preconceived context, as that which, 'opaque' and 'bereft of
language', resists the 'pressure' of identity in its very muteness,
from the selfhood which Adorno describes in *Aesthetic Theory* as
the non-signifying moment of language, and which he alludes
to in *Negative Dialectics* when speaking of 'the inner' and the
way in which the non-identical 'comes into its own'. Language
is not a preconceived context, it does not replace the spirit
which establishes this context and substitutes it for language.
Language helps what remains without a context to find articulation, to find a voice: but this, the non-identical, cannot be external to language, something to which the latter would simply
refer. The non-identical is not the external point of reference
for linguistic communication. In order to characterise the movement of the non-identical Adorno introduces the concept of
constellation:

> The inner of the non-identical is its relationship to that
> which it itself is not, that which its fabricated and frozen
> identity withholds. The non-identical comes into its own
> only in self-externalisation, but not in self-ossification. This
> can still be learned from Hegel without conceding anything
> to the repressive moments of his doctrine of self-externalisa-
> tion. The object opens itself to a monadological emphasis
> which is the consciousness of the constellation in which it
> stands: the possibility of immersing oneself in the inner
> requires that external moment. (ND:165; ET:163)

Movement and difference

The notions of 'inner' and 'outer', of 'opening-up' and 'self-ossi-
fication', of 'immersion' and 'externalisation', of 'subject' and
'object', are misleading ones; insofar as they represent more
than simply the characteristic diremptions of the understanding,
they are all governed by the law of speculative-dialectical
mediation. If Adorno emphasises that 'the chorismos of inner
and outer is historically conditioned', then from his perspective
this conditioned character must equally hold for the mediating

sublation of oppositions. The non-identical which comes into 'its own' enters a constellation; more precisely: the experience of the non-identical is the experience that it has always already entered into constellation, that it is nothing but constellation, a movement of differing, of entering into constellation. One certainly cannot identify the non-identical as an indeterminate identity which would finally appear, through its externalisation, as something mediated. Constellation, a movement of differing which only reveals a 'unifying moment' (ND:164; ET:162) to the extent that it no longer presupposes an original unity, is itself original. It is a movement of language. At the beginning of his lectures on *Philosophical Terminology* Adorno writes: 'The language of philosophy is essential to it, and philosophical problems are largely problems of its own language. The separation of language from the object of thought, which can be encountered in the so-called positive sciences, does not hold of philosophy to the same degree.'[81] Even if Adorno does not mention the relationship of language to positive science in the narrow sense in *Negative Dialectics* − where he speaks of the relationship of constellations and thus of language to science and knowledge in general and to sociological positivism − a certain change of emphasis can nonetheless be discerned: 'How objects are to be disclosed through constellations is not to be derived from philosophy, which has shown little interest in this, but rather from important scientific investigations; fully accomplished scientific work has often enough proved to be in advance of its own philosophical self-understanding as scientism' (ND:166; ET:164). The differing movement of the non-identical, the constellation, is linguistic in essence, although one should not therefore regard philosophy as the unique domain which is privileged to reveal this essence. The insight into the linguistic essence of constellations is not affected by the way Adorno employs the concept of 'science' or 'knowledge' in the passage quoted − by the possibility that it means more and something else than just positive scientific knowledge. Of course, Adorno's thought here once again exposes itself to misunderstanding. For it is difficult to reconcile the claim that language is supposedly the other of speculative dialectic − an other that, if it does wrest itself free of dialectical appropriation, is never negative enough − with the thesis that language is merely a 'model' of constellation: 'The constellation illuminates the specific aspect of the object which is either indifferent or disturbing to all classificatory procedure. The behaviour of language is a model for this. Language is not just a system of signs appropriate for the cognitive functions. Whenever language essentially appears as language, becomes presentation, it does not define its concepts' (ND:164; ET:162). As presentation the non-identical is the movement of the unsublatable antithesis of thought. The concept that fails to secure its identity – its own as well as the identity of what is to be grasped – enters into constellation: this entrance is the emergence of language in its essence as 'configurative language'. To think an 'object' is to think the concept in the movement which is released by the unsublatable antithesis of thought and which is itself the movement of presentation or presentation as movement. Presentation here is precisely not what it was for Hegel, namely the self-(re)presentation of the absolute, just as the movement of the concept here is not a progressive advance but a dynamic entrance into the field of constellations. This does not imply, however, that definitions remain something alien to presentation. Rather they emerge from the unfolding of 'configurative language', from the 'process' of thought, from the changing play of constellations: 'A thinking which would be unable to generate definitions as it developed, and which would be incapable even momentarily of letting the thing appear with linguistic succinctness, would be as sterile as a thinking that contented itself with providing verbal definitions' (ND:167; ET:165). At this point language appears as the language of life itself: Adorno is here opposing unfruitfulness, opposing death. In the lectures on *Philosophical Terminology* he repudiates definitions which betray a 'circumscribing and limiting thought', and does so in the name of Nietzsche who, in his eyes, deserves 'unqualified' agreement: 'For one can do no justice to the life of the thing, indeed to life itself, by simply transfixing our concepts for the sake of the idols of univocity and clean distinctions.'[82] The 'unifying moment' of speculative dialectics which proves incapable of protecting life from sterility and death – though speculative dialectic is of course not a procedure based on definitions and classifications – 'survives' in negative dialectics; it survives 'without the negation of the negation'. Only negative dialectics can bestow life upon the concept: a life-in-constellation, a life as constellation, one that is neither the spiritual life of consciousness nor the life of vitalist metaphysics.

Double reading

If Adorno's exposition is misleading, this is because the terminology remains all too beholden to the schema of representation or representational thinking. The thought exposed here should in fact liberate language from the schema of representational thinking, at least in those passages where Adorno thinks the 'logic' of the non-identical in accordance with its most radical implications. He expresses the connection between the constellation and the unsublatable antithesis of thought as follows: 'Constellations alone represent, from without, what the concept has cut away within. The concept has cut away the surplus it seeks to attain, a surplus it seeks to attain all the more the less it can actually attain it. Insofar as concepts gather around the object or the thing which is to be recognised, they potentially determine the inner character of this object or thing, and thus attain in the process of thinking what thought has necessarily eradicated from itself' (ND:164f.; ET:162). The concept which would be more than it can be enters into a constellation – with other concepts – because it necessarily fails to secure its own unity. The 'object' or 'thing' in question is not, as Adorno's remarks here might suggest, something that could be separated from the constellation. Otherwise the non-identical would be an identically persisting substrate, whose non-identity would consist only in resisting the act of identification. It would fall prey to the 'logic' of what is 'opaque and lacking language', to a 'selfhood' that would not be the selfhood of a life-in-constellation but simply its duplication in and through identificatory thought.

The – intrinsically linguistic – movement of the non-identical knows no distinction between 'inside' and 'outside'. The 'inside' and the 'outside' are precarious conceptual determinations and their inadequacy is precisely what the constellation reveals. But since the concept is never pure, since its essential failure involves an original impurity and since Adorno is attempting to topple the 'idol of clean distinctions', its determinations always continue to be effective at the very moment in which they are suspended. The concept which affirms itself even as it is posited affirms 'the chorismos of inner and outer' or the mediation of the terms of this binary opposition. The movement of the non-identical, which can never be laid to rest, can still be denied or forgotten, it can still be brought to a standstill. Hence it is possible to produce a double reading of negative dialectics, to read Adorno (as reading) in a double fashion. Every reading which claims hegemony unintentionally enhances the reading it would exclude.

The concept calls forth an oblivion or a denial of constellations. But the name does the same: the denial and oblivion that it calls forth turn language into jargon. There is no jargon that would not be a jargon of authenticity: 'Words become those of jargon only through the constellation which they deny, through the gesture of uniqueness which belongs to each. What the singular word lost in magic is now procured for it, autocratically, by special measures.'[83]

The movement of entering into constellation, which is a movement without a presupposition, facilitates the denial or oblivion of the constellation since no ideality can secure it. It is the movement of historical time: 'To become aware of the constellation in which the object or the thing stands, amounts to deciphering the constellation which a singularity bears within itself as something historically produced ... The history in the object can only be released by a knowledge mindful of the historical value of the object in its relation to other objects. Such a focusing actualisation of something we already know, transforms it' (ND:165; ET:163). Every 'object' appears as something to be grasped conceptually or as a name; every object appears as something isolated, as something opaque which lacks language and which conceals its historical genesis, and also as something which is unique and immune to change because of its singularity. In the face of such an isolated and unique existence we forget that there is no simple 'object', that the 'object' only finds a place in the – linguistic – movement of constellation, that it is not simply something which stands over against us as ob-ject. Object and concept disintegrate: the movement of negative dialectics, no longer reconcilable with Hegel, 'is not directed towards the identity which supposedly lies in the difference of every object with regard to its concept. Rather, negative dialectics is suspicious of everything identical. Its logic is one of disintegration: the disintegration of the armoured and objectified shape of the concepts which the knowing subject seems to find over against itself' (ND:148; ET:145). The difference between object and concept, of course, is not that between the concept and what appears to be 'opaque and lacking language'. It is rather the difference which cleaves the concept and constitutes the movement of constellations as language. Thus, to the extent that the object is isolated or unique, to the extent that it stands over against the concept or coincides with the name, it has brought the movement of constellation to a standstill, putting an end to language, becoming, history, and the logic of disintegration. But this standstill reveals itself to be historical. It is only a moment of the movement, though not in the speculative sense. The movement splits apart in its very origin.

Language as event

If all thinking is 'exaggeration'[84] (and how could it be otherwise if thinking is intrinsically and essentially antithetic?), if only those thoughts which fail to understand themselves are true[85] (and are thoughts not always and already marked by the antithesis of thought?), then such exaggeration, and such a constitutive absence of understanding, harbour the possibility of that 'delusion' or 'madness' which Adorno associates with the will to system, to totality, to closure. History is the openness, the vertiginous abyss, the differing of the antithesis of thought in which 'delusion' and truth continually inscribe themselves: 'The potential of both truth and delusion nests within this difference between thought and its fulfilment. Delusion can thus always appeal to the fact that there is no guarantee which would protect thought from disappointing the expectation which it contains.'[86] Delusion can be recognised by its inability to endure the antithesis of thought, its readiness to forget and deny it. Such denial occurs either in the realm of concepts, or in the domain of names, assumes either the shape of a will to system or that of the abandonment and denunciation of thought. The standstill, which produces the opposition of the object, proves to be incompatible with the standstill which, in his 'theses on the concept of history', Benjamin describes as a 'messianic stilling of events', as an event which suddenly halts thought and object alike. Benjamin does not separate thought and object; they are both brought to a halt 'in a constellation fraught with tensions'. The 'messianic stilling' gives them a 'shock' or 'blow' which makes them crystallise and become 'monads'.

Adorno says that to release history is to actualise 'something already known' and thus to 'transform' it. But if indeed the movement of constellation is not a movement of the concept or of knowledge, if indeed it constitutes a 'logic of disintegration', then the constellation finds its origin in something unforgettable and immemorial that can never be actualised. It lies at the source of all actualisation and transformation, not as a foundation or principle but as an unrepresentable and vertiginous abyss. Adorno's insistence that the movement of constellation is a movement of language suggests that what escapes all actualisation, being unforgettable and immemorial, is the 'gift of language' of which Benjamin speaks, a gift without which there would be no language and which can therefore never be recuperated by language. The 'language of names' (whose ineffable sign is the antithesis of thought precisely because the abstraction which separates it from the signified exposes it to its own effacement) already presupposes the 'gift of language' and merely 'reflects' the linguistic actuality of God (an actuality which itself is only realised through the gift of language and is interrupted by this gift in the process of its realisation).[87] To release history means not only that the object is liberated from its isolation, but also that history is freed from clinging to itself. A constellation always appears when one conceives of an 'object' and experiences something which cannot be actualised within the constellation. Which is to say that the standstill, without which the constellation would remain invisible, allows us to recognise the uncognisable origin of the movement that precedes all knowledge. Such an appearing is an event and crystallises in the monad of the dialectical image which Benjamin distinguishes from the 'eternal image' of historicism. The dialectical image is that which is most profoundly penetrated by history and which penetrates history more profoundly than any other image. According to Adorno, Benjamin defines 'dialectical images' as those 'objective crystallisations of historical movement' which 'determine the newest as the figure of the most ancient'.[88] The most ancient is on the one hand myth, but it is also, more ancient than myth itself, the unforgettable and immemorial from which the constellation springs.[89] The unforgettable and immemorial 'gift of language' harbours the possibility of myth since it interrupts actuality in the moment it brings it about; but it also communicates itself as an event through the 'shock' or the 'blow' provoked by the appearing of a constellation.

Undecidedness

If speculative dialectics were indeed 'bereft of language', Adorno's own approach would be impossible to understand. Negative dialectics would necessarily forfeit 'determinacy' altogether. For one would have to ask oneself why negative dialectics declares its solidarity with an overthrown and fallen metaphysics, why it continues to describe itself as a kind of dialectics at all. And what other name is appropriate to metaphysics if not that of speculative dialectics? The movement of negative dialectics would be impossible to trace: how can we even conceive of the total independence of the concept from language, from the constellation, from the antithesis of thought? In the last of his *Three Studies on Hegel* Adorno subjected the relationship between speculative dialectics and language to a closer examination, uncovering an indeterminacy in those sections of Hegel's writings 'where it remains undecided what precisely is at issue', an indeterminacy which is not merely accidental. Speculative dialectics appears as a movement of the concept that is no such thing – and this is what brings it closer to language: 'Hegel disempowers individual concepts, uses them as though they were the imageless images of what they intend. Hence the Goethean "residue of absurdity" in the philosophy of absolute spirit. What is meant to allow speculative dialectics to go beyond the concept is also what it keeps subsuming under the concept in particular instances.'[90] How is the expression 'imageless images' to be understood here? A few pages before the passage in which the expression occurs Adorno writes: 'The demand for clarity constantly and vainly expects of language that it immediately provide something which mere words and sentences cannot possibly provide. It can be provided only by their configuration, and even then it will remain fragmentary. Hence it would be far better to proceed by carefully avoiding the simple positing of verbal definitions, and by attempting to mould the concepts as truthfully as possible upon what they say in language: virtually as names.'[91] The use of concepts as 'image-less images' is a kind of 'moulding' upon the name – which is certainly not to claim that the concept reflects, reproduces or imitates the name. The concepts here are 'imageless images' precisely by virtue of the fact that they are concepts and not images; but above all because the name in its immediacy says nothing. It is only in its unsublatable antithetic relationship to the concept that the name appears as that which expresses the unsayable, that which the concept cannot say. The ban on images and the impossibility of naming the name are as insepar-able from the image and the name as are the expectation that the name might finally say what it does not say and the constantly disappointed attempt to 'mould' the concept upon the name. The concept thus asserts itself on the basis of this necessary disappointment. It is driven beyond itself by the name and at the same time subjugates the name that is supposed to name the non-identical. This is why thought 'as constellation circles and turns around the concept and seeks to disclose it, hoping that it might spring open like the locks of carefully maintained strong-boxes: not through a particular key, or an individual number, but through a numerical combination' (ND:166; ET:163). The concept that 'springs open' enters into a constellation for it is precisely the constellation and the move-ment of self-transcendence which it triggers that the concept has tried to resist. Adorno's 'definition' of philosophy is that of the antithesis of thought: 'Philosophy could be defined, if at all, as the effort to say that of which one cannot speak; to help the non-identical to expression, although expression always still identifies it.'[92] Nothing is finally settled in the constellation, nothing is finally revealed in configurative language, not even language itself. Language as configuration can lay no claim to transparency.

The death of intention

The idea of constellation and of language as configuration can already be found in Adorno's early writings. In his inaugural lecture 'The Actuality of Philosophy', written in 1931, Adorno claims that 'history is no longer the site from which ideas arise, autonomously detach themselves, and then disappear'. It is on the basis of this claim that he introduces the concept of the 'historical image'. Historical images, he says, resemble 'ideas whose inter-connection constitutes truth without being intentionally directed at it; thus truth does not occur in history as something intended'.[93] There is no doubt Adorno is alluding here to the 'epistemo-critical preface' of Benjamin's work on the *Origin of German Tragic Drama*, which he cites elsewhere in his lecture. Benjamin defines truth as 'an intentionless being formed out of ideas': 'the comportment appropriate to truth is consequently not an intending in the process of knowing, but a willingness to enter into and disappear within it. Truth is the death of inten-tion.'[94] The ideas that constitute such truth appear to be 'eternal constellations', 'configurations' of the thingly elements of phenomena. Concepts are to serve the presentation of these ideas. If the 'historical images' of which Adorno speaks form a context and perhaps a constellation, then each one of them is also a context, a construction which allows the concepts and the 'isolated elements of reality' to enter into constellations. The image is not a 'mere given', and the context from which it arises, from which an image-like 'figure' emerges, is not an 'indifferent and ungraspable context that consists of nothing but discon-nected determinations of particular instances'. For, as Adorno emphasises in his lecture on 'The Idea of Natural History' from 1932, the constellation ensures that the 'moments' which evade thought are not simply considered 'in their pure there-ness' and then subsequently transformed into 'universal concepts'.

Adorno polemically stresses the artificial character of 'histori-cal images', the fact that they have been produced, in order to distinguish them from the archaic aspect of 'mythical arche-types': 'The historical images, which do not constitute the meaning of existence, but answer and also dissolve its questions ... do not already lie there organically in history. On the contrary: they must be brought forth by human beings and can

ultimately be justified only if a sudden and striking clarity
makes reality gather around them.'[95] Reality itself becomes an
image, and the image becomes reality. It is these constructed,
non-organic images, which Adorno calls 'models' and which
allow 'reason to approach reality tentatively and experimentally,
to approach a reality which does not surrender itself to a law'.
The model is capable of 'imitating' this reality if the model is
'properly shaped'. Does the constellation imitate what is for its
part an 'intentionless reality', a reality which is transformed into
a constellation through the imitation, and only then presents
itself as a constellation? How can the intentionless character of
the 'historical images' be reconciled with the intentional character of a shaping construction that makes them susceptible to
'imitation'? Does the 'sudden and striking clarity' result from
the 'death of intention' through which the 'historical images'
relate to truth, or are the models still intentional when they
function as 'magnetic centres' which seem 'objectively to attract
objective being'? Adorno does not provide unambiguous
answers to these questions, not even in *Negative Dialectics*: 'The
context established [by subjective production], that is, the
"constellation", can be read as a sign of objectivity or of the
spiritual content. What lets such constellations appear so similar
to writing is the way in which what has been subjectively
thought and gathered together suddenly reverts to objectivity
by virtue of language' (ND:167f.; ET:165). When a sudden
reversal happens, when it does so with a 'sudden and striking
clarity', what has been gathered together by thought can no
longer be something which has simply been 'gathered together'.
Thus all depends on what is meant by 'objectivity' and 'spiritual
content', therefore on how one reads the constellation and its
similarity with writing. It should be noted that Adorno
expressly conceives of this reversal in terms of language. But it
also seems that the more he insists upon the produced character
of the 'models', the less he is inclined to place language in the
foreground. Although it is true that at the end of 'The Actuality
of Philosophy' he briefly mentions the essay as form, the lecture
does not refer to language as the essence or site of the reversal.
It is instructive in this respect to consider the text called 'Theses
on the Language of Philosophers', which Adorno is thought to
have written in the early 1930s and which can thus be compared

directly with the two lectures under discussion here. That the reversal transpires 'by virtue of language' is not supposed to imply the reduction of language to an 'instrument', at least if we assume that the eighth thesis is a valid one and regard it as a claim about language in general: 'Over against the traditional words and a subjective intention that lacks language, configuration is a third element. But not a third element through mediation. For it is not as if the intention is objectified by means of language. Rather configurative language signifies a third element as a dialectically intensified unity of concept and thing which cannot be dissolved in explicative terms.'[96] Adorno does not explain why this unity cannot be dissolved through explication. He merely adds that this fact is responsible for 'the radical difficulty involved in all serious philosophical language'. Strictly speaking, language is not simply configurative because it organises its words in constellations, but because it is already, in itself, the movement which brings forth the 'unity of concept and thing' as something which 'cannot be dissolved in explicative terms', as an antithetical unity traversed by a disunity. The non-identical, which seeks to find a voice in thought and which is not oriented towards the primacy of identity, is the antithetical movement of language of which concept and name partake. This means that concept and name both divide language and are divided by it. Is not the 'death of intention', with which all 'intending in the process of knowing' expires, the moment of uttermost tension in which constellations come to a standstill and become 'determinate signs' and 'readable writing'?[97] It is in this moment that the gift of language is experienced, in a moment which belongs to an intentionless reading that does not read (anything), because it does nothing but read, nothing but read the unreadable that sustains and prevents reading. The unreadable is that which cannot be grasped with respect to a constellation, that which constitutes the essence of all readability. It is therefore not opposed to readability. To the extent that it is writing, a constellation mortifies intention.

Enigma and solution, question and answer

The task of philosophy, Adorno claims in the lecture on 'The Actuality of Philosophy', is to read the inevitably incomplete text of the world. Because being is essentially fractured within itself, the existent becomes an 'enigmatic figure' which demands interpretation. But the enigma entails a perilous blindness: 'The text which philosophy is called upon to read is incomplete, contradictory and fractured, and there is much in it that could be consigned to blind demonism. Perhaps it is our task to read in order that in reading we might learn to recognise and exorcise the demonic powers.'[98] Adorno thus identifies interpretative reading as a means of defence against 'blind demonism'. But if we are not supposed even to attempt the restitution of an essentially fractured existence, an essentially fractured text, if it is not the 'task of philosophy' to 'reveal or to justify reality as "meaningful"' since its fractured character forbids such justification in principle – what then does define the task? Adorno describes the demonic as blind. Or is it blindness that is demonic? In a later essay on 'The World of Images in Weber's *Freischütz*' Adorno connects blindness and the demonic with the downfall and ruin of life: 'Life as unconscious urge permanently overtakes itself: in its mighty leaps it already harbours its own downfall.'[99] Adorno had already traced this connection in an early piece on Schubert which dates from 1928. Just before mentioning the 'demonic function of the depths', Adorno writes: 'Following the emptily falling words, not their clarifying intention, the wanderer walks into the depths … Here nature is no longer the meaningful object of the inner human feeling for nature. The images of nature are rather the allegories of chthonic depth itself, as intrinsically inaccessible as the poetic word.'[100] Along with blindness, ruin and empty falling, the demonic is inseparable from the absence of intention. Is reading then directed towards an enigmatic intentionless reality which it duplicates in the act of interpretation? Is it essentially spiritual because it succours a reality which is so fractured that its intentionless character wreaks destruction? Does it create a bulwark against the throng of 'demonic powers'?

It is quite clear that the reading Adorno has in mind is not merely a constative act, the impartial duplication of a given text. This reading is rather a performative reading, one which brings forth what is read, constructing figures and images out of 'the isolated elements of reality' and allowing the concepts to enter into constellations. That is why the enigmas make their appearance: they arise only in the interpretation. Adorno finds himself driven towards this paradoxical thought because he denies any meaning to reality. If reading merely interpreted an already given 'enigmatic figure', and contented itself with duplicating it, this would inevitably result in justifying reality as 'meaningful' in the first place. The 'fractured character of being', a being which, since it cannot be 'meaningful', is not 'meaningless' either, and which is 'fractured' for this very reason, enforces the construction of an enigma that immediately consumes itself. Interpretation repudiates 'the assumption of a second world, a world beyond or behind this world, which would be disclosed by the analysis of the apparent world'.[101] It is impossible to overlook the allusion to Nietzsche in this passage. Adorno would like to break with a certain Platonism which 'was indeed first ascribed to Plato from a post-Kantian perspective':

> The interpreter who moves beyond the phenomenal world in order to find another world, one that would sustain and explain the former, one that would be the world in itself, acts like someone who searches the enigma for the reflection of a being that lies behind it and sustains it. But the function of a solution to an enigma is to dissolve the enigmatic figure by illuminating it in a flash, not to remain hidden behind it and to resemble it. Genuine philosophical interpretation does not identify a persistent meaning that already lies behind the question, but suddenly and momentarily illuminates the meaning even as it consumes it.

If 'enigmas are questions of a particular kind',[102] then Adorno may be justified in replacing the enigma with the question, even though he does not say why he uses both terms as synonymous. Philosophy as interpretation, as interpretative reading, deals with questions which do not precede the answers that can be given to them; the answers do not conceal themselves behind the questions as if they preceded the preceding questions. In his lecture 'The Actuality of Philosophy' Adorno thematizes the difference between scientific research and philosophical interpretation in terms of their respective relationship to question and answer. Perhaps the 'reduction of the question to given elements

that are known in advance', a reduction that supposedly characterises scientific research, is based upon the 'first/then' schema
which is rejected in *Negative Dialectics* as one inappropriate to
philosophy: 'In philosophy the authentic question almost always
includes its answer within itself. Unlike scientific research,
philosophy does not know the schema of first question, then
answer' (ND:71; ET:63). But the answer is neither given nor
produced. It neither lies behind the question, nor does it result
from an act of subjective positing. Such positing would represent a return to idealism or involve a radical perspectivism. But
the experience of an enigma is ultimately alien to both idealism
and perspectivism, since idealism always and already dissolves it,
and perspectivism totalises it. The answer must consume the
question, and the solution the enigma, for the meaning cannot
exist independently of the enigma and the question. It is in this
very consumption that question and answer, enigma and solution, become suddenly manifest and appear as if they were illuminated. Enigma and solution are not laid down in advance,
they possess no permanent shape. The solution is not a piece of
knowledge at one's disposal once the enigma has been
consumed, for this would again result in justification. The solution is an experience without knowledge: the enigma does not
resolve itself in knowledge. The enigma and the solution are
embedded in the movement of constellations and depend upon
its ungraspable and uncontrollable originality. This uncontrollability is constitutive of both the enigma and the solution. It is
only when the solution consumes the enigma that one can speak
of an enigma at all.

There must be a distance, however small, which separates
enigma and solution. The possibility of a chronological schema
of question and answer is therefore contained in the essence of
the enigma. If the chronological schema involves a mimetic
relationship, if the answer follows the question because it
conceals itself behind the latter and is its original and exemplary
image, an image whose reflected after-image must appear as the
question, then perhaps this 'first/then' schema is the condition of
a 'poetic word' which strives to sound the 'chthonic depths' that
are beyond the grasp of all intention. At the same time the
enigma only appears once the solution already consumes it and
disturbs the chronology. The consuming allows the movement

of constellation to stand still and is itself simultaneously recuperated by the constellation. Thus the experience of the enigma is unique only at the cost of its repetition. Every solution consumes the enigma, yet it also leaves it untouched; the enigma is no more capable of being an enigma when separated from the solution than it is when united with it. Hence the irreducible disparity: 'An enigma does not desire an answer in the sense of a solution that lends itself to an already prescribed path.'[103] As the experience of a moving constellation the consuming is the linguistic experience of the 'fracturedness of being'. It is the experience of language as language: namely as the self-withdrawing gift. The enigma, the mark of the solution which consumes it, already presupposes this experience, presupposes it as a forgotten experience; otherwise the construction of the enigma would be an arbitrary fabrication: 'Thinking which does not assert itself as origin ... reproduces what it already possesses; for thinking is an experience' (ND:71; ET:63). The path of the enigma leads from that forgotten and never appropriated presupposition to the experience of language in the consuming solution. Only if the experience of the gift of language or of language as language has been forgotten can there be a path and an enigma. To recall an observation from *Aesthetic Theory* concerning the work of art, one could say that the enigmatic character peers out differently from every constellation: 'as if the answer, like that of the Sphinx, were always the same, albeit only through the difference, and not through the unity which the enigma, perhaps deceptively, promises' (AT:193; ET:127).

Falling

Reading is dragged into a movement of falling because the appearance of a solution which consumes the enigma signifies the death of intention. Where the fall encounters no resistance, where the moving constellation is consigned to forgetfulness, reading finds itself given over to the demonic. The demonic perpetuates the falling of reading and precipitates its downfall. Adorno's reference to the unconscious urge of perpetually self-overtaking life is modelled on Schopenhauer. But the perpetuation of the vital urge can also, as Heidegger makes clear in his interpretation of Nietzsche, transpire as a 'schematisation of chaos': 'In the essence of the urge which surges forward beyond itself there lies something appropriate to it, that is, something itself urgent in character that urges *against* submitting to the surge, that urges a *standing* within the latter, if only in order to *be* urgeable at all, and to be capable of surging forward beyond *itself*.'[104]

The task of recognising and exorcising the demonic is the task of remaining within the moving constellation and not abandoning the non-identical. This task becomes apparent at the moment when reading starts falling and is transformed into an intentionless reading. There is such a task because the demonic cannot in principle be exorcised, because reading must fall. It is in the movement of falling, not in the act of fabricating, that the reader experiences 'the openness', that is to say, the meaning which, to the extent that it is fabricated, proves to be a mere 'fiction': 'That which might without humiliation claim the name of meaning is to be found in the domain of the open, not in the domain of what is closed upon itself' (ND:370; ET:377). One cannot simply appeal to meaning: life is not meaningful, nor is it without meaning. In *Negative Dialectics* Adorno counters every attempt to justify the meaningfulness of life and ignore the 'fracturedness of being': 'A meaningful life would not raise the question of meaning' (ND:369; ET:377). But Adorno also stresses that those who herald the 'abstract nihilism' which doubts all meaning have 'no answer to the counter-question: why do you yourself continue to live?' (ND:370; ET:377). Adorno thus uncovers the symmetry which exists between the two answers to the question concerning meaning. He does so by confronting the hypostasis of both meaning and meaninglessness with the heterogeneity of the question. One who raises the question of meaning has already lost meaning, is asking too much or too little. One can speak of meaning only where meaning has not rigidified and turned either into the positivity of meaningfulness or into the negativity of 'abstract nihilism'; one can speak of meaning only where question and answer remain in the openness of moving constellations and where the question which resists its destruction is formed in the destruction effected by the answer. 'The answer', as Adorno explicates in his inaugural lecture, 'stands in strict antithesis to the enigma; it

needs to be constructed from the enigmatic elements, and annihilates the enigma, which is not meaningful, but meaningless, as
soon as the devastating answer is given.'[105] The answer both is
and is not the meaning of the question. It is the meaning of the
question because the question calls for an answer, and does not
exist prior to the answer. But it is not the meaning of the question because the question does not include the answer within
itself 'as something intended', and because the answer annihilates
the question. If, in his lecture, Adorno occasionally substitutes
the concept of sublation for the notion of annihilation, then,
according to the antithetical 'logic' of his own argument, the
answer established by such a sublation of the question must be
sharply distinguished from the meaningfulness which can be
attributed to positive knowledge. The meaning of the answer is
not a form of knowledge that has secured its positivity or that
does so in a sudden reversal. Reading falls when the still
enfolded question is unfolded and rendered 'transparent', when
it has become so pressing a question that it already reverts into
the illuminating and annihilating answer. The question into the
answer 'in a flash'; it does not follow the rhythm of an organic
development, as the idea of a progressive unfolding might
suggest. The answer consumes the question without which it
would annihilate itself; it consumes the question which, as long
as it remains enfolded, is not a question yet.

The cunning of the name

In its antithetical relationship to the concept, the name marks
the death of intention. However, since it is too close to what it
names and therefore remains too distant from it to possess a
cognitive function, the name is also an instance of identity and
identification. As far as cognition is concerned it can be said
that the closer the bond between name and named proves to
be, the closer the name stands to the concept that severs that
bond. The name is thus by no means indivisible and is singular
only to the extent that it is also divided. This is nowhere more
vividly presented than in that section of *Dialectic of Enlightenment* where Adorno – after ratifying the ban on images and the
prohibition against naming the name – interprets the cunning
of the name:

The subject called Odysseus denies his own identity, which makes him a subject, and keeps himself alive by imitating the amorphous. He calls himself Nobody because Polyphemus is not a self, and the confusion of name and thing prevents the deluded savage from evading the ruse: his call for retribution remains, as such, magically bound to the name of the one on whom he would be avenged, and this name condemns the call to impotence. For by bestowing intention upon the name, Odysseus tries to withdraw it from the domain of magic. (DdA:86f.; ET:67–8)

The dissociation of the name makes cunning possible: it is the antithesis of thought which structurally involves the possibility of cunning. The cunning of the name is not simply a further instance of the cunning of Odysseus, one cunning amongst others. Rather it is the cunning of all cunning, an original cunning: 'The adaptation of *ratio* to its contrary, a state of consciousness in which no firm identity has as yet begun to crystallise ... perfects itself however in the cunning of the name' (DdA:86; ET:67). The name identical with the named is not the name of the subject identical with itself. Polyphemus confuses name (Odysseus) and intention (Nobody) since he is himself no subject: he is Nobody, that is, 'the amorphous' which the subject is compelled to imitate in order to secure its own identity. Polyphemus does not recognise Odysseus because in fact Odysseus fundamentally betrays the law of the dissociated name, the law of cunning. In bestowing intention upon the name and calling himself Nobody, Odysseus becomes invisible, and in this invisibility all the more visible: he objectively reminds the Cyclops that he himself is nobody, holds up to him his own mirror-image. The cunning consists in the fact that it makes itself known, but cannot be known by one who never recognises himself. For recognition presupposes the dissociation of the name. Only he who can lose his name, only he who can assume another name – the name of the other – finds himself in a position to appropriate his own name. Odysseus dissociates the name of Polyphemus by calling himself Nobody, by dissociating his own name. The enterprise is risky because it renders a first and sudden recognition possible.

Dissociation thus results as the bestowal of intention upon the

name. Once separated from the named, the name can identify
the latter and simultaneously turn upon itself in order to assert
itself through self-denial. But the name is also endangered by its
dissociation:

> He who calls himself Nobody for his own sake and manipu-
> lates adaptation to the state of nature as a means of mastering
> nature, falls victim to hubris. Yet the cunning Odysseus can
> do no other. In flight as he is, still exposed to the jurisdiction
> of the giant's flailing hands, he does not merely ridicule him,
> he also reveals his real name and origin; as if the primitive
> world still enjoyed so much power over the one who has
> just managed to escape from it, that after calling himself
> Nobody, he must, lest he become Nobody once again,
> restore his own identity by recourse to the magic word
> already dissociated from rational identity. (DdA:87; ET:68)

Insofar as there is a name which must be preserved before all
other names, insofar as the identity of the subject must continue
to cling to the magic of the name, this identity is already an
identity which has been shattered – which has been shattered by
intention. If the name were nothing but intention, were wholly
confirmed in this its conventional character, if the principle of
equivalence were unlimited, and every name the substitute for a
second, then no identity could ever be achieved. The total principle of equivalence, to which language is subjected, ends up
placing the magic name in the place of the disenchanted one:
'Terms themselves become impenetrable; they acquire a striking
force, a power of adhesion and repulsion, which makes them
resemble the absolute opposite: incantations ... The name as
such – to which magic most readily associates itself – is under-
going something of a chemical transformation: a metamorphosis
into arbitrary and manipulable designations, whose effect is now
admittedly calculable, but which for that very reason is just as
autonomous and despotic as that of the archaic name'
(DdA:188; ET:164–5). Intention, without which the identity of
the subject cannot even begin to form, does not guarantee that
identity. The name outlasts it: it persists as a name detached
from the intending subject. But the name which outlasts the
intention is, at the same time, the impenetrable, the not yet

dissociated name, the name of Polyphemus. This is why its form resembles the shape of the subject which cannot recognise itself in that shape: 'The Cyclops Polyphemus sports with his cartwheel-sized eye a trace of the same prehistoric world: the single eye recalls the nose and mouth, more primitive than the symmetry of eyes and ears which, as a unity of two sources of perception successfully combined, first effects identification, depth, objectivity in general' (DdA:83; ET:64).

Stupidity of the subject

Horkheimer and Adorno describe the blindness that is constitutive of the subject as stupidity. If cunning results from adaptation to the shape of the blind and stupid, to the 'amorphous' which presents itself to the cunning Odysseus in the shape of the Cyclops, then it must also relinquish this shape and confess itself as cunning. Otherwise the adaptation threatens to annihilate the cunning. The unnamed name must be named in the end. That is the blind spot of cunning, and its stupidity: the demonic which effects the subject's downfall.

In a footnote concerning their interpretation of the encounter with the Cyclops, whose thought process is described as 'lawless, unsystematic and rhapsodic', Horkheimer and Adorno appeal to Wilamowitz for whom the Cyclops are in fact animals (DdA:83; ET:64). It is thus hardly surprising that the authors of *Dialectic of Enlightenment* draw a connection between stupidity and animality in the short text on 'the genesis of stupidity' which concludes the book. The less developed a living being is, the more obviously it displays features of stupidity: for 'stupidity is a scar' (DdA:295; ET:257). Stupidity arises when body and intellect expose themselves, only to find themselves crippled by 'physical injury' and 'terror'. As Horkheimer and Adorno remark: 'The more developed animals owe their existence to this greater freedom; their mere presence proves that once their feelers groped out in new paths and were not withdrawn. Each of their species is a monument to the countless others whose attempts to develop were doomed in their beginnings.' In an analogous fashion, every thought is the announcement of a further thought that could not be thought after all. The concept which stumbles at the name, and the name which

stumbles at the concept, are blinded. Concept and name are
scars of thought. By virtue of its own essentially antithetical
structure thought constantly exposes itself to the danger of
becoming, like the frightened animal, 'timid, frightened and
dumb'. In man the scar of stupidity is called character. For does
not character generally presuppose a measure of inurement
without which it could never have developed in the first place?
Character is the result of a poverty of experience now transformed into a richness, is the frightened animal which has not
been permanently paralysed by its fear. It uses the expressions of
this fear as an occasion for finding another path, a path it does
not immediately have to retrace, out of fright, in the opposite
direction. Can we not ascribe the ban on images to these prohi-
bitions which leave behind them the scars out of which character is formed? 'And not only the forbidden question, but also
the scorned mimesis, the forbidden tears, the forbidden daring
and risk of play, can lead to such scars. Like the species of the
animal order, the mental stages within the human species, and
the blind spots within the human individual, represent the
stations at which hope was stilled. Their very petrifaction bears
witness to the fact that everything that lives lies under a spell'
(DdA:296; ET:258). The antithesis of thought itself harbours the
possibility of 'evil, defiance and fanaticism' to which character
remains originally related. For it owes its own firmness to those
'inconspicuous scars' that can lead to 'blindness and impotence'
as easily as they can lead to disaster, to rage, to the demonic. Is
not the demonic the blind movement of falling and ruin, at
least in Adorno's eyes? Thus it is not surprising that Horkheimer and Adorno find a certain 'reconciliatory' moment in the
conduct of Polyphemus: 'The behaviour of the giant has not
yet objectified itself and become a character' (DdA:85; ET:66).

Too much talk: fatefulness of enlightenment

The stupidity which is inseparable from the cunning subject
reveals itself in the dialectic of eloquence. Horkheimer and
Adorno describe this dialectic as follows:

> Speech, though it deceives physical force [as with Polyphe-
> mus], knows no restraint. Its flow is a parody accompanying

the stream of consciousness, thought itself, whose unswerving autonomy turns into foolishness and reveals its manic aspect. It does so when it enters reality in the form of discourse, as if thinking corresponded with reality. In fact, however, thought exercises power over reality only by virtue of distance. But this distance is also the experience of suffering. That is why the clever one, contrary to proverbial wisdom, is always tempted to speak too much. He is objectively conditioned by the fear that if he does not unfailingly affirm the powerless superiority of the word over force, that superiority will once again be wrested from him by force. For the word knows that it is weaker than the nature it has deceived. Too much talk allows force and injustice to prevail as the actual principle, and therefore invariably prompts those who are feared to commit the very deed that is feared. The mythic compulsion of the word in prehistory is perpetuated in the disaster which the enlightened word draws down upon itself. (DdA:87f.; ET:68–9)

He who is tempted to speak too much is tempted to find an elliptical conclusion to his speech, one that would open it up to what it circumscribes, without ever succeeding in doing so.[106] There can be no enlightened spirit who fails to provoke the charge of obscurantism, and provoke it all the more violently the more beholden to enlightenment this spirit knows itself to be. Any consistent enlightenment finds itself entangled in that guilt of concept and of name that it seeks to reveal for what it is. Enlightenment falls victim to the name and the concept, to the enlightenment which takes up with the concept, to the counter-enlightenment which isolates the name. Just as on the one hand the name which is inscribed in the unsublatable antithesis of thought reveals itself to be the magnet which both repels and fruitlessly attracts the concept, so on the other hand the concept proves to be the pole which the name must reach but may not touch, if it is to be made accessible to experience at all. For the coincidence of the name and the named does not represent a liberation from a mythic past that perpetuates itself in conceptual identification; it also represents 'the mythic compulsion of the word'. Enlightenment can never fully conceptualise the double movement of concept and name which challenges it and procures its right to existence. It can never call this movement by its proper name. Hence the dialectic of enlightenment is called forth by the antithesis of thought. Perhaps it is misleading to describe the movement of concept and name as 'antithetical', since it severs the unity of the two opposed and mutually attracting poles of thought and thereby destroys any position or opposition that would present itself as final. This does not mean that thought can now pass over into an essentially dialectical result. The dialectic of enlightenment does not exhibit the form of a result, and negativity itself is not simply the result of this dialectic. Thus the 'foolishness' of thinking calls forth the force of the 'feared deed', but it equally calls forth laughter: and how should it represent 'foolishness' otherwise? Horkheimer and Adorno reveal a link between laughter and names; to recognise this link means to become aware of the double sense and ambiguity of both laughter and names. The ambiguity of the name consists in its possessing the violent power of identification, but it also grants the possibility of acquiring self-understanding. Such understanding can be acquired through the act of naming which as an 'original act' is inseparable from the 'gift of language', at least according to Benjamin:

> Even though laughter is still the sign of violence, of escape from blind and obdurate nature, it also contains the opposite element. It is through laughter that blind nature can become aware of itself, and thereby renounces its destructive violence. This double-sense of laughter resembles that of the name, and perhaps names are nothing but frozen laughter, as is obvious today in the case of nicknames – the only ones that still bear something of the original act of naming. Laughter is marked by the guilt of subjectivity, but in the suspension of rights and statutes which it denotes and announces, laughter also points beyond its entanglement with guilt. (DdA:96f.; ET:76–7)

The task of thinking is to liberate the laughter petrified in the names.

Mimesis

The Jew personifies the very type of the crafty individual who owes his cunning to eloquence. Hence the Jew can also be recognised in Odysseus who calls himself *udeis* or 'nobody' and therefore has to speak too much. The Greek 'already bears the features of the Jew who when gripped by the fear of death still insists on a superiority which derives from his fear of death. The revenge upon the middleman transpires not only at the end of bourgeois society, but also at its inception: it is the negative utopia towards which violent force always tends' (DdA:88; ET:69). The middleman functions as the Jew who invites violence upon himself through his eloquence. The Jews have been so long caught up within the sphere of circulation that 'they could not avoid mirroring in their being the hatred which they had borne from time immemorial' (DdA:198f.; ET:174). Violence directs itself against eloquence, against enlightenment, not only in a bourgeois and capitalist society but generally. The Jew is the type which arises from the indissoluble entanglement of enlightenment and violence. Violence as violence against the word has its origin in thought – in its antithesis. This origin has taken on shape in the Jew. Thus whoever thinks ineluctably becomes a Jew and an agent of enlightenment who fears destruction and insists upon the superiority of enlightenment and its project.

Speech and discourse as parody of thought escape the 'domination of the subject' which nonetheless needs them in order to assert itself as subject. They thereby come to represent something to which idiosyncrasy can attach itself. The function of idiosyncrasy is explored by Horkheimer and Adorno in the chapter entitled 'Elements of Anti-Semitism'. The two authors perceive the essence of idiosyncrasy as an experience of something that lies outside the dominant control of the subject. It is a question of nature: insofar as individual organs respond to 'biologically fundamental stimuli' and thereby reveal their independence, they remind the subject that it is not wholly in control of the nature within itself. The subject reacts idiosyncratically because its power to control is threatened. And not merely by inner nature, but by outer nature as well. For the organs which cannot be directly controlled by the subject 'accomplish its adaptation to the immobile natural surroundings' (DdA:204; ET:180). The moments of such adaptation are 'moments of biological prehistory' which constantly return; for instance, when we perceive 'signs of danger at whose sound the hair once stood on end and the heart once froze'.[107] Terror thus becomes the paradigm of idiosyncrasy. Idiosyncrasy is the repulsion arising from the terror that substantiates the subject's experience of destitution. But the subject also constitutes itself in the moment of its destitution, in the ever-returning moment of its adaptation to that which seems to threaten its survival. Petrifaction, the reaction of 'reflectory mimesis', is an 'archaic schema of self-preservation'.

What *Dialectic of Enlightenment* describes by the name of 'nature' stands metonymically for the relationship to otherness. The reconciliation which 'the remembrance of nature in the subject' (DdA:58; ET:40) is supposed to effect, must be thought in conjunction with the ban on images and the prohibition against uttering the name of the other. Is the act of naming already a transgression, or does the name not rather designate the transcendence of the named? There can be no simple answer to this question. The ban on images is itself an instrument of domination (DdA:205; ET:180–1). As a prohibition it inevitably prejudges the relationship to the other and offers itself up to an alien and heteronomous purpose. And yet 'the remembrance of nature in the subject' can only be properly accomplished through the 'faithful fulfilment' which respects the ban on images. For if it stood within the power of the subject alone to expiate its guilt through its own resources, the idea of guilt, the 'guilt of thought' which calls for the self-reflection of enlightenment, would have no meaning, and the subject could never experience itself as guilty.

One cannot clearly distinguish between openness and reduction in the experience of the other. The opening to the other is already a reduction of its otherness. Thus Horkheimer and Adorno emphasise that the adaptation to 'immobile natural surroundings' or to what is 'dead' also involves the subject's inurement to nature: 'Just like Daphne, living beings strive to transform themselves into immobile nature when they attain the very highest state of excitement. But immobile nature permits only the most external relations, those which characterise space' (DdA:205; ET:180). Yet no relation to otherness would be possible without that terror which sets the mechanism of 'reflectory mimesis' in motion and leads to the sacrifice of otherness. In the moment of the original experience of otherness there can be no question of establishing an alternative between a 'reflectory mimesis' and an 'organic melding with the other'. In the moment of constituting destitution and destituting constitution – of *de-constitution* – there is no 'authentic mimetic relationship' that could be opposed to an inauthentic or 'reflectory mimesis'. Opening and reduction form no abstract relation of mutual opposition here. The otherness of the other implies the possibility of terror. If the God of the Jews intensifies 'the terror of the incommensurable', is his name then just another 'name' of the other, or is it, as a name which should never be pronounced, the name itself? Is it the Jews who experience the terror of the other in the most penetrating fashion of all? Can the ban on names and images be detached from its Jewish origin? Adorno confirms the hypothesis that terror belongs to the structure of otherness when he claims that every work of art is a 'manifestation of otherness' which repeats the 'shudder of prehistorical times' (AT:123f.; ET:79f.). In *Dialectic of Enlightenment* guilt is traced back to terror as the original experience of the other: 'The constellation within which equality is produced, the immediate equality of mimesis and the mediated one of synthesis, the equality resulting from an adaptation to objects in the blind process of life and the one resulting from a reifying act of comparison in the scientific process of concept-formation, remains the constellation of terror' (DdA:205; ET:181). The principle of equivalence is irreducible, if not absolute: for indeed the reduction of otherness is simultaneously an opening to the other. This opening can, in turn, bear the features of reduction, indeed always bears them if opening and reduction cannot be clearly distinguished. The features of reduction are particularly striking where the rationalisation of idiosyncrasy produces the 'authoritarian relinquishment of the forbidden' and permits the imitation of what incites revulsion. It thus appears that idiosyncrasy – which derives from the de-constitution of the subject, from its 'logic of disintegration' – is not wholly withdrawn from the domain of subjective intervention and manipulation. It can be rationalised and thus facilitate the repetition of the mimetic act which underlies it. 'The imitation of what he calls a Jew is in the blood of the anti-semite' (DdA:208; ET:184). Horkheimer and Adorno provide several examples of 'mimetic symptoms' of anti-Semitism, like the 'argumentative gesturing with the hands' and the 'singing tone of voice which paints a vivid picture of object and affect independently of the capacity for conceptual judgement'. The 'singing tone of voice' recalls the movement through which speech and discourse detach themselves and become independent. For a discourse which has thus detached itself and assumed independence relates to thinking – to 'the capacity for conceptual judgement' – as does the relatively independent organ to the body in general. In his *Essay on Wagner* Adorno stresses how the 'uninhibited volubility' of the composer, which could be 'reconstructed on the basis of his prose writings if it had not already been as clearly reported as his equally exaggerated gestures',[108] reflects the law of anti-Semitism as idiosyncrasy. For such idiosyncrasy announces itself precisely through the process of mimetic repetition.

Speech detaches itself and becomes independent because it is incapable of bridging a gulf which it could only ever bridge at the cost of its own relinquishment. It becomes independent not only in relation to its object, but also and above all in relation to itself. Idiosyncrasy clings to a discourse which has become independent all the more so the more it parodies the thinking on which the identity of the subject and its domination over nature depend. Never is the subject more acutely aware of its own loss of control than at the moment when discourse becomes independent. This is why idiosyncrasy here immediately represents its own rationalisation, the process through which the de-constituted subject exposes itself to the uncontrollable in order simultaneously to regulate it. The protagonist of enlightenment is a Jew and a persecutor: as a Jew he persecutes himself, exacts upon himself what he struggles against.

Constructing the totality

From a structural point of view, the originary de-constitution corresponds to the unsublatable antithesis of thought. Reflectory mimesis serves the cause of self-preservation: the self-preserving subject identifies the other by virtue of its own adaptation to otherness – to nature. It adapts itself to its immobile natural surroundings or to that which moves and cannot be controlled, as the cunning manipulation of reflectory mimesis reveals. The names which identify mythic space bear witness to 'the shudder of prehistoric times'. There is no name that would be free of such a shuddering. The concept presupposes the capacity for identification which differentiates itself as 'reflectory mimesis' and as cunning. The concept identifies the other, opens itself up to it and reduces it at the same time. This opening, this adaptation which precedes the possibility of comparing anything and without which the concept could never identify the other, exposes it to the name. Released from its relation to the concept, the name is just as blind as Polyphemus and presents itself as an index of something prior to all identification. It is for this reason that 'rationality cannot be *less* than self-preservation', and that it cannot transcend self-preservation other than 'through self-preservation'.[109] Thinking itself is only conceivable as de-constitution. This is the guilt of thought: 'It can be said of philosophy, of theoretical thought in general, that it suffers from an idealist pre-conception insofar as it only has concepts at its disposal. It is only through concepts that thinking deals with what is to be thought, while never possessing it. Its Sisyphan labour lies in this: to reflect on, and where possible to correct, the untruth and the guilt whose burden it thereby incurs' (AT:382; ET:258).[110] Such reflection leads to the insight that the concept does not simply preclude access to the non-identical, since the non-identical consists in the movement provoked by the concept and the name, in the movement of constellations.

If guilt cannot be represented as a decline from the origin, since it is as original as the originary de-constitution, then history must inevitably become an extension of the mythic context of guilt already instituted by the principle of equivalence. The originary de-constitution turns myth and history into a context of guilt. Fate cannot be averted: it is indeed given along with the domination of nature. As something 'construable', as positive totality, history reveals itself not as 'what is good' but rather as 'horror' (DdA:255; ET:225). Adorno takes up this thought from *Dialectic of Enlightenment* in

Negative Dialectics. He retains the idea of constructing a totality. But the totality to be constructed is a negative one: 'Universal history is to be construed and denied. After the catastrophes experienced and in view of future ones it would be cynical to assert that some world-plan towards the better manifests itself in history and constitutes its unified significance. But that is no reason to deny the unity which hammers the discontinuous, chaotically splintered moments and phases of history together, namely the unity of natural domination, advancing in its control over human beings, and finally over inner nature as well' (ND:314; ET:320). Adorno has given a name to history: to a history which proves to be the path of a world-spirit that forever perpetuates catastrophe. This name is 'Auschwitz'. Auschwitz designates a realm 'from which even today there emanates such horror that one hesitates to name it'.[111] But if 'Auschwitz has irrefutably demonstrated the failure of culture' (ND:359; ET:366), if in Auschwitz a 'radically guilty' culture has revealed itself as barbarism, if Auschwitz has rendered the principle of equivalence absolute and if genocide must henceforth be regarded as an 'absolute integration which announces itself wherever human beings are radically assimilated to each other' and 'literally eliminated because they differ from the concept of their total insignificance' (ND:355; ET:362) — then Auschwitz is the name which retrospectively institutes the negative unity of history, which first and still makes possible the construction of a universal history of negativity. A construction which does not conceal or reduce this negativity is possible only where the dialectic of enlightenment reached its end-point. At the same time, though, its possibility also depends on a catastrophic past which is yet to come, and on the fact that 'the unspeakable' remains unspoken — 'the unspeakable which, if world-historical standards are applied, culminated in Auschwitz'.[112] Auschwitz is unique, but it is also the 'first specimen' of a teleological tendency which is driving towards the destruction of the non-identical (ND:355; ET:362). The logic of Adorno's arguments here permits a paradoxical conclusion. The name 'Auschwitz', which has a metonymic function, is the name of an event that has — always already — happened and nonetheless has yet to happen. The dreams of 'the spared survivor' reveal something about precisely this disquieting impossibility of distinguishing the event, an impossibility which bestows significance upon the event and simultaneously deprives it of significance. 'The survivor requires a coldness which is the fundamental principle of bourgeois subjectivity and without which Auschwitz would never have been possible. This is the drastic guilt of the spared survivor. In retribution he is haunted by dreams like the one in which he learns he is no longer alive because he was gassed in 1940: his entire subsequent existence appeared to be merely imaginary, an expression of the deluded wish of one murdered twenty years before' (ND:355f.; ET:363). To the extent that 'Auschwitz' is a metonymically employed name – the name of the world-spirit – all those who survive are 'spared ones'. The death of death which, according to Adorno, transpired at Auschwitz and robbed experience – the experience of consciousness – of its identity, corresponds to a life that has forfeited its referential character, a life that can no longer be distinguished from death or dream and wish, a life that is no longer aware of itself or that is no longer the life of a conscious subject.[113]

If the construction of a negative totality of history requires us to think the final event as an event that is yet to come, it also compels us to represent the inaugurating event as a contingent one – as an event that never happened, at least according to the kind of necessity which is demanded by a 'philosophy of history'. Thus Adorno says that the 'dawning catastrophe' – the catastrophe of all catastrophes, the catastrophe which perpetuates its own permanence – calls for 'the hypothesis of an irrational catastrophe in the very beginning' (ND:317; ET:323). The criteria are those of rationality. The 'dawning catastrophe' is ultimately itself a contingent one: only if it could have transpired otherwise, can it still be different one day, but only if it can be different one day, could it have transpired otherwise before. Adorno writes: 'The vanished possibility that things might be otherwise has today contracted into that of averting the catastrophe in spite of everything.' The originary de-constitution is an originary de-construction. We can descry the possibility of the catastrophe in the originary de-constitution (it could always have happened this way, it has always happened this way), but not its pure necessity, destructive of all possibilities (it could *only* have happened this way, it *only* happened this way). Hence the origin is never intact and can never be distinguished in its purity from pure catastrophe: 'The goal is not to return to the origin, to the phantom of an essentially benign nature. For what may be called an origin belongs to the goal and constitutes itself only once the goal has been reached. There is no origin beyond the life of the ephemeral' (ND:158; ET:155–6). The goal itself is no necessary goal, but solely a possible one.

Following Adorno and taking the antithesis of thought as a point of departure, the naming of history can be characterised as an act of privileging. The name would wish the concept to be forgotten. But not only is the name inscribed in an antithetical movement which forces it to expose itself and give itself away to the concept; not only must the event which receives the name of Auschwitz submit itself to a systematic and scientific analysis, to historical, sociological and psychoanalytic research, to economic studies and linguistic investigations. The concept itself also divides the name, thus opening up the possibility of other namings, of other names, of other names for other events and of other names for the other in the event.

The new barbarism

In this intermediate realm of a catastrophe both past and future, self-preservation cannot but serve the averting of the catastrophe. Hence 'the vanished possibility that things might be otherwise', vanished not merely because the 'practical transition' failed, but because after this failure Auschwitz took place, remains bound up with the guilt of a spectral self-preservation: 'The guilty urge for self-preservation has survived, perhaps has even strengthened itself through the constant presence of threat. But self-preservation must fear lest the life to which it clings transform itself into that which terrifies it, into a spectre, a fragment of the world of spirits which conscious awareness recognises as non-existent' (ND:357; ET:364). In the sketch for a 'theory of ghosts' appended to *Dialectic of Enlightenment*, Horkheimer and Adorno speak about a 'proper relationship to the dead', about the relationship which such 'conscious awareness' has to the deceased. This relationship is supposed to be based upon an undiminished awareness of the 'horror provoked by the prospect of annihilation' (DdA:243; ET:215). But if one has already died, if the annihilation belongs both to the past and the future, one can never become sufficiently aware of the horror. For the ghost there is no 'proper relationship to the dead' because it has no consciousness. Philosophy itself becomes a ghost, although not because thought is characterised by that distance which removes it from what it would grasp. Rather it appears as a ghost precisely where truth is no longer the truth of speculative thinking, where thought must dispense with the edifying and elevating 'promise of its truth' (ND:357; ET:364). The definitive and conclusive character of the event possesses such overpowering evidence that, in the very moment the essential is 'unveiled', the 'most trivial and superficial interpretations' can prove to be more convincing than those 'which attempt to penetrate the essence'. There is no event in the emphatic sense that would not bring barbarism with it: the 'impoverishment of experience' and the 'new barbarism', of which Benjamin spoke after the First World War,[114] are the signs of any and every event. After Auschwitz even the barbarism is still too weak; for if a certain 'elevation' is already implicit in self-preservation as such, then it is precisely 'the most trivial and superficial interpretations' which are lost to those who have survived – to the barbarians.

Those who live after Auschwitz turn into ghosts because life rests upon a preliminary decision, an 'idealist preconception' which it can never recuperate. This raises the question of how it is possible to write about Auschwitz – after Auschwitz. In the foreword to the 'critical models' included in the collection entitled *Catchwords*, Adorno writes that language fails whenever one tries to 'write properly' about Auschwitz.[115] Anyone who writes about Auschwitz, anyone who writes after Auschwitz, must renounce linguistic 'differentiation'. But this renunciation is required in the name of 'differentiation' itself, in the name of the 'impulses' of difference. Adorno warns of the danger involved in such renunciation, warns of the 'universal regression' which it endorses. Does this mean that what must be renounced can only be granted to the one who renounces, who runs the risk of falling prey to this tendency towards 'universal regression'?

Writing after Auschwitz

In the third part of *Minima Moralia*, written between 1946 and 1947, Adorno investigates 'the decay of nuance'. This decay can be halted only if one renounces the attempt to halt it:

> The consequence to be drawn from the decay of nuance is not to cling obstinately to the decaying nuances. It would also be wrong to extirpate them altogether. Rather one should outdo the nuances by writing in an even more nuanced way and by pushing them to the limit where a reversal takes place, where they lose their subjective shading and become the pure and specific determination of an object. The writer must ensure that the word expresses nothing but the object it refers to, and that it does so without sidelong glances. He must combine the tightest control over the word with a patient effort to check every single expression, to tap at its surface and to listen to language itself in order to find out which words are still meaningful.[116]

This detection, this speleological hearkening, intensifies control, but is not identical with it; for the attempt to listen to language is combined here with the control over what a word means. Language itself speaks, as it were, and communicates itself to the writer who listens to the words. An experience of language, however historically mediated it may be, is thus the condition for acquiring control over language. That which proves to be linguistically meaningless cannot refer to an object, cannot purely define it. But it is impossible to control the condition which allows for language to be controlled. Otherwise the hearkening to language would simply coincide with the control over it. If, as Adorno demands in the foreword to *Catchwords*, control itself is to be renounced in the name of control and of a 'differentiation' which arises only from control, it would seem that the linguistic experience of the one who, after Auschwitz, writes about Auschwitz is the experience of a dialectic of renunciation, the experience of an exaggeration and of an outdoing which permits the appropriation of what has been exaggerated and outdone. Were this the case, were the renunciation in question to effect an intensification, then life could

finally be reconciled once more with life. The name of Auschwitz would designate a moment belonging to a dialectical
movement. However, the demand to renounce 'differentiation'
and control, in the name of both, can be interpreted in various
ways: (1) we must renounce 'differentiation' because it is no
longer possible to differentiate – and that is the only possibility
of saving difference; (2) we must violate the rule of 'writing
properly' and outdo difference all the more, the less one can
differentiate: it is only such outdoing, itself a symptom of
'regression', that can save difference. No attempt at dialectical
mediation will secure the transition from renunciation or
outdoing to difference, if indeed the name 'Auschwitz' imposes
the demand for renunciation and outdoing. For this name
means nothing that could be meant – nothing that could be
made present, and nothing of which one could become aware:
'The guilt of a life which as a pure fact already deprives other
life of life can no longer be reconciled with life at all. Statistics
supplement an overwhelming number of murdered victims
with the minimal number of individuals saved, as if the calculus
of probability had been applied. Such guilt reproduces itself
without cease because it can never be wholly presented to
consciousness at any one moment. This and only this drives us
to philosophy' (ND:357; ET:364).[117] Philosophical thought finds
its very definition, one that defies all definition, in a guilt
which permits no representation and therefore no expiation
either. But would a represented guilt, a guilt made present to
consciousness, indeed be expiated? Does not guilt remain ever
incommensurable?[118]

Jaspers on the question of guilt

In 1945 Karl Jaspers speaks of the guilt of the German people,
or rather: lets the German people speak of their guilt. 'That we
are alive makes us guilty', he says. The remark occurs in his text
'On the Question of Guilt', an essay that arose 'from a series of
lectures concerning the spiritual situation in Germany'.[119] Every
German is guilty 'in some fashion or other', for every German,
'who really is a German', or who exists 'in an authentic
manner', proves to be 'the German people'. The German and
the German people share the same name for Jaspers. How does

he explain the possibility that the Germans could become guilty without simply burdening them with a collective guilt? 'What broke out in Germany was a crisis of the spirit, a crisis of faith, that was already at work in the Western world as a whole.'[120] The idea of spirit here defines the guilt of the Germans because it defines their essence, and that means the essence of the German language: 'Thus the German, that is the German-speaking human being, feels intrinsically affected by everything which arises for the German. It is not one's liability as a citizen, but the fact of being intrinsically affected that creates the basis for an intangible guilt which is somehow analogous to a shared responsibility. One is intrinsically affected as a human being who belongs to German spiritual and cultural life, who shares the same language, the same origin and the same fate.'[121] The less tangible the guilt and the less 'objectifiable' the responsibility, the more deeply they penetrate the essence of the Germans and their life, the linguistic spirit which constitutes that essence or their 'life in the mother-tongue'. Of course, the fact that the crisis of spirit has affected Germany in a way unmatched by any other country is not supposed to reduce the guilt of the Germans themselves. But Germany does thereby come to present an 'instructive' example 'to the others'. The Germans must lay particular emphasis upon their relationship to other countries and states: 'How Germany stands in the world, what it is that occurs in the world, the way in which others relate to Germany, these questions are all more relevant to Germany insofar as it is characterised by an unprotected geographical location. Because of its location in the middle, or in the centre, it is much more exposed to the effects of world events than other countries.' Germany is unprotected not only because it is centrally located, that is, on the grounds of its external borders, but also because of its own inner inconstancy. It has been unable to form a 'spiritual centre wherein all Germans could meet'. There has never been a 'permanently valid focus' of life. Within Germany 'dominion, though sometimes exercised by Germans, has always basically consisted in foreigners dominating the people'. Germany has found itself condemned to impotence on account of its 'fragmented' character: 'Our classical literature and philosophy has yet to become a possession of the entire people, still belonging as it does to a small cultural elite.

This elite did indeed reach out beyond the political borders of Germany but it did not reach further than those places where the German language was spoken. And there is not even agreement here as to what deserves to be recognised for its greatness.'[122] The fragmentation and dissemination may certainly have helped the German spirit to gain recognition amongst German-speaking circles abroad (do these circles 'lead a life' within the mother-tongue?); yet the very openness of Germany 'on all sides' has also prevented 'the recognition of greatness'. The 'greatness' of the German heritage has enjoyed a purely particular life both inside and outside of Germany. And where the spirit which is the essence of the German people does allow certain 'transient centres of interest' to arise, it is still incapable of commanding any shared recognition of its greatness. This is why 'a single irresponsible leader' has been able 'to destroy Germany and the state politically for ever'. It would be a misunderstanding, however, to assume that Jaspers is attempting to derive the 'absolute necessity' of the outbreak of a spiritual crisis on the basis of geographical conditions. For Jaspers also rejects all recourse to the idea of some 'naturally given character of a people' as a vain attempt to find refuge in an *asylum ignorantiae* and as an easy means of 'sustaining false values, whether they be expressions of elevation or disparagement'.[123] Since the Germans know 'almost nothing' about their 'naturally given character', they can only presume that 'the naturally given basis of [their] vital existence harbours something that exercises certain effects that penetrate the highest spheres of spirit'. Thus, when rejecting the hypostasis of the 'character of a people', Jaspers does not reject the possibility of there being such a character. He mentions geographical location and the naturally given character of the people in relation to spirit. Location and character are not factors that could be considered as the causes of a crisis which 'has seized hold of the entire Western world'. At most they contribute to the releasing of this crisis in Germany.

The crisis of spirit

How then does Jaspers describe this crisis of spirit in the overall world-historical context?

The declining power of the Christian and biblical faith in general; the loss of faith that seeks for substitutes; the social transformation provoked by technology and particular methods of labour which lead ineluctably to socialistic structures, to structures do justice to the masses and which allow everyone to live a truly human life – these changes are all underway. Everywhere conditions are more or less such that people are saying: things must be different. In this situation those who are most profoundly affected, those who are most acutely aware of their dissatisfaction, tend to appeal to premature, overhasty, deceptive and deluding solutions.[124]

The 'crisis of spirit' has almost brought about 'the complete destruction of the German essence'.[125] It is true that this is a universal crisis of the West. But if the geographical conditions and the 'naturally given character of a people' have to be grasped according to their spiritual significance, then there must be something within the German heritage that threatens it: 'within our heritage as a people' there is 'something powerful and threatening that constitutes our ethical corruption'.[126] The Germans are 'the most heavily affected' people. They must assume the 'guilt of their fathers' because their own spiritual essence, their language, already harbours within itself the possibility of turning upon itself, of turning upon its own greatness. Put differently: the spirit of the Germans is an essentially guilty spirit. Jaspers does not actually draw this conclusion, but it is implied in his line of argument. He says nothing about the guilt in question here: it resists subsumption under any of the four concepts of guilt which serve him as the guiding thread of his analysis. Even 'metaphysical guilt' must be distinguished from the guilt of the German spirit. Jaspers defines it as follows: 'The fact that I am still living, when such things have happened, lies upon me as an inexpungible guilt.'[127] This 'metaphysical guilt' – which is neither criminal or political nor moral – remains bound to the idea of a responsibility which is grounded in 'the solidarity between human beings as human beings'. It does not refer to conscience, or to the 'communication with friend and neighbour' to which 'moral guilt' refers, but rather to 'God alone'. One must not confuse the shared responsibility towards the other human being, a responsibility which justifies itself in the face of God, with the shared responsibility towards the other German. The moment that guilt essentially belongs to the German spirit, to 'the spiritual conditions of German life', and does not merely specify the guilt of the human being as such, the shared German responsibility proves to be more than just a specification of universal responsibility.

The 'crisis of spirit' has not completely destroyed 'the German essence' because this essence resists its destruction. And it does so for reasons which are not simply empirical. 'Being German' is not an 'invariant component' of one's existence but a 'task'. In my relationship to foreigners (Jaspers names the Jews, the Dutch and the English in a single breath) 'the fact of being German, and that means essentially the fact of living within the mother-tongue, is something so persistent that I feel a shared responsibility for what Germans do and have done, in a way that cannot be grasped rationally and that must even be refuted from a rational point of view'. The distinctiveness of 'being German' lies in this rational refutation through knowledge: from the perspective of knowledge there is no guilty German spirit. Spirit and knowledge are not synonymous. Spirit institutes a closeness which cannot be known. It calls upon the Germans of future generations and reveals to them the being that they both are and are not – the being that they have to assume as a task: 'I feel myself closer to those Germans who also feel this way – without wishing to derive any false pathos from the fact – and feel myself more remote from those whose minds would seem to deny this connection. And this closeness signifies, above all, the shared and exhilarating task not to be German as one is German now. We should become German, be German in a way we are not yet German, listen to the call of our great predecessors and disregard the history of national idols.' The call and the task of spirit, then, precede knowledge. Those who do not sojourn in this spiritual closeness, in this aurora, those who would seek knowledge and transform the 'fact' of 'being German' into an 'invariant component', deny the 'German essence'. Was it not the intention of those most heavily affected by the 'crisis of spirit' to take upon themselves the task of actually becoming the German people? Are not the consequences arising from collective guilt, which no philosopher can ultimately account for, marked by the same formal status as those 'deluding solutions' that have entangled the German people in such guilt? Does not the source of this fatal feature lie in the fact that Jaspers defines the German spirit as intrinsically critical and vertiginous in character?

A telling historical sign

The Germans who live in accordance with their essence when they live 'within the mother-tongue', come into their own when they lose their language. This loss is a sign that they truly live within the mother tongue:

> Because we feel the collective guilt, we also feel the enormous task of renewing human existing from out of its origin – the task which all human beings on this earth share together, though it manifests itself more urgently, and more feelingly, there where a people that has become guilty stands before nothingness. This task is decisive since it concerns being itself. It would seem that as a philosopher I have now abandoned myself wholly to the realm of feeling, that I have forfeited conceptual understanding. And in fact language comes to an end here; we can only recall negatively that our distinctions must not become a resting place for thought, even if we deem them to be true and cannot therefore repudiate them.[128]

Since the philosopher locates the crisis of spirit in the spirit of the German people itself in order to provide some response to the question of guilt, he cannot avoid transforming this guilt into a privilege, into the privilege of 'the eternal essence of our soul'. This transformation takes place in spite of all the disclaimers and independently of the goal which represents the task the German people is supposed to fulfil. The German people reveals itself as privileged insofar as it undergoes the experience of nothingness – an argument which cannot but trigger its own reversal. The privilege rests ultimately upon the experience of being: 'The weakest being of all finds its only support in the world as a whole. Confronted by nothingness, it reaches out for the origin, for the all-encompassing. That is why the extraordinary significance of this anticipation [of the world-order] manifests itself precisely to the German. Our own future in the world is conditioned by the world-order which is not yet established in Nürnberg, but to which Nürnberg points as a sign.'[129] For the Germans, their guilt represents the kind of intimating or telling historical sign that Kant speaks about in *The Conflict of Faculties*.[130] Irrespective of all the different effects which it causes, a great historical event also calls our attention to a 'tendency on the part of the human race as a whole, that is, not considered in terms of individuals alone'. This is something that can be grasped from the 'enthusiasm' which the event produces amongst the spectators who do no more than 'wishfully' participate in what is taking place. The philosopher Jaspers who cannot as such participate directly in the event is thus the figure which allows the Germans to become spectators and witnesses of their own event. Doubtless it is hardly a positive enthusiasm that is at stake here. But if an 'extraordinary significance' can indeed be connected with the name of Nürnberg, then 'the idea of an affectively perceived Good' remains fundamentally intact, even if the affect in question is a divided one. From Jaspers's perspective the terrible ambivalence of German guilt is capable of deciding the character of the 'world-order'. The guilt thus acquires a significance which can never be grasped unambiguously:

> The essential question is whether the Nürnberg trial becomes a link in a sequence of meaningful and constructive political acts, however often these may be thwarted by error, irrationality, heartlessness and hatred – or whether, through the standard here applied to humanity as a whole, the powers which created this standard are themselves rejected in the end. The powers which have instituted Nürnberg show that what they have in common is the wish to form a world-government, for they submit themselves to the world-order. They show that, having proved victorious, they now really want to assume responsibility for humanity, and not merely for their own states. Such evidence must not be false'[131]

Just as Kant separates the event of the French Revolution both from its success and from the 'wretchedness' and 'acts of violence' which accompany it, so Jaspers would not see the chain of sense disrupted, would see rather the purity of evidence maintained.

But what of those distinctions which reveal the fundamental impossibility of such an undertaking? Do they contribute to that 'fraying of the concept of guilt' which conceals 'the origin and the unity' in order to liberate us from guilt?[132]

The question of guilt as an introduction to metaphysics

Hugo Ott reports that Jaspers sent Heidegger his essay on 'The Question of Guilt' in 1950. 'Heidegger's response was a rather mean-spirited defence, erected on the basis of various factual claims which were partly misleading in themselves, and which prove to be completely inadequate when placed within a broader context.' Ott's remark prefaces a quotation from the response which Heidegger wrote a few days after receiving the essay.[133] However one chooses to evaluate this response, it seems unlikely that Heidegger failed to perceive in the essay of his former friend a distinctive transformation of central themes characteristic of his own thinking – themes which can be identified by recourse to the texts. This observation is not intended to obscure the undeniable differences between the two thinkers. Such differences emerge, for example, when the status of America is in question. The freedom 'which has been wrested by mankind in the West' would, according to Jaspers, be finally and decisively destroyed in the event of an American dictatorship 'in the style of Hitler'. But do we not read in Heidegger's *Introduction to Metaphysics* that the German people, that is, the 'metaphysical people', must 'unfold new and historically *spiritual* powers from out of the midst' if the 'mighty decision concerning Europe is not to be reached by way of destruction'? Does this not presuppose that this destruction depends upon that people that finds itself more imperilled than any other? Is it not to this people, confronted as it is by a 'loss of spiritual power', that there falls the task of grasping 'its heritage in a creative fashion'?[134]

National consciousness and guilt

Even more surprising than the perceptible affinities between Jaspers's essay on 'The Question of Guilt' and Heidegger's *Introduction to Metaphysics* are the convergences that can be detected when Heidegger, Jaspers and Adorno each separately raises the question of the essence of Germanness. During the 1950s Adorno participated in the so-called 'group experiments' of the Institute for Social Research and contributed a chapter on 'Guilt and Defensiveness' to the project. One cannot simply read this chapter as a philosophical response to the 'question of guilt'. Nonetheless, the theoretical and philosophical implications involved in the interpretation of facts always require careful analysis, as Adorno himself constantly emphasised. In the section entitled 'Acknowledgement of German Guilt' Adorno justifies a particularly instructive distinction by referring to the results of empirical research:

> There is by no means any simple identity between national consciousness and the defensive denial of guilt. One would probably get closer to the truth on the assumption that individuals who struggle to evade the consciousness of guilt are also generally those who simulate and exaggerate their national consciousness precisely because they are incapable of any substantial solidarity with other human beings; whereas those who still have some real sense for the concept of a people are precisely those capable of taking upon themselves the things which affect a people in its entirety.[135]

A national consciousness which does not require the fiction of itself, which involves a 'substantial solidarity' with others and indeed has such solidarity as its basis, is therefore irreconcilable with the defensive denial of guilt. Adorno anchors the concept of the people in a national consciousness which is capable of constituting itself as a consciousness of guilt. The concept of the people must be delimited over against the fiction of a people, but it must also be distinguished from the idea that a people can adequately be defined by collecting any number of external characteristics. In order to have a 'real sense' or feeling for the concept, as those do for whom national consciousness and consciousness of guilt are not incompatible, a people must represent more than any such collection. A people is neither a fiction, nor an empirical fact. There is therefore a 'philosophical' truth to a people, one that is accessible to 'feeling'. However, Adorno says nothing further about it here.[136]

He returns to the problem of nationalism and fiction in a

lecture from 1965 which is entitled 'Concerning the Question: What is German?' Adorno is not asking himself what 'German' means; rather he is responding to a question which has been addressed to him, and is reflecting upon its significance. For the answer which suggests itself, and is taken on along with the question, conflates ideal and idealisation. One must therefore distinguish between Germanness as an ideal and Germanness as an idealising wish. Otherwise the 'ideal' merely serves the cause of 'idealisation'.[137] But an idealising answer only suggests itself because the idealisation already dwells within the question and perhaps within the ideal, too. The question answers to the wish for idealisation, and idealises what is German before the idealising effect of a possible answer can do so, and before a more discriminating answer can oppose such an effect. Hence the question alone already creates its context. It is marked by a context and it generates a context. But a context-generating question can only really be posed as one that is taken over – as a question released from itself and from the questioner. The question which Adorno takes over 'violates by virtue of its pure form the irrevocable experiences of the last couple of decades' – and that also means that it turns against the experience of guilt. It 'detaches an essential collective entity which is called "German" and suggests that this entity must be characterised according to its essential features'. 'Essential collective entities' exist only insofar as they are detached and rendered autonomous through the constantly repeated question: 'What is ... ?' One can therefore recognise nationalism in the very shape of the question; one can recognise it before it allows itself to be recognised in an answer. This question is not a philosophical question, for it 'remains within the domain of those stereotypes which thought is called upon to dissolve. It is quite uncertain whether there is such a thing as a German person or Germanness at all, or anything similar in other nations.' But what explanation can Adorno offer for the process of idealisation if he doubts the pertinence of his own distinctions, of the distinction between an 'ideal' and an 'idealisation'? Germanness is neither a fictitious 'essential collective entity', nor an empirical datum:

> What is true and better in any people is rather to be found in what does *not* accommodate itself to the collective subject,

and where possible resists it. The formation of stereotypes, however, only promotes collective narcissism. What one identifies with, the essence of one's own group, unwittingly becomes the good; the alien group, the others, become the bad. The reverse is also true, for the image of everything German amongst other people is not exempted from this mechanism. But since the ideology of the primacy of the collective subject over the individual created such utter disaster under National Socialism, there is all the more reason in Germany to avoid any regression to the stereotyped imagery of adulatory self-sacralisation.

The almost imperceivable but nonetheless identifiable tendencies which suggested the possibility of just such a 'regression' expressly prompted Adorno to write his lecture. The examples he selects clearly indicate what he is warning against: the image of a country and a people fragmented and divided within themselves, riven by artificial borders, and estranged from their original vocation. Adorno mentions the political problems of reunification, the question concerning the Oder–Neisse demarcation and the claims of those who were expelled from their homelands. 'Further pretexts are supplied here by a purely imaginary international ostracism of what is German, and by the no less fictitious lack of that national self-confidence which many would so gladly encourage in us.'[138] Imagination and fiction are both mentioned in this passage. The lack of national self-confidence is fictitious because in Germany – can one speak of 'Germany' in 1965 without already making a geo-political decision? – there should no longer be any reason to sense a lack of 'national self-confidence' and to attempt to strengthen what is allegedly lacking. But also because nationalism arises from the fiction of lack, from the fiction of a totality that previously existed within its natural borders and now finds itself divided: 'Because German unification was historically accomplished at such a late stage, and in so precarious and unstable a fashion, there is a tendency, in order to feel like a nation at all, to over-emphasise national consciousness and react angrily by punishing any deviation from it.' Adorno uses the language of psychoanalysis to describe the nationalistic effects of the fiction he denounces. Over against the 'fictitious lack' of unity he appeals

to the despised remains of a unified and divided German tradition that has sunk to the status of a neutralised cultural possession. He appeals to a Kantian concept of autonomy, and to 'the
duty of renouncing collective obedience and all self-idolisa-
tion'.[139] For Adorno nationalism amounts to 'collective narcissism' and indicates a regression to a form of tribal consciousness,
'to archaic conditions of pre-individual existence'. Though he
does not refer to them explicitly, he alludes to Freud's writings
on mass psychology and cultural theory. According to Freud,
the narcissistic self-contentment of the mass is secured through a
double bonding: 'Many identical individuals, who can all identify with one another, and one unique individual superior to all
of them, that is the situation which we find realised in the mass
capable of surviving as such.'[140] The life of the mass appears to
Freud as the 'resurgence of the primal horde'. Is the relationship
of the mass to its own ideal not rooted in an irreducible
ambivalence? Does the ideal of the mass not represent the
murdered and at the same time yearningly missed father? Does
not the elevation which creates a father–ideal presuppose a 'fictitious lack' which betrays the thought of murder? One could
summarise the ultimate consequences of Adorno's argument as
follows: no national consciousness without guilt.

Double-bind

The 'functional reversal' of the question 'What is German?' is
certainly not exhausted in the critique of that stereotypical
thinking that promotes regression. Adorno wishes to uncover
the 'truth' behind the stereotypes: 'If one can suppose anything
to be specifically German, then it is this intrication of the great,
of what refuses to abide within any conventionally established
boundary, with the monstrous. When crossing boundaries, it
seeks to subjugate what it encounters, just as idealist philoso-
phies and works of art could tolerate nothing which resisted
absorption within the commanding reach of their own identity.'[141] In order to prevent a possible misunderstanding, Adorno
carefully specifies that 'even the tension between these
moments' does not constitute some 'original givenness', or 'so-
called national character'. The 'specifically German' entwinement of 'the great' with 'the monstrous' is based upon the back-

wardness of German society in relation to those advanced exchange economies in which the commodity character is said to have spread much earlier 'over all [social] spheres', including the 'spiritual' sphere. Adorno is just as cautious when he analyses the 'particular elective affinity' which exists between the German language and speculative philosophy. He ascribes to the German language a certain 'metaphysical excess' which manifests itself both in the impossibility of adequately translating speculative concepts, especially the concept of *Geist* or 'spirit', and in the necessity of using German as a means of presenting philosophical arguments. For during its history the German language has acquired the capacity of articulating the expressive moment of phenomena which exceeds their 'positivity' and their 'givenness'. It is precisely this expressive moment that lets Germanness become German, and the truth true. However, the 'metaphysical linguistic character' of Germanness does not guarantee the truth of any particular metaphysics or of 'metaphysics in general'. This metaphysical character constitutes, as Adorno clearly states, no special 'privilege'.[142] The German language tends to assert itself as a language of names: Adorno's idea of 'constellation' – of configurative language – is consequently directed against 'the immanent drift of its words towards saying more than they do say'. The 'metaphysical excess' which liberates philosophy from positivism seduces the philosopher into relinquishing the concept for the sake of the name. Truth and fiction are inseparable and are indeed inscribed in the German language as its 'specific' feature. That spirit, the absolute, can suddenly revert to 'absolute horror', that the radicality of spirit, its tendency to cross all limits, is permanently entwined with the possibility of regression, that the language of truth is essentially the language of untruth: this is the 'German' *double-bind* which constitutes no 'national character' and dislocates every concept – even the Kantian concept of autonomy[143] – and which Adorno derives from the fact that a 'stock of untapped and quasi-natural forces' has survived in Germany.[144] It is impossible to decide what the nature of these quasi-natural (and not: natural) forces is: they are neither good nor evil, neither normal nor monstrous, neither simply natural nor unnatural 'forces'. 'Quasi-natural' is thus an expression Adorno uses to designate what is not delimitable in terms of identity or

opposition, but renders determinations of identity and opposition possible. It is for structural reasons therefore that there is
no unambiguous answer to the question 'What is German?':
Germanness is the twofold effect of a *double-bind* structure.[145]
But if the idea of the absolute and of 'absolute horror' does
refer to a specific feature of Germanness and the German
language, if Germanness and the German language are characterised by their essential relation to truth and to untruth, a relation which is doubtless problematic, then the privileging which
opens the way to nationalism can no longer be excluded here
either. Though in his discourse he tries to resist such conclusions, Adorno has no argument which would allow him to
reject the connection of socio-economic and historical factors
with the privilege of a 'stock of quasi-natural forces'. The
'metaphysical excess' is necessarily itself a privilege. From this
perspective it would be possible to trace the experience of guilt
back to those 'forces' which precede all presence. For this
experience is the experience of a guilt which, in *Negative Dialectics*, Adorno associates with the name of Auschwitz and with
the constant postponement of the act that would render it
present and bring about a full awareness of it. The fact that
national consciousness does not exclude the experience of guilt
can now be understood in a different way, in a way which is
incompatible with what Adorno intends this fact to mean. And
here one can no longer deny the proximity to Jaspers and to
Heidegger.

You shall never be remembered

To the extent that the event exceeds experience and thus eludes
its own presentation one cannot avoid bearing the guilt of
missing the event. Consciousness is not the site where an event
can be taken in, but rather one which distorts its character.
Adorno comprehends Auschwitz in the same way in which he
comprehends the name itself, the name which cannot be uttered
because a ban has been placed upon it. He comprehends it as an
absolute event and that means in spite of everything:
as an event of the absolute in which the absolute consumes
itself. But where is the place for such comprehension, if anyone
who speaks of Auschwitz after Auschwitz is necessarily

condemned to euphemism? 'One can only speak euphemistically about what is incommensurable with all experience; thus, in Germany, people speak of the murder of the Jews. This incommensurability has now become a total *a priori*, so that the devastated consciousness can no longer find a place from which it might reflect upon it.'[146] The construction of a negative historical totality is a sign that Auschwitz is both acknowledged and denied as event. The euphemism cannot be avoided or rephrased. For it is not the one who asserts the uniqueness of Auschwitz that first transforms what has happened into an event. After all, uniqueness is not a category of historiography. Every time the name 'Auschwitz' is used or mentioned, the possibility of meaning, of experience, of language, and thus also the possibility of euphemism, is given. Perhaps the act of naming is itself already a euphemism, though this does not mean that one could safely imagine oneself immune from euphemism by remaining silent. Quite the contrary. But because the antithesis of thought as originary de-constitution is an opening to something other, we must understand Adorno's categorical imperative – according to which Auschwitz must never be repeated (ND:358; ET:365) – to mean that all the concepts at our disposal must be thought from the indeterminate site of the event. Even the negative construction of the historical totality reveals itself as all too euphemistic. Thought is always guilty and constantly remains indebted. The characterisation of Heidegger's philosophy as a 'highly developed system of credit' is also valid for Adorno's own thinking of the non-identical, irrespective of its contextual specificity, its import as a critique of ideology and its translation into the language of guilt and debts.

In his studies on Husserl, Adorno identifies phenomenology with epistemology and anticipates his later comparison by linking phenomenology to a 'system of credit':

> In spite of its static and descriptive tenor, apparently so removed from all speculation, Husserl's epistemology is also caught up in a context of guilt. His epistemological system resembles, to use a more modern language, a system of credit. Its concepts form a constellation in which each is supposed to redeem the debts of the others, although the presen-

tation itself obscures the process which obtains between them. Expressions of Husserl's such as 'fulfilment' (as of contractual conditions), 'evidence' (as of factual proof), 'judgement' (as of a trial) unwittingly construct an epistemology in analogy with a universal system of legal right.[147]

What is striking in this passage is the translation of the language of guilt and debts into the language of constellation. Does not the movement of constellations reveal the essential asymmetry inherent in the process of exchange which both sustains and thwarts the principle of equivalence? Does not this principle arise from an oblivion of the constellation which is harboured in its very movement? If 'even the most enlightened epistemology' participates 'in the myth of first principles through the figure of a never fulfilled, and therefore infinite and ineluctably self-renewing contract', then this myth is produced by the movement of constellations and points to its essence. Adorno accuses Heidegger of just such a dependence upon myth. Heidegger transforms the name into myth, into a mythic first principle, because 'he seeks to reestablish the power of the name through a ritual of naming' (ND:117; ET:111). On the one hand, Adorno rejects what Scholem calls the 'teutonising cabbalism' of the 'philosophy of origins'. On the other hand, he denounces the false modesty of a thinking which no longer names (anything) and which for this very reason remains ritualistic. Heidegger owes the name. His thought does not repay its borrowed credit. 'In the end this thought hardly dares to predicate anything even of Being. What this manifests is less a mystical meditation than the need and difficulty of a thought which wants to approach its other, but cannot allow itself anything for fear lest it thereby lose what it claims. Philosophy thus tends to become a ritualistic gesture. Of course there is also something true about this gesture: the fact that philosophy falls silent' (ND:86; ET:78). The question of the validity of such a critique of Heidegger may be left open here. What is significant is not only that Adorno does not denounce or reject 'the philosopher of origins' as a mystic, but also and above all that he traces Heidegger's 'highly developed system of credit' back to a 'need and a difficulty of thought'. In what sense can silence and muteness be 'true'? Muteness can interrupt thought. The language of thought can remain silent as to 'its own silence'. [148] But silence and muteness are not, however, the last word of thought. In the event the muteness perhaps coincides with the gift of language. But what language is (still) given to us after Auschwitz? To the extent that an event is a destruction and an opening, and that it cannot be (re)presented as an event, thought is memory, the memory of a destruction, of an opening, of a guilt which always exceeds the memory of thought.

Horkheimer and Adorno see the human relationship to death as mankind's relationship to itself: 'The dead are subjected to what the Jews once regarded as the most terrible of curses: you shall never be remembered. No longer mindful and caring of themselves, human beings work out their own despair upon the dead' (DdA:244; ET:216). What can be said of a human being who is entirely uncertain of his humanity, who, not recognising himself in an identity or in a language, can think of himself only as bereft of all security and as completely dispossessed of himself? He remains mute, he is not attached to conditions or presuppositions, he does not reveal or affirm anything, he does not assert himself when he appears to say: here I am, this is me. [149]

PART II
Inaugurations

We are caught up into a dialogue which brings language to language, and indeed not merely as something arbitrary or incidental but as the task that is laid upon the maiden, is laid upon Germania: 'Name, O daughter, thou . . .'

Martin Heidegger

But where art is present in its highest consummation, it actually contains, precisely in the medium of the sensuous image, the form of presentation which is the most essential and the most appropriate for the content of truth. So it was amongst the Greeks, for example, that art represented the highest form in which the people imaged forth the gods and bestowed upon themselves a consciousness of truth. That is why the poets and artists became for the Greeks the creators of their gods, that is, the artists bestowed upon the nation the specific images and ideas of the divine in all its action, life and power, that is to say, bestowed the specific content of religion itself. But not indeed in such a way that such images and teachings were simply presented in an abstract conscious fashion, *prior* to poetry itself, as so many universal religious propositions and intellectual conclusions which would then merely require the artists to clothe them in images and embellish them externally with the splendours of poetry. The manner of artistic production here consisted rather in this, that the poets could bring forth what stirred within them *only* in the form of art and poetry.

G. W. F. Hegel

1

Counter-Turning of the Beginning

Storm

Heidegger introduces his lectures on Hölderlin's hymns 'Germania' and 'Der Rhein', given during the winter semester of 1934/5, with the question concerning 'beginnings'. He starts precisely by distinguishing commencement [*Beginn*] from beginning [*Anfang*], and then determining the latter as origin. And here he introduces two examples, the first of which — in its connection with the second — appears less innocuous than it might initially seem. It precedes his attempt to define the distinguishing feature which gives a concrete contour to his second example:

> 'Commencement' — this is something different from 'beginning'. A new weather situation, for example, commences with a storm, whereas its beginning is the already active and complete transformation in the state of the air itself. The commencement is that with which something starts, the beginning is that from which something arises and originates. The world war began centuries ago within the spiritual and political history of the West. The world war commenced with border skirmishes. The commencement is soon left behind, and disappears as the happening advances. The beginning, the origin, on the other hand, only comes to appearance in the happening, and is fully there only at its end. (GRh:3)

The collocation of 'storm' and 'world war' may well remind us of Ernst Jünger's *Stahlgewitter* ['Tempests of Steel']. Does the beginning always begin with a storm? Is the storm the commencement of the beginning? Is it in the storm of commencement that beginning, as a radical transformation of hitherto existing arrangements and conditions, comes to light as collapse?

Beginning, greatness, stand

Perhaps the storm allows us to recognise the commencement in its greatness. The Rectoral Address of 1933 at least would seem to suggest as much. The beginning of something great, as Heidegger explains it there, is itself the greatest of the great. The great is all the greater, the more originally it belongs to the beginning. Greatness itself is therefore, in accordance with its essence, something of a beginning. This is why it reveals itself as temporal in character: 'The beginning, as what is greatest, has already passed over everything that is to come, and thus over ourselves as well. The beginning has fallen into our future, it stands there as a distant command, as the distant demand upon us to recuperate its greatness.'[1] The greatest of the great, the great as that which demands and commands, is the beginning as something that stands in the future. The beginning is so remote from the commencement, is released so far into the past and into the future, that, more imminent than everything yet to come, it remains constantly in imminence. Only that which has always already passed by, can constantly remain in imminence and demand recuperation. In the Rectoral Address Heidegger draws no distinction between beginning and commencement. But when the great first reveals itself as what it is, the beginning, as the greatest, has already gone beyond the former: what commences has begun. The imminent beginning is 'the breaking forth of Greek philosophy': 'It is here that Western man first stands forth out of a folkdom by virtue of his language. He stands forth against *beings as a whole*, questioning and grasping beings as the beings that they are.'[2] It is in heeding the demand or command of the imminent beginning, and in allowing itself to be empowered by it, that what is great repeats the beginning of that which breaks forth and sets out. What now sets out in this repetition stands out questioningly before the 'danger of constant uncertainty concerning the world', a danger that is rooted in the constant concealment of beings as a whole. The people that owes its power to language stands in the storm. Because it transforms the future into a standing-place, the beginning that breaks into the future lays its demand upon the German people that stands steadfast in the storm, and that in standing forth and setting out wills itself in this forth-standing and this out-setting: 'But we shall only fully understand the splendour and the greatness of this breaking forth if we sustain within ourselves that far-reaching and profound thoughtfulness in which the ancient wisdom of the Greeks found utterance: "Everything great stands in the storm…"'. Does not the rather singular translation of this sentence from Plato's *Republic*, which concludes the address and is first cited in the original Greek, presuppose the entire context and connection already established between 'beginning', 'greatness' and 'standing'? Philippe Lacoue-Labarthe, who has expressly examined the significance of the idea of 'standing' and 'placing' in Heidegger's thought, speaks here of an 'all too obvious ideological-political overde-termination' of language.[3] Hugo Ott has also drawn attention to what he calls the 'final drum-roll' of the Rectoral Address. But if it is true that the translation, problematic as it may be, accords with the 'logic' of the beginning expounded in the address, then it is not enough to interpret it merely as a case of linguistic manipulation intended as an 'accommodation' to the current 'rhetoric of struggle'.[4] Such a claim inevitably reduces the over-determination of the translation itself.

Imminence

It is Hölderlin, according to Heidegger, who has brought poetry back to 'its original essence'. As the poets' poet, as the poet of poetic composition itself, Hölderlin is 'still too far ahead' and 'even today still too early' (GRh:219). The one who inaugurates, who allows us to experience the power of the origin, of the beginning, comes too early. That is why he remains unrecognised and thus also comes too late: 'What is always of today rushes past him, pacifies itself with its own complacency, one in which everything would seem already to have been decided.' Heidegger shows that because of its temporal structure such inauguration, originary in its essence, can only enter experience as it were unseasonably, at the wrong time. The wrong time of inauguration cannot become the proper moment, since inauguration and beginning are more than a mere occurrence only insofar as they are imminent, always yet to come. It is true that the beginning determines what happens, but it threatens simultaneously to escape its own determination. And the commencement can do nothing to alter this either. The beginning requires the commencement in order to emerge from the concealedness to which its temporal structure consigns it. But it is precisely this structure – as a structure of determining – which leads what happens to lose the traces of the beginning, which are also the traces of the beginning. What allows the commencement to disappear constitutes both the power and the powerlessness of the beginning. The commencement announces that what happens is in truth the happening of the beginning. As such – as commencement – the beginning leaves itself behind. The commencement, or more precisely: the beginning, must extinguish itself if it is to affirm itself in the happening. But since the fullness of its presence is only vouchsafed with the end, the happening which unfolds between the commencement and the end is most expressly marked by the beginning – the happening no longer requires the commencement – and is most strongly endangered by the forgetting of the beginning – the comencement no longer announces the beginning, the end has not yet emerged. The beginning exposes itself in its imminence – between the commencement and the end.

In the Rectoral Address the will is the factor that is to prevent the loss or the forgetting of the beginning. Hence one could define it as 'the will to the end', as the will of the people that wills itself and that in a certain sense is satisfied with itself, if indeed the beginning is 'fully there' only at its end. And since the beginning essentially comes at the wrong time, since it cannot securely establish its own fullness and presence, the idea of a will to the end provokes the objection that it rests upon a de-temporalisation of the beginning.

Blindness of the philosopher

In his essay on Kafka, Walter Benjamin cites the words which the writer ascribes to the grandfather in the short text entitled *The Next Village*: 'Life is astoundingly short. To me, looking back over it, life seems so foreshortened that I scarcely understand, for instance, how a young man can decide to ride over to the next village without being afraid that even the span of a normal happy life may already fall far short of the time needed for such a journey – quite independently of unfortunate acident.'[5] Benjamin does not attempt to interpret the grandfather's words. He contents himself with naming their object – the distortions of time: 'For indeed no one says that the distortions which the Messiah will one day appear to set right are merely distortions of the space we inhabit'. But amongst Benjamin's notes there is one passage which presents an interpretation ascribed to Brecht: 'This story forms a kind of counterpart to that of Achilles and the Tortoise. He may ignore all incidents along the way, he will still not arrive at the next village as long as he divides the ride or the journey into its tiniest parts. Then life is too short for this journey. But the mistake lies in the singular "a". For just as the ride is analysed into its parts, so too is the rider. And just as the unity of life is lost, so too is its shortness. It can be as short as one likes, it makes no difference, because the one who arrives in the village is not the one who rode out in the first place.'[6] It is only for the one who looks back upon it – only for the grandfather – that life appears as a unifying interconnection at all. The reflection which grasps life as a whole constitutes the identity of that life. In this context it is largely irrelevant whether this retrospection actually transpires at the end of life or takes the shape of an anticipated future. The unity of life is always that produced by the grandfather. Yet reflection simultaneously dissolves this unity. Life does not constitute a closed unity because it is too short. Reflection presents the living individual as one crippled at birth. One who dies even before beginning to live. There is no unitary subject for which a unity of life could present itself, or fail to present itself. The shortness of life cannot possibly be experienced as such. In order to speak reflectively of the shortness of life, one must already have arrived at the next village. That is why the grandfather indeed has arrived at the next village, not as the grandfather but as another: as a young man. The anticipation of the future which proves impossible for all wisdom (not because it must reckon with unforeseen 'incidents' but because it recognises that the coming future transcends the time at our disposal) can be achieved only by the one who is free of care and concern since he has already decided and has already arrived in the next village. Just as such youthful freedom presupposes a certain unity, however alien in nature it is to all reflection, wisdom involves that freedom from care and concern as its unsublatable other: as its blind spot. Only he who is free from care and concern is able to hear the voice of wisdom. For the grandfather the Messiah is the coming one who comes too late: life is insufficient to experience the coming of the Messiah. For the young man the Messiah is the one who has already come, has come too early: life is not short enough to allow the experience of his coming. Both wisdom and freedom from care and concern alike are subjected to a distorted and distorting time.

Precisely this subjection can be expressed with Heidegger in relation to the coming beginning. The contemporary world, careless and unconcerned, ignores the beginning that comes too early, while the philosopher, consumed with care and concern, recognises that the beginning comes too late. Hence he attempts to recuperate that beginning, by denying wisdom and abandoning it to blindness, although not without attempting to interpret this as an anticipation, as will to the end. On the last page of the Rectoral Address Heidegger writes as follows:

> But no one will ask us whether we do or do not will, when the spiritual strength of the West fails and the joints of the world no longer hold, when this moribund semblance of a culture caves in and drags all that remains strong into confusion and lets it suffocate in madness. Whether this will happen or not depends alone on whether or not we, as a historical-spiritual people, still and once again will ourselves. Every individual *participates* in this decision, even he, and indeed especially he, who evades it. But we do will that our people fulfil its historic mission. We do will ourselves. For the young and the youngest strength of the people, which already reaches beyond us, *has* by now *decided* the matter.[7]

The decision which is to be shared is already a divided decision: prior to all deciding, prior to all evading. The philosopher thus abandons himself to the blindness of an otherness he cannot sublate, bestowing upon this blindness, in a final philosophical act, a transparency which he does and does not have at his disposal. The youngest wills the beginning and the dawning: that is the word which the philosopher as philosopher still speaks and can no longer speak.

Genius of forgetting

The philosopher is a philosopher there where he has distanced himself from 'scientific teachings concerning the nature of the people and its traditions': there in the solitude of the 'creative landscape' which relieves him of the busy stress of the contemporary world − of the large city. A few months after he assumed the rectorship Heidegger justified his rejection of a continued academic career in Berlin. He chooses rather to remain in the provinces: 'When in the night of winter a wild snowstorm roars and buffets about the hut, obscuring and over-shadowing everything, *then* is the high time for philosophy. *Then* its questioning must become a simple and essential questioning. The laborious exploration of every thought cannot but be hard and keen. The struggle for expression in language is like the force with which the towering pine trees withstand the storm.'[8] Language is the greatness which stands in the storm. Essential questioning and the affirmation of Western humanity 'from out of a folkdom' both transpire 'by virtue of its language'. Can one tread a path other than that taken by Heidegger in the Rectoral Address in order to recuperate the coming beginning? Benjamin regards the restoration of what is distorted neither as alternative nor as amalgam:

> Amongst the Chassidim there is a saying about the coming world which tells us that everything there will be arranged in just the same way as it is with us. In the coming world our little room shall also be the same as it is now; in the coming world our child shall also sleep just as it sleeps now; in the coming world we shall also wear what our body wears in this one. Everything will be as it is here − but just a little different. This is what imagination suggests. It merely draws a veil over the remoteness. Everything there can be as it is now, but the veil begins to heave, and everything it con-

ceals shifts imperceptibly. There is a change and an exchange;
nothing remains and nothing vanishes.[9]

In the libretto to Adorno's *Singspiel* 'The Treasure of Joe the
Indian' we find the sentence: 'Almost nothing has made everything good again', and in *Negative Dialectics* Adorno returns to
the conception of the coming world to which Benjamin refers.
Faithful to the ban on images, Adorno radicalises this conception and excludes any relation to the achievements of imagination: 'In the right state of things everything would be, in
accordance with the Jewish theologoumenon, only ever so
slightly different from the way it is now, but it is impossible to
imagine how even the most irrelevant thing will look'
(ND:294; ET:299). Perhaps the imagination can help us there
where we can content ourselves with neither one possibility nor
the other, and where no mediation is possible. But imagination
represents nothing since, as Benjamin elucidates in an early fragment, it is essentially a 'sense for an emerging disfigurement'
and owes its existence to the 'genius of forgetting'.[10] Is it not
just such a genius that is lacking in the Rectoral Address?

Poetry and thought

The distinction between God and man is also correlated with
that between beginning and commencement. The beginning is
divine, the commencement is not: 'Now we human beings can
never of course begin with the beginning – only a god can do
that – but must rather commence, that is, take our start from
something that first leads towards the origin, or points towards
it' (GRh:3f.). The commencement itself cannot of course be a
merely arbitrary starting. If the commencement is not already
determined by the beginning, then it remains bound up with a
multiplicity and dispersion which completely separate it from
the beginning: 'He who commences many things often never
reaches the beginning'. Thus the commencement, which unlike
the beginning must disappear, cannot but be unique. The
uniqueness of the commencement consists precisely in the fact
that it can be left behind, because it cannot be deflected. The
commencement marked by multiplicity constantly stands before
the beginning and thus obstructs access to the latter. That is

why it is insufficient merely to distinguish between beginning and commencement: one must also be able to separate the commencement that deflects from the commencement that points. The human being is divine and can lead to the origin to the degree that he cannot act like a god, that he is exposed to the danger of that deflection which signifies the loss of the divine. This danger is inscribed in language.

It would be rather pointless to attempt to isolate what Heidegger says in his own name from what he presents in the name of Hölderlin, and to do so as a matter of principle. For if Hölderlin's poetry (and here that means the hymns 'Germanien' and 'Der Rhein') is supposed to lead us towards the beginning, if the labour of thinking demands that 'Hölderlin himself should commence and determine' this thinking, then the difference between commentary and commentated, between the explication which leads us further and that which merely leads us into the text and reproduces it, finds itself continuously disrupted. This does not mean that this difference is entirely lost from view or forfeits every trace of validity: but it means in the last analysis that it does not govern the relationship between thinker and poetry. In answer to the question whether the thinker's language does not necessarily deflect the poetic commencement from the beginning – whether thought does not itself endanger the poetry which leads to the beginning, and with it the divine – Heidegger says: 'If any poet demands a *thinking* conquest of his poetry, that poet is Hölderlin, and that by no means because he was incidentally "also a philosopher", one indeed whom we may easily place alongside Schelling and Hegel; but rather Hölderlin is one of our greatest *thinkers*, that is one of those most important for our future, because he is our greatest *poet*. The poetical approach to his work is only possible as a *thinking* encounter with the *revelation of being* that is accomplished in this poetry' (GRh:5f.). Thinking is not external to poetry, as the idea of a conquest might perhaps suggest: it is rather the self-relation of poetry itself. If greatness is that which cannot be exhausted in the present, this self-relation of greatness is an open one: it turns towards the beginning from which it first receives its essential determination. This turning towards the beginning is what makes thinking and poetry – the poetry that relates to itself, to the beginning, in thinking – an originary beginning. That is why Hölderlin is not merely a great poet – and thinker – but rather the greatest one. Such a conclusion already permits the distinction between the great and the greatest which plays a role in the Rectoral Address.

Heidegger adds a qualification to his remarks concerning the relationship between poetry and thinking: 'The appearance and indeed the danger of an empty thinking and talking about poetry will constantly accompany our work, and will do so all the more, the less we know of *poetry*, *thinking* and *saying*, the less we have experienced how and why these three powers belong most intimately to our original historical existence.' Thinking now appears as something foreign to the self-relation of poetry, something that threatens the turn to the beginning. Insofar as poetry relates to itself in the poetic turning of thought itself – and only thus can it turn to the beginning if thinking is indeed essential to poetry – it simultaneously relates to an other that turns it away from the beginning. It is now clear why Heidegger should speak of 'conquest' here: the turning in question is never a pure or inner self-relation. It is not merely Heidegger's attempt to effect a poetic turning on the part of thinking that is dangerous, but rather the relationship to thinking that is grounded in poetry itself: for the 'revelation of being' is by no means something which has merely fallen into the lap of poetry as it were, but something that poetry itself has 'accomplished'. Of course the repetition of what the poet has thought poetically must be more than a duplication. Thought itself has entered into the poetry of the beginning. But because the beginning is still imminent (and with it the originary poetry that begins), because the self-relation is an open one that is turned towards the beginning (poetry is also a commencement), the thinking repetition of poetry proves to be necessary. Thought has never therefore fully entered into poetry without remainder. The more poetry turns towards the beginning and the more open its self-relation remains, the more endangered it finds itself to be, the more urgently this self-relation – in its constitutive openness – requires its restitution through the repetition of thinking. Thought is the repeated conquest of the poetry that as beginning founds 'original historical existence'. Along with Hölderlin, Heidegger claims that 'the historical existence of peoples, their rise and consummation and fall, arises out of poetry, as does the authentic knowing of philosophy, and from both of these the effective existence of a people as a people through the state – the political' (GRh:51). The thinking repetition does not duplicate, but holds open what otherwise threatens to fall prey to mere appearance – for instance, to the idea of a 'world-view' that would somehow be peculiar to Hölderlin. This threat results from the openness itself. Hence the repetition is a performative act – to use a vocabulary alien to Heidegger – and does not content itself with being a constative act which refers to something already stated.

The power and force of language, the truth of a people

The danger of deviation and deflection belongs to the essence of language. This danger is experienced in the very moment that poetry relates to itself as its own other, as thinking, in order to accomplish the 'revelation of being', and that means its own language. The expression 'by virtue of language' or 'through the power and force of language' [*kraft der Sprache*], familiar to us from the Rectoral Address, also recurs in the lecture on Hölderlin:

> It is in language that the revelation of beings happens, not simply as an emphatic expression of what is unveiled, but rather as the original unveiling itself, but therefore also precisely as veiling and the prevailing degeneration of the same, as mere appearance or *semblance*. By virtue or through the power and force of language man is the witness of being. He stands in for being, stands up before being, and falls victim to being. Where there is no language, as with the animal or plant, there is no openness of being in spite of the presence of life, and therefore also no non-being and no emptiness of the nothing. Plant and animal stand before the threshold of all this, blind desire and inchoate flight alone prevail here. Only where there is language does world hold sway. Only where there is world, that is, language, is the highest danger, *the* danger itself, the threat to being as such through non-being. Language is not only dangerous because it brings the human being into some danger or other, but is rather *what is*

> *most dangerous of all*, the danger of dangers, because it is language which first creates the possibility of the threat to being and language alone which holds this threat open. Because man *is* in and through language, he creates this danger and procures the destruction that lurks there. As what is most dangerous of all, language is what is most ambivalent and ambiguous of all. It places man in the domain of the highest struggle and accomplishment, and holds him at the same time within the realm of abyssal degeneration. (GRh:62)

The power and force of language allow man to experience the revelation, the manifestation and the openness of being. Perhaps it is particularly necessary here, where Heidegger avails himself of the quasi-theological language of being and beings, to guard against any premature attempt to regard him as a theologian reluctant to confess himself as such. Of more decisive significance than the over-determined language is the fact that Heidegger is drawing attention to the inaugural movement which itself underlies the theological reading itself. For the reference back to fundamental ontology is undeniable here. In *Being and Time* Heidegger had written: 'But because speech [*Rede*] is constitutive for the being of the there, that is for state of mind and understanding, and Dasein thus signifies being-in-the-world – Dasein has already announced itself as being-in that speaks. Dasein has language.'[11] In accordance with the Greek word *logos*, Heidegger defines speech as a process of 'making manifest'; the phenomenon, that which shows itself of itself and in which appearance and semblance are founded, is the 'manifest'.[12] In the lecture on Hölderlin, Heidegger does not differentiate between 'speech' and 'language' – language is always the already uttered articulation of speech, its 'wordly' being. If one disregards this distinction for the moment, the common element is clearly revealed: no time holds sway between language and world, between language and the revelation or manifestation of beings, which presupposes the essential possibility of the openness of being as far as Dasein is concerned. Language – insofar as it is not distinguished from speech – is the inauguration by virtue of which, through the power of which, any revealing and manifesting can transpire and has already transpired.

In *Being and Time* (1927) Dasein has language, is a speaking being which exists 'insofar as it dis-covers world and Dasein itself'. In the Rectoral Address (1933) the power of language belongs to the human being as a member of his 'people': the people itself wishes to stand up questioningly before 'beings as a whole' because language bestows upon it the power and the force to do so. The people does not allow itself to be overwhelmed by the 'uncertainty of the world', by what is hidden from it. Language is determined here in a way that seems to go beyond the analyses initially advanced in *Being and Time*. In the lecture on Hölderlin (1934/5) the emphasis appears to have shifted from the process of dis-covering and willing towards that of 'witnessing'. The human being existing in and through language is as such the 'witness of being'. But this shift of emphasis − if that is what it really is − by no means excludes a connection with the essential themes of the Rectoral Address. Perhaps the shift is better identified by the fact that here − in contrast to the Rectoral Address − the poet is accorded a priority rather than the thinker: 'The truth of the people is the corresponding openness of being as a whole, in accordance with which the sustaining, the commanding and leading powers receive their worth and standing and achieve their unanimity. The truth of a people is that openness of being from out of which a people knows what it wills historically, insofar as it wills *itself*, and wills to be itself. The fundamental attunement, and that means the truth of the existence of a people, is originally founded by the poet' (GRh:144).

Concepts and political determination

If the historical existence of peoples arises from poetry, if philosophy and politics alike are founded in poetry, the language of poetry is not originally a particular language which can be distinguished from others by a series of specific traits, but rather language itself in its origin. To look upon poetry as one specific linguistic domain is to falsify not simply the essence of poetry, but the essence of language itself, and with it the openness of being which constitutes the truth of the historical existence of a people. Language is, according to its essence, poetic. One must ask, therefore, what Heidegger − drawing here upon Hölderlin

– understands by poetry, rather than hastily presupposing the usual concept of the same. The poet, however, is only able to assert a certain priority to the degree in which the thinker – and as a poet he too must be and yet cannot be a thinker – grasps the original inauguration of the opening: 'But the being of beings thus unveiled is *grasped* [*begriffen*] and articulated as being, and thereby first inaugurated, by the thinker.' The repetition of the beginning, which is accomplished by the thinker, is also and above all no mere duplication, precisely because this repetition – and not already poetry itself – brings the beginning to conceptual grasp. The poet can only be the greatest 'thinker' if he assigns the repetition of the original inauguration to the thinker who is to come. The poet does not think the beginning which he inaugurates: he leaves it as the task for the thinker – to understand the beginning as task is thus to understand it as repetition. Only insofar as it is opaque to itself can the beginning remain imminent and yet to come. Thus Heidegger says about the fragment in which Hölderlin describes language as 'the most dangerous of gifts': 'This fragment is laden with a metaphysics that has not been thought through to the end, and precisely because the beginning of this metaphysics has not even been "thought" at all, that is, has not thinkingly been placed within the context of our historical existence' (GRh:61). If the determination of the beginning excludes transparency, if a transparent beginning cannot but immediately consume itself and constitute its own end, then the beginning harbours metaphysics within itself as its own concealment. Conversely, the thinker could never think the beginning at all if poetic inauguration had not already taken thinking up into itself and related to it in its own self-relation. However, the concept itself proves to be all too indeterminate: 'Being that has been grasped and conceived is only brought within the full earnestness of beings, that is, within the *determinate* historical truth, insofar as the people is brought to itself as a people. This transpires through the creation of the state determined in accordance with the essence of the people on the part of the creator of the state.' A poetic inauguration – an inauguration of the fundamental attunement – which were not grasped by thought and determined by politics would immediately degenerate into another particular language. The commencement requires the concept and the political determination which cannot themselves conceive or determine anything independently of poetry in the first place.

The incalculable

That the beginning remains yet to come means that its time can never be calculated, that there is no time *before* the beginning. Poetry, thinking and politics are therefore subject to no temporal sequence, and form no successive series of now-points:

> The powers of poetry, of thinking, of state-founding, exercise an effect, especially in ages of unfolded history, both backwards and forwards, and do not belong to the order of the calculable. They may lie unacknowledged for a long time, without bridges from one to the other, and yet they can exert an effect upon one another, in accordance with the variously powerful unfoldings of poetry, thinking and political action, and within a more or less comprehensive public space. These three creative forces of historical existence effect that alone to which we may ascribe greatness. (GRh:144)

The creative happening which establishes a beginning creates the space in which such greatness can unfold itself. To recognise the power of the great means to recognise its resistance to inscription within a temporal sequence. Heidegger does not speak of the 'storms' of poetry as a metaphor for an actual transition within a constituted spatio-temporal continuum, but rather in order to mark the irreducible discontinuity of the beginning, that which places it beyond the well-worn tangibility of the everyday: 'From year to year Hölderlin's poems become more inexhaustible, ever greater, ever stranger – and they cannot be accommodated in an ultimate definitive sense. They still lack the real, historical and spiritual space. This space cannot be dispensed from the outside, and they themselves will have to create it for themselves. If we are not prepared in future to persist and endure the storms of this poetry, this attempt remains indeed nothing but an inquisitive exercise' (GRh:23). Calculable time – which belongs to the spatio-temporal continuum as the forgetting of the beginning – is the time of the individual, even if the latter succeeds in liberating himself somehow from its power. The time of peoples, on the other hand, does not fall in this time:

> It is possible to envisage the years which belong to the brief existence of the individual. We can calculate this time and locate it between the figures that mark the date of birth and the date of death. The time which belongs to the years of the peoples is hidden from us. But when someone surges out beyond his own time and all its calculable contemporaneity, surges out freely into the open as the poet does, he must estrange himself from those amongst whom he belongs in his own life-time. He never recognises his own and represents an offence in their eyes. Asking after the true time for the sake of his own time, he excludes himself from the time of the contemporary. (GRh:50)

The beginning is necessarily misunderstood since it can only be a beginning insofar as it thwarts the familiar. Such misunderstanding is rooted in a misunderstanding of our own essence: the individuals whose 'life-time' knows nothing of the 'world-hour' of the people do not know who they are. Thus the time of a people is not the aggregate sum of various individual 'life-times': 'Not only do we not know who we are, but we must, in the end, participate in poetry in order to create the necessary condition for the time of the "event of truth" to come, the time in which we shall be able to experience who we are' (GRh:58).

If we pursue the thought that the 'life-time' of the individual and the time of the people, whose 'world-hour' strikes when the calculable dissolves away, are incompatible with one another, we are forced to draw a twofold conclusion. First, the beginning is always the beginning of a people. For this hour can never be calculated. But the incalculable hour is precisely the 'world-hour'. Second, the individual who is caught up in his own life-time, and thus in the contemporary, fails to attain his essence, fails to participate in it, until and unless he experiences his belonging to the original essence of the people as inaugurated through poetry. This participation must not be conflated with the appropriation of some existing knowledge that would teach us who we are. On the contrary, we only experience who we are insofar as we participate in the poetical. This 'who' is no anthropological determination, not even an existentiell determination of the ontic, at least if 'the existentiell is only the intensification of the role of anthropology which takes place within metaphysics when it reaches its completion'.[13] One enters into the time of the people, a time which concerns and touches the world, precisely in freeing oneself from what one is. The time of the people does not extend the individual 'life-time', which being calculable is always too short for an individual to free himself from what he is, but rather interrupts it.

Misunderstood and as yet unrecognised, the poet is the inaugurator of the beginning, one who commences: for the commencement, which the beginning leaves behind, unites within itself the transience of the 'life-time' which does not survive the event with the endurance of the beginning. This commencemnt can be ascribed neither to the time of the individual nor to the time of the people. It is the interruption of the 'life-time' which allows the turning to the beginning, to the divine from which the time of the people arises. 'Wrapped in the word' the poet brings the 'lightning-bolt' of the divine into the existence of the people which he inaugurates: 'Storm and lightning are the language of the gods, and the poet is the one who must stand fast unyieldingly before this language, must capture it and bring it into the existence of the people' (GRh:31). The experience of poetry is the experience of a danger that is at its greatest between the commencement and the end. And the one who commences, who strives to inaugurate the beginning, must abandon himself without reserve to this danger.

The most dangerous of gifts

As the inaugurator of the beginning the poet occupies an intermediate role – that of the 'half-god' – and is not himself identical – like the god – with the beginning. The poet is, one could say, the ecstasis of the beginning, the beginning that is coming, that is a commencement. But only as ecstasis is there beginning at all. The beginning is its own postponement. In the shape of the poet who inaugurates an original language or language in its beginning, the god – the beginning – is beyond and beside himself. But it is this self-exteriority alone which constitutes the originary. The opposition of calculable and incalculable time – of 'life-time' and the time of the people – does not hold for the poet, because he exposes himself to the incalculable – and that also means to the thinking and politics in which the self-relation of poetry consists – rather than attempting to apply to it a measure that is drawn from the calculable. That is precisely why the poet experiences a splitting and an interruption within the incalculable itself, experiences the danger of language without which there would be no self-exposure. The individual 'life-time' and the time of the people, the commencement which leads away from the beginning and that which leads towards it, are distinctions which belong to the beginning, and for this very reason are always precarious. If the beginning is essentially ecstatic in itself, then whatever comes into its proximity must ineluctably turn away from it – not because of some presumption or hubris to be punished by destruction, but because of the structure of the beginning itself. What is wholly turned away may be just as originary, may belong just as much to the beginning as that which turns towards the beginning. Hence, contrary to Heidegger's intention but as a strict consequence of his thought, the beginning is to be sought in the 'life-time', in the prose and even the idle talk to which language in its beginning is closed. Language is closed to such talk since, as we read in *Being and Time*, it allows us 'to understand everything without a foregoing appropriation of the issue', protecting us from the danger of 'failing to achieve such an appropriation'. Heidegger's seminar on *Time and Being* contains a reference to the Janus-faced character of the forgetfulness of being, a formulation which clearly expresses the precarious nature of the distinctions. It is language that endangers language. Language is neither an instrument nor a specific faculty of the human being, but is rather the original exposure of existence. Turned at once both towards and away from the intrinsic counter-turning of the beginning, the human being can neither inaugurate without destroying, nor destroy without inaugurating. It is no accident that Heidegger speaks here of the 'inward character' of this conflict of language with itself. For at the end of the lecture and after attempting to interpret this Hölderlinian expression within 'the horizon of the Heraclitean thought of a 'conflictual harmony', Heidegger brings this 'inwardness', which 'does not merely describe the "inwardness" of sensibility', into direct connection with the enmity that holds sway within the origin:

> To utter an essential word is already and intrinsically to deliver this word over to the realm of misinterpretation, of misuse and of deception, to the danger of transforming it into the most immediate opposite of its own determination. Everything whatever, the purest and most obscure, as well as the cheapest and most common, can be captured in some approachable turn of phrase. The dangerousness of language is thus essentially a doubled one, each pole of which is fundamentally different from the other: on the one hand the danger of the highest proximity to the gods, and thus to the measureless destruction they wreak, on the other hand the danger of the cheapest entanglement in the vacuities of idle talk and its deceptive appearance. The inner pairing of these two conflicting dangers, the danger of the essence that is so hard to endure and the danger of carelessly losing the essence altogether, intensifies the dangerousness of language to its utmost. The dangerousness of language is its *most original essential determination*. Its purest essence unfolds itself in an originary manner in poetry. Poetry is the *original language of a people*. But poetic saying degenerates, turns into genuine and then into spurious 'prose', and finally becomes idle talk. (GRh:63f.)

In his lecture Heidegger denounces the 'entanglement in idle talk' when he says: 'It is not so long ago that the underground psychoanalytical depths of poetry were being sought out; now everything is dripping with blood, soil and folkdom, but everything still remains as it was' (GRh:254). But is this 'entanglement' a consequence of the dangerousness of language? Is it language which forces Heidegger, who had spoken of 'struggle' [*Kampf*] in the Rectoral Address of 1933, to expose himself to a potential misunderstanding, so much so that in a report of 1945 he has to clarify and explain his use of words? How far can a thinker who expressly recognises 'dangerousness' as the 'most original essential determination of language' expose himself to the former without thereby neglecting the effort to counter the inevitable misunderstandings?

On poetry: the over-poetic

The people, according to Heidegger, exists insofar as it is poetically com-posed. It is inaugurated by poetry as original language – and thereby also already destroyed: in prose and idle talk it loses the language-given unity which poetry bestows upon it. Inasmuch as Heidegger mentions prose, and even distinguishes 'genuine' from 'spurious' prose, he erects a hierarchy of genres, even if he does not appeal to the traditionally established limits which define not only the individual genres but also what constitutes a genre as such. The poetic word, which is not the word belonging to one particular realm of language, is the word of the beginning itself, a beginning already touched by prose and idle talk. The simplicity of the originary can only be maintained in the counter-turning which ensures that the beginning remains to come. The beginning is intrinsically a counter-turning because it must both turn away from and strive to return to itself. This is why poetry can never be regarded as a unified or simple determination. It always reveals itself to be over-poetic. In his lecture on Hölderlin's hymn 'Remembrance', delivered in the winter semester of 1941/2, Heidegger focused explicitly upon this self-overtaking movement of poetry:

> The word of poetry is over-poetic with regard to itself and the poet – it opens up and obscures a wealth which is inexhaustible precisely because it possesses the character of the originary, that is, of the single and simple. Now we might attempt to approach this word by trying to describe the world of images and ideas as it was once 'subjectively sensed' by Hölderlin, and thus transpose ourselves into his psychological and emotional condition. But then one would certainly remain, in many ways, quite outside the realm opened up by the word of poetry. The poetically com-posed is by no means identical with what Hölderlin intended of himself to imagine and represent, but is rather that which intended the poet himself when it called him to his poetic task. In the

strict sense, therefore, we must say that the poet is first com-
posed by what he has poetically to compose.[14]

The inauguration accomplished by the poet is thus no act of
subjective spontaneity, but is a response to language itself
which, in the counter-turning of the beginning, has already
inaugurated and destroyed itself as language. Thus there is
always already a language that is always yet to be. Or expressed
in a different way: the poet is not the subject who inaugurates
and composes, it is rather composing and inaugurating as the
essence of originary language which, on account of its constitutive counter-turning, needs the poet and inaugurator, and
produces the latter through a peculiar hyperbolic and excessive
movement. Inauguration thus universally possesses the paradoxical form of an original supplementarity. This implies that the
inauguration belonging to the poet is not, as representational
thinking would have it, a secondary inauguration which could
subsequently be added on externally to what has already been
inaugurated. It is the supplement of inauguration involved in
inauguration, or to be more precise: it is inauguration as its
own supplement. Herein lies the significance of the commencement as the division and supplementation of the beginning
which properly belongs to it from the start. What begins, what
begins in and as language, is, as we have seen, a movement that
turns away in turning towards and turns towards in turning
away.

What begins in and as language

But why must we think of language and beginning, of language
and inauguration, of the word of poetry and the origin as being
intrinsically linked? Why is that which begins always that
which begins in and as language? For what reason is language
something which begins, and, as something which begins,
poetry? It is obvious that the beginning can be nothing but an
inauguration: where something begins, where something transpires which is other than anything that has taken place before,
something has been inaugurated. Inauguration is the opening up
of something other, and thus a beginning as the emergence of
what was not revealed before. In order to understand the rela-

tionship between beginning as inauguration and as language, one must seek for the essential character of language in the power of naming.[15] For every naming is effectively an inaugurating, just as every inaugurating is likewise a naming. Naming brings what it names to appearance, it shows forth what has been called (by name), it allows it to be seen.

Although Heidegger does not examine naming explicitly in the lecture (as he will later on in *What Is Called Thinking?*), he emphasises right from the very beginning that poetic 'composing' signifies – if we consider the origins of the word – an act of revealing: 'Composing: a saying which shows and reveals' (GRh:30).[16] What transpires 'by virtue of language', through its 'power and force', transpires through the naming power in which the essential character of language is gathered. At the close of the lecture course, in a section which bears the title 'The Metaphysical Site of Hölderlin's Poetry', Heidegger tries to think language and people, poetry and thinking, origin and poetry, as united through naming. 'This people itself [the German people] must ground and inaugurate its existence, that is, it must once more and originally name being, in inaugurating it poetically and thinkingly' (GRh:289). Now if the beginning or what begins in and as language is hostile towards itself, is turned against itself within itself, then the 'archi-originary naming power' of the word (GRh:195) must allow for an 'effective power' of the word which does not itself 'show and reveal' but nonetheless remains inscribed within the 'archi-originary naming power': 'Unambiguous clarity of speech and accuracy of words are required. When language is turned into an instrument in the service of traffic, it must adapt itself to the character of traffic systems and regulations. In order to save time and increase the effective power of the word, the latter is gathered up to appear as a compressed fascicle of letters. The word becomes a traffic sign like an arrow, a circle with a line through it, or a triangle.'[17] In *What Is Called Thinking?*, a lecture course presented during the winter semester 1951/2, Heidegger regards the 'unambiguous clarity of concepts and terms' as an expression of a 'one-track kind of thinking': 'Although it might initially appear as something quite external, we can see the ubiquitous increase of terms which consist in abbreviated words or collocations of the initial letters of words as a sign of the growing power of one-track thinking.'[18] It would be overhasty to interpret passages like these simply as a typical expression of conservative cultural criticism. And why? Because Heidegger is not pursuing cultural criticism at all here: it is not a question of lamenting the decline of language. In the context of Heidegger's early lecture on Hölderlin one could say that naming is divided by the counter-turning of what begins in and as language. But then again the very themes which one is tempted to ascribe to a conservative critique of culture also make an appearance in another kind of critique which is not at all conservative: in the critique of ideology as practised by critical theory. The theme in question at once fulfils and fails to fulfil the function with which it has been identified – and perhaps this is also true in the context of a single framework of thought, and not merely in comparing one framework of thought in relation to another.

Two examples can be adduced here. (1) Adorno sees through the 'jargon of authenticity' as a 'socially necessary illusion' which reacts 'in its objective impossibility to the emerging impossibility of language itself'.[19] He describes this jargon as a language of 'words which snap like so many signals'. In Adorno's eyes, it is precisely because Heidegger freezes the movement of constellations and uses words as names – 'everyday language is used here and now as if it were a holy language'[20] – that his language transforms itself into a jargon, into a language of signals, into one of 'traffic signs'. Presentation is peculiar to philosophy since 'all of its words say more than any one word says'. In order to preserve this excess, by virtue of which philosophy is presentation – and thereby is philosophy at all, Adorno's critique of ideology is directed against the language of signals and the signals of language: against language as signal. (2) Marcuse observes that 'functionalised, abbreviated and standardised language is the language of one-dimensional thinking'.[21] Perhaps the affinity between the expressions 'one-track thinking' and 'one-dimensional thinking' represents more than merely a linguistic or terminological affinity. The 'functionalisation' of language – its adaptation to 'traffic regulations' – prevents thought:

> The 'thing identified with its function' is more real than the thing distinguished from its function, and the linguistic

expression of this identification (in the functional noun, and in the many forms of syntactic abridgement) creates a basic vocabulary and a syntax which stand in the way of differentiation, separation and distinction. This language, which constantly imposes *images*, militates against the development and expression of *concepts*. In its immediacy and directness, it impedes conceptual thinking; thus it impedes thinking. For the concept does *not* identify the thing and its function ... Prior to its operational usage, the concept *denies* the identification of the thing with its function; it distinguishes that which the thing *is* from the contingent functions of the thing in the established reality.[22]

Heidegger, Adorno and Marcuse all regard the operationalisation and functionalisation of language (the 'jargon of authenticity' stamps words into 'tokens') as a kind of ritualisation which is incompatible with true thinking: the signal and the image substitute for that which makes − critical − thought possible.[23]

'Aestheticisation of politics' or 'politicisation of aesthetics'?

In his essay on 'The Work of Art in the Era of Mechanical Reproduction', Benjamin locates the origin of the political changes accompanying the process of operationalisation and functionalisation − the increase in univocity and availablity of meaning − in the 'crisis undergone by the conditions of exhibition'. This crisis has resulted in 'a new process of selection': 'a selection accomplished by the apparatus, from which the champion, the celebrity star, and the dictator have emerged as victors'.[24] Does not the technology of mechanical reproduction, which establishes the priority of controllability and detaches the reproduced object from ritual to ground it upon politics instead, lead to a certain ritualisation, too? Can we even imagine a process of 'selection' that did not produce a ritual effect? It is quite true that the 'cult value' that is formed in the context of rituals tends to maintain the object in a sphere of concealment − at least this is Benjamin's thesis. It is also true that authenticity and aura remain bound up with the cult value, and stand in opposition to technical reproducibility which implies the principle of universal exhibition as far as the reproduced object is concerned. Yet, as the 'new selection' reveals, the tense relationship between cult and exhibition value does not exclude the possibility that 'the crisis in the conditions of exhibition' brought on by universalising technology – Jünger would say: by the process of 'total mobilisation' – amounts to a ritualisation. It is only the introduction of a strictly codified language, which reduces the ambiguous to the unambiguous, to the repetition of practised signs and gestures, that can attempt a 'possible exhibition of controllable and indeed properly surveyable accomplishments under specific social conditions'. An unambiguous and univocal language is language completely exhibited. Benjamin identifies the 'crisis in the conditions of exhibition' with a 'crisis of democracy'. The operationalisation and functionalisation of language always possess a conservative and a progressive aspect: both are inseparable from one another, and it is precisely this inseparability which Benjamin calls politics. Just as an authoritarian and anti-democratic aspect attaches to the limitation of equality and equal distribution inherent in an ambiguity which is more than virtual univocity, so too the lack of ambiguity plunges democracy into a crisis where the demagogue who knows how to exploit the apparatus most skilfully gains the upper hand. The path which leads from the theatre to the technological reproduction of events – film, photography and radio – is the path from democracy to dictatorship: 'The parliaments are withering together with the theatres'. The 'aestheticisation of politics' of which Benjamin speaks reflects the fact that under Fascism mankind exhibits its own destruction. The 'politicisation of art' effected by communism is also, according to Benjamin, a way of exhibiting humanity, but not as the alienated mass which mankind has become in the age of technical reproduction. Rather, mankind is exhibited as a mass that has understood 'the interest of self-knowledge, and thus the interest of a knowledge based on class consciousness'.[25] But are the 'politicisation of art' and the 'aestheticisation of politics' not inextricably entwined with one another, since politics results from the intrication of the progressive and conservative aspects which belong to the functionalisation and operationalisation of language?

Having time

Heidegger refers us to the economic perspective: time is saved by transforming the word into a 'compressed fascicle of letters'. If we turn to *Being and Time*, the signal-language which allows us to save time can be understood as the language of inauthentic existence. If 'the inauthentically existing individual constantly loses the time that he never possesses as such',[26] then wanting to save time is a characteristic feature of his behaviour. In order to save time, one must relate to it in a calculating fashion, one must constantly lose time. Is it not the individual 'life-time' as the time of calculation – the time of signal-language – that corresponds to 'inauthentic existence', while 'authentic existence' on the other hand must be ascribed to the people and its time? This double attribution does not simply denote an amalgamation of the argument of the lecture course on Hölderlin with that of fundamental ontology. On the contrary, the connection is already implied in fundamental ontology and its conception of time. In *Being and Time* Heidegger bases the 'distinctive temporality of authentic existence' on the fact that, guided by 'resoluteness', such existence 'never loses time and always "has time"'. The authentically existing and resolutely disclosed self always has time 'for whatever the situation demands of him':

> The self's resoluteness against the inconstancy of distraction, is in itself a *steadiness which has been stretched along* – the steadiness with which Dasein as fate 'incorporates' into its existence birth and death and their 'between', and holds them as thus 'incorporated', so that in such constancy Dasein is indeed in a moment of vision for what is world-historical in its current situation. In the fateful repetition of possibilities that have been, Dasein brings itself back 'immediately' – that is to say in a way that is temporally ecstatical – to what already has been before it. But when its heritage is thus handed down to itself, its 'birth' is *caught up into its existence* in coming back from the possibility of death (the possibility which is not to be outstripped), if only so that this existence may accept the throwness of its own 'there' in a way which is more free from illusion.[27]

Throwness delivers Dasein over to itself and its potentiality for being, 'but does so as being-in-the-world'; to the extent that it is thrown, Dasein necessarily referred to a world and exists factually with others. The 'making-present of the situation' in the moment, the disclosing of the there as situation, the having time for what the situation demands and for the moment of world-history, is what makes it possible for Dasein to pass on its heritage, to pass itself on as heritage, at least insofar as it remains bound to the future and the 'foregoing anticipation of death': 'Only that being which is essentially *futural* in its being, so that, free for its death, it can be shattered upon it and be thrown back upon its factical there, that is to say, only that being which as futural is equally originally a *having-been* can, in passing on the inherited possibility to itself, take over its own throwness and be *momentarily* for "its time".'[28] The fate of authentic temporality, and thus the historicity of a Dasein held out into the 'future that has been', is a 'destiny': 'If fated Dasein as being-in-the-world exists essentially as being-with with others, then its happening is a happening-with that is determined as destiny. We thereby describe the happening of the community, the happening of the people. The destiny is not compounded from the individual fates, any more than being-with-one-another can be grasped as the multiple occurrence of several subjects.'[29] Just as the time of the people is not simply compounded from the calculable 'life-time' of its individuals, the destiny here is not only no sum of fates, but also no sum of existences which reckon with their own time. It is only in the temporality of authentic existence, which is essentially a destiny, that birth and death can be wrested from the public time with which one reckons; the publicised and 'exhibited' time of calculation that characterises being-with-one-another must not be confused with the time of a destiny. The time of fate as destiny is free from illusion, whereas the public time of calculation as lost and spared time of existence is governed by illusion. It is the determination of fate as destiny, therefore, that opens up the path which leads from fundamental ontology and its understanding of time to that expressed in the lecture on Hölderlin. One cannot overlook the analogy here, however much the emphasis along this path may shift from fate to destiny. The temporality of Dasein intrinsically contains both the possibility of a fateful existence marked by a destiny and the possibility of an existence which reckons with time in the domain of public time. The counter-turning of what begins in and as language brings it about that the turning-towards produced by the word of poetry in the time of the people is a turning-away which finds expression in the weakening of the naming power – in the 'impossibility of calling upon the ancient gods' (GRh:95) and in the language of signals – as well as in the calculability of time.

The 'Graeco-German mission'

But the decisive difference lies in the fact that Heidegger's lecture on Hölderlin interprets the transmission of the heritage – the repetition of what has been – specifically as a 'Graeco-German mission'. He calls the heritage by name, and equally those who shall inherit it. He thereby concretises the interpretation of fate as destiny – or of Dasein as a people – in a way that cannot adequately be explained as long as we simply content ourselves with identifying this interpretation and analysing it in the light of historically determined ideological motivations. Philosophy, the supplement of poetry in its self-relation, can only be this supplement when it follows 'its ownmost necessities': 'that is, in the Graeco-German mission from which thought, out of its own origin, steps into the original dialogue with poetry and its need' (GRh:151). For thinking and poetry have their own origin – how could thinking otherwise be a supplement to poetry? – and yet this very difference in origin points to the origin itself, to the commencement which both inaugurate. For like the thinker, the poet – Hölderlin – enjoys 'a historical place and mission that is unique in kind' (GRh:220). He is 'the poet who first composes the Germans', and as such the misunderstood one who, beyond the oppositions of Christianity and paganism, experiences the coming of the gods that fled. But it is not simply the relation between thinking and poetry, on the one hand, and the beginning, on the other, that allows the thinker and the poet to enter upon an 'original dialogue'. The beginning, as what is to come, takes on the form of 'the Graeco-German mission'. Heidegger *names* what is Greek and what is German: this naming necessarily lives off the naming power of inauguration. That is why the experience of the word of poetry is decisive for Heidegger's conception of the 'Graeco-German' mission. It is only the engagement with poetry – with Hölderlin – that can fulfil the claims that have already initially been advanced – in the Rectoral Address, for example. When we ask after the connection between fundamental ontology and the thinking of National Socialism, we must ask after the power of naming. In the lecture which Habermas dedicates to Heidegger's thought in his *Philosophical Discourse on Modernity*, he writes: 'Because [Heidegger] had identified "Dasein" with the existence of the people, the authentic potentiality for being with the [Nazi] seizure of power, and freedom with the will of the "Führer"; because he had projected the National Socialist revolution as well as its labour, military and academic service into the question of being itself, this established a kind of internal connection between his philosophy and contemporary events which could not easily be disguised.'[30] Whether this explanation is particularly plausible cannot be decided here. But it is strange, to say the least, that a 'projection' alone should suffice to establish an 'internal connection'. Could one not equally claim from an 'immanent' perspective that such an act of identification is actually an arbitrary and external one? Insofar as he speaks of an act of identification, Habermas himself must implicitly refer to the significance of the power of naming. The establishment of what he describes as an 'internal' philosophical connection depends upon the possibility of denomination. In the Rectoral Address, to which Habermas is alluding, the 'National-Socialist revolution' does indeed mark the decisive departure, the setting out and breaking forth with which the repetition of the beginning begins: it marks the 'Graeco-German mission'.

Naming the name

In order to bestow a name upon the people and its destiny or sending, in order to place history under a certain name – under the name of the Greeks and the Germans – it is not of course sufficient merely to appeal to a universal and semi-abstract naming power of language in general. Naming must be grasped as the essence of language, and language, i.e. poetry, must be grasped as beginning and inauguration. Above all, however, the beginning must already bear a name: we can only descry the naming power of language because the Greek and the German languages bring us along the path towards it, while the Latin and the English languages, for example, obscure our access to this essential realm. Naming already possesses a name. This is why Heidegger – the thinker, the poet, the statesman – can only bestow the name that naming bears. *The naming must be named if one is to speak of a 'Graeco-German mission' in the first place.* In his posthumously published *Spiegel* interview, which by virtue of the delayed publication that he had requested fulfils the function of a testament, Heidegger still locates the double name of naming within the Greek and the German languages – naming bears a double name because the beginning is its own repetition. The political relevance of such a location becomes intelligible once we have recognised what it is that makes all 'acts of identification' possible.[31]

Original language and 'the final solution'

The privileging of Greek and German, the combining or pairing of Greek and German within the framework of a mission, implies the exclusion of other names. The linguist Jean-Claude Milner has described the event of language, something that cannot be grasped by the methods of positive science, as a kind of original co-incidence:

> What is resistant here is an event: the co-incidence in which a flurry of sound and a flurry of images have chanced to come together and have firmly attached themselves to one another; in a manner indeed which seems all the more unchangeable since there is no reason for such a co-incidence, and therefore equally no reason for a separation. There is no doubt that this event lacks a substance that could be uttered; for one would have to identify, in language, the moment which immediately precedes language. But that is not decisive: the thinking of language can bestow no other form upon itself than the form without content which is at stake here. What is decisive is that this form can only exist in the dimension of forgetting.[32]

From the conception of the event of language as presented here Milner concludes that 'revisionism' – which he also characterises as 'negationism' – does not think the forgetting, thereby missing the original co-incidence in which the event of language consists:

> In this respect the particular discourse and vocabulary of the final solution represents more than one of those habitual attempts to cover up something. One must be so bold as to claim that it represents, as it were, a parable of language itself; one must reflect that every word in every language relates to the conjunction through which it can identify its 'signified' in the same way in which the word *Endlösung* ['final solution'] relates to the decision through which it arises and which it must bury and forget for ever. In its clearest and most vivid shape negationism denies this config- uration: according to the former there is no forgetting, and especially no forgetting that would be constitutive of lan- guage: every word designates what it wants to designate.[33]

The naming and the power of naming which Heidegger has in view cannot possibly, according to the claim invested in them, be subjected to any theoretical semiotic analysis. The terminol- ogy of linguistic science is inappropriate to an exposition of such naming, even if it is employed for the purpose of describ- ing the event of language which precedes all linguistic science. One is tempted, nevertheless, to follow Milner in speaking of a co-incidence of the name and the named. But it is also necessary to radicalise this thought of co-incidence. Name and named do not precede it. This co-incidence which first allows the name to be, and the named to appear – for the name and the named are not separate prior to the co-incidence – happens as event in the original linguistic inauguration. The poet inaugurates the 'origi- nal language of the people': he stands up before the language of the gods, which is the original linguistic inauguration and marks out the inauguration of the 'original language of the people', he captures it and brings it into the existence of the people as their original language. But he does not create it out of nothing. What begins in and as language is yet to come: that is why the beginning – the original linguistic inauguration – is the event that has always already happened. Language is in advance of itself; every inauguration is its own repetition. Because language is an event, a beginning, and thus also a counter-turning within itself, forgetting characterises language – the power of naming – in the beginning. The function of the name which naming bears is now clearly revealed: it is to work against forgetting. It is only when the naming power is named that one can understand the repetition of the beginning as appropriation, and understand the beginning itself as mission. The counter-turning of originary language indeed divides the power of naming and multiplies the languages. There is a Graeco-German mission because the originary language demands another language that can remember the forgetting and bring the forgotten to language once again. Already in the beginning the beginning is another beginning in another language. The immemorial co-incidence of a name and a named is an event that has happened, has programmed the event in a language – and not merely in language as such. Ever since the beginning one speaks in a language that has other languages alongside itself.

One does not speak of the power of naming in language as such: that is why it is impossible to speak in German about the power of naming without privileging the German language, and without relinquishing this privilege in the very same moment. The name of the naming power protects from this relinquishment of privilege, from the multiplication of languages and from the self-repeating repetition of the beginning. But insofar as the name stabilises the counter-turning of originary language it also denies the event of language – and thus provides the foundation for negationism and revisionism. All other names are excluded *a priori* because the name governs in advance the co-incidence of name and named, and no forgetting of language is permitted to transform the 'most dangerous of goods'. On the one hand, therefore, it is clear that Habermas cannot succeed in establishing the 'internal' philosophical connection between fundamental ontology and the ideas of National Socialism: at least to the extent that he has failed to clarify the connection between the power of naming and the logic of the beginning. On the other hand, one must ask whether the task of the Rectoral Address – the 'spiritual task of the German people' that 'effectively acts with regard to its fate'[34] – can really be separated from the task and fate of 'the will to will'. What is the relation between Heidegger's remarks in *The Overcoming of Metaphysics* (1936–46), where 'the language of "task"' is described as an invention of 'the will to will', and the Rectoral Address itself, where Heidegger discusses the repetition of the Greek beginning in the setting-forth of the German people? Is it an invention or a task that is at stake here, an invention of a task or a task without invention?

> Because the will to will intrinsically denies every goal, and only permits goals as willing and deliberate means of over-playing itself, as means of setting up the open space to play in, but also because the will to will must not appear as the anarchic catastrophe which it is when it sets itself up amongst beings, the will to will still needs to legitimate itself. And here it invents the language of the 'task'. The latter is not thought here with regard to the beginning and its preservation, but as a goal dispensed from the standpoint of 'fate' and one which shall thereby justify the will to will.[35]

The word 'being'

What does Heidegger mean by the standpoint of 'fate'? Are the quotation marks within which the word is placed meant to suggest that one can also think fate 'with regard to the beginning', indeed that one must think its originary essence in order to understand the function of the quotation marks, in order to understand 'task' and 'fate? What is the relationship between name and fate?

In the *Introduction to Metaphysics*, which pursues the philosophical opening up of the beginning, Heidegger says that 'the fate of a historical people and its work' is a matter of 'greatness'. Fate does not determine knowledge; rather knowledge itself is revealed as fateful: 'There is fate only there where true knowing concerning things prevails in Dasein. But it is philosophy which opens up the paths and perspectives of such knowing.' Like that effected through poetry, the opening up accomplished through philosophy is an untimely one: 'All essential questioning on the part of philosophy necessarily remains untimely. And that because philosophy is either cast forward far beyond its contemporary now, or because it binds the now back to what has earlier been in an *originary* manner. Philosophising has always been a knowing which is not only incapable of being made timely, but is one which rather brings time under its own measure.'[36] In the winter semester of 1934/5, Heidegger is occupied with Hölderlin's 'understanding of fate'. He dedicates several pages to this 'fate' which he explicitly distinguishes both from 'Asian *fatum*' and from the Greek idea of '*moira*'. ('For the first time, and in a specific way that could not be repeated, the Greeks accomplished the overcoming of the Asian notion of fatedness [*Fatum*] ... But we should not equate Hölderlin's understanding of fate [*Schicksal*] with that of the Greeks. We must learn to use this essential German word in an essential manner as a naming of an essential being [*Seyn*] in its true German content, and that also means: to use it seldom' [GRh: 173].) Very shortly afterwards, in the summer semester of 1935, Heidegger delivers his lecture course entitled *Introduction to Metaphysics*. Does philosophy here come to occupy the position which was formerly ascribed to poetry? Is original inauguration replaced here with the opening up in and through knowing? Is the hierarchy reversed here? At the end of the first lecture Heidegger claims that 'being is now for us simply an empty word and a vanishing vapour'. For 'everyone goes on speaking and writing away without more ado, and above all without being *endangered*, in language'.[37] This emphasis upon the danger which is threatened by language itself, precisely because language no longer reveals itself as a danger at all and appears as a 'means of communication, as indifferent as a public means of traffic', undoubtedly contains a reference to Hölderlin. The 'emptiness of the word "being"' results from the 'total disappearance of its naming power': one speaks without danger, therefore, when naming arises from a forgetting or an inadequate knowledge of the essence of language, and of its constitutive dangerousness. The word being, the 'uniqueness of this name and its naming',[38] marks all names and every process of naming: 'Let us assume that the indeterminate meaning of being did not exist, and that we had no understanding of what this meaning signifies. What then? Would being be merely a name and a verb within our language? No. *For then there would be no language at all.'*[39] If we are to speak at all, we find that we have always already named being: the 'naming power' has always already accrued to or grown upon us. Being is a being-ahead-of-itself of language or the name. The 'uniqueness' of being rests upon the fact that it is a name before the name, a name that one names before one names anything. One must guard here against the misunderstanding that 'being' is itself another name: it is rather the original opening and gathering of the name, the name as such in its nameability and in its being named. But this original gathering of the 'naming power' is, as we have seen, a movement of division; being must still be called by name and thus inaugurated. There is no 'purification' that is capable of restituting the 'naming power': 'The organisations dedicated to the purification of language and the prevention of further abuse deserve attention here. But such measures only serve in the final analysis to demonstrate that we no longer know what is at stake with language. It is because the fate of language is grounded in the particular *relation* of a people to *being* that the question concerning *being* is so intimately bound up with the question concerning *language*.' People and language alike have a fate. The fate of the people lies in the knowledge concerning the beginning, a knowledge which philosophy discloses through asking the question concerning being. But philosophy can only ask after being if it has already received the 'naming power' through which the word being is neither an 'empty name' nor a 'vanishing vapour'. The possibility of philosophical knowing depends, therefore, upon the experience of naming as an experience of linguistic danger, as an experience of the danger of language.

The experience of naming decides upon the fate of language: it is here that the 'relation of a people to being' is grounded. Is it not the experience of language as poetry?

> In the question concerning the essence of language we are constantly confronted by the question concerning the origin of language. The answer has been sought in the most remarkable of ways. And here too the first and decisive answer to the question concerning the origin of language is this: this origin remains a secret, a mystery; not because people have not been canny enough up till now, but because

all canniness and all cleverness have gone astray even before they set to work. This secret mysterious character belongs to the essence of the origin of language. But this also implies: language can only have begun and come to be from out of the domain of the overwhelming and the uncanny, within the human departure and setting forth into being. In this setting forth language was the coming into word of being: poetry. Language is the original poetry in which a people composes being.

Such poetic composing is a naming:

> The word, the naming, sets the beings that open up back into their being from out of the immediate and overwhelming thronging, and preserves them in this openness, delimitation and standing. Naming does not subsequently supply beings that are otherwise already open and manifest with a mark or designation, called the word, but rather the other way around: the word sinks down from the height of its original deed of violence [*Gewalt-tat*] in the opening up of being to become a mere sign, so much so indeed, that the sign itself then obtrudes itself before beings'.[40]

Heidegger credits the Greek people with the unity which the German people has yet to win and accomplish for itself. Must one regard the 'original poetry' as the 'great poetry' through which 'a people enters into history' and begins 'to give shape to its language'? 'The Greeks created and experienced this poetry through Homer.' At the same time they too are subject to the counter-turning of the beginning – of what begins in and as language. The unity of the Greek people must ultimately – and in spite of all essential differences – be inaugurated through the repetition of the beginning, that is, through the German people assuming its own 'historical mission'[41] and thereby acquiring its own unity.

History and the multiplication of languages

The 'danger of a growing darkness of the world',[42] the danger of language itself, threatens the German people to the degree that this people 'exposes the history of the West, from out the midst of its future happening, into the original realm of the powers of being'.[43] The question concerning being, inseparable from the violent deed of the word that first opens up being, must repeat what begins in and as language, if being is indeed being ahead of itself: the being ahead of itself of language, which divides itself in its original supplementarity. It is because language is ahead of itself that the 'deed of violence' is over-powered before it can overmaster the thronging to which it is exposed. Divided and afflicted with forgetting, what begins in and as language ascribes the repetition of the beginning and the question concerning being to a language, to a people, thereby opening up the way for a repetition of this repetition in another language. The division of what begins in and as language or of the naming power must be understood as the multiplication of languages, one which necessarily precedes the constitution of the unity of any single language. For otherwise, indeed, Heidegger's discourse on the 'Graeco-German mission' or on the necessity of 'assuming the historical mission of our people in the midst of the West' would remain unintelligible. Language multiplies itself from the first, in the very beginning. Every inauguration is at once a repetition, and a repetition of a repetition. That is why there is only inauguration in an essentially plural sense. Inauguration is infinite, but in a finite manner. This infinite finitude is what is called history:

To ask: how do matters stand with being? means nothing less than to repeat or *retrieve* [*wieder-holen*] the beginning of our historical-spiritual existence, in order to transform it into another beginning. Such a thing is possible. It is indeed the exemplary form of history precisely because it takes its departure from a fundamental transpiring or happening. A beginning is not repeated by forcing oneself back to something supposedly past and now familiar which merely needs to be imitated; but rather by re-beginning the beginning in a more original manner, and along indeed with everything strange, obscure and uncertain that a true beginning involves. Repetition as we understand it here is anything but the improved continuation of what has so far prevailed with the means of what has prevailed so far.[44]

And Heidegger adds: 'The beginning, insofar as it begins, must in a certain sense leave itself behind. (Thus it necessarily conceals itself, although this concealment is not nothing.) The beginning cannot once or ever preserve the beginning as immediately as it began, but only as it can be preserved, namely as the re-petition of its originary character in a more original manner.'[45] The event of history happens as the repetition of the beginning, a repetition which the beginning prescribes for itself. In itself the repetition is open to the event of the beginning, is indeed openness, caesura rather than continuous extension and imitation of what has already been opened up. What repetition openly reveals is the alterity of the beginning, that otherness of language with which history always and necessarily commences. That the beginning is ahead of itself, that it leaves itself behind, implies that the event of history happens in the beginning, in what begins in and as language. The beginning is history itself, the 'fundamental transpiring and happening', the 'primal history' that does not lie there somewhere in the past as a present to be retrieved. It is rather the coming inscribed in a repetition, a coming which is utterly different from the coming of something future. It indicates the possibility that the event of history continues to happen again and again. Thus, the naming of the 'naming power' is what effectively thwarts history.

Repetition

In his remarks on *The Overcoming of Metaphysics*, Heidegger speaks about an 'end of philosophy' which would mark a 'transition to another beginning' rather than simply 'the end of thinking' as such.[46] This transition must be therefore grasped as a repetition. For repetition, as the experience of the otherness of the counter-turning beginning, is always a 'transition to another beginning', and not the duplication of something already present at hand. In the *Introduction to Metaphysics*, or more precisely in the interpretation of the chorus from *Antigone* which this lecture course includes, we can recognise the beginning in a 'relinquishment of firm ground', in a setting-forth or breaking-out which takes place in the midst of the 'winter storm'. And is not 'the tireless breaking into the indestructible sway of the earth' also such a breaking-out that relinquishes? If breaking-out is a breaking-in and breaking-in is a breaking-out, if there can be no breaking in without a breaking-out, no breaking out without a breaking-in, then the deed of violence cannot simply be thought as a breaking-out or as a breaking-in – the deed of violence which is always the 'violent deed' of the word that stands 'like a pillar' and strives to withstand what proves to be overpowering. The deed of violence is a breaking-in that breaks out, and a breaking-out that breaks in; as such, it seeks to defy what is overpowering: the 'self-consuming wildness of the sea' and, at the same time, in the course of the selfsame movement, the tireless burgeoning of the earth. Beginning, greatness and storm are once again brought together at this point. What is at stake here is a Dasein which is uncanny, is strangely homeless, to the degree that it abandons its familiar homeland and breaks out to transgress its borders, to break into what proves to be overpowering and master it through the word. 'Violently asserting itself within the overpowering', the homeless and uncanny Dasein holds itself, beyond all wilfulness and savagery, in the prevailing sway and violence of the beginning, which in its sway, as a counter-turning, demands the mastering word – and how could anything that would not turn against itself ever hold sway? The sway is a task: the beginning gives itself up and gives itself over in its counter-turning, gives over to Dasein the task of its repetition, a repetition that gives up the beginning, gives it over once again, because it must necessarily take place within one particular language. Just as originary language bears within itself the possibility of operationalised language, so too everything great bears within it the marks of its own distorted shape:

The beginning is the most uncanny and the most mighty power and violence. What comes afterwards is not development, but the flattening out of mere dissemination, an inability to hold inwardly to the beginning, a process in which the beginning is at once trivialised and inflated to become that distorted shape of greatness which presents itself as numerical and quantitative magnitude and extension. The uncanniest *is* what it is *because* it harbours such a beginning, one in which everything breaks out by virtue of an excess into what is overpowering and needs to be mastered. The inexplicable character of this beginning is no defect or failure on the part of our knowledge of history. The genuine greatness of historical knowing lies rather in the understanding of the secret and mysterious character of this beginning.[47]

If the 'inability inwardly to hold to the beginning' is not a matter of development or progressive unfolding, its immediacy cannot be interpreted as the initial or preliminary stage of a dialectical process of knowledge. But it would be equally misleading to identify the understanding of the 'secret and mysterious character' of the beginning with the possession of some special arcane knowledge, or to suggest by a kind of symmetrical reversal some irrationalism of origins here. The beginning eludes knowing because it turns against itself within itself. It is not something actually concealed that constitutes its 'secret and mysterious character', but rather the concealment which interrupts knowing and thereby fate as well. If this interruption inaugurates history as the forgetting of the beginning – of the origin, of being, of language – it is still possible to claim with Heidegger that it is only such an interruption that permits the transformation of fate into a 'standpoint'. For we can recognise the coming of the beginning and of history in the distorted shape itself. The more original the repetition, the more it exposes itself to the counter-turning and the less it abandons itself to the latter. The most original of all repetitions, repetition itself, would have to repeat the counter-turning as counter-turning, repeat language as language. Such repetition could enjoy no site within an actual language. Perhaps Heidegger's idea of the 'end of the history of being' – discussed in the seminar connected with lecture on *Time and Being* he gave in 1962 – alludes precisely to this repetition: 'The event of appropriation [*Ereignis*] indeed harbours possibilities of manifestation which thought cannot make out, and in this sense it certainly cannot be said that the entering or the retreat of thinking into the event will put a "stop" to the sendings of being. But we must still consider whether after this entering or this retreat we can continue to speak of being and thus of the history of being, assuming that the history of being is understood as the history of sendings in which the event conceals itself.'[48]

The naming of naming thwarts history, and is itself no

'entering or retreat into the event'. The 'entering or retreat into the event' cannot be accomplished through a naming of naming precisely because such a naming receives a particular name.

2

Rise and Downfall

Semblance of regression

If it were indeed clear from the start that the beginning secures itself in its own coming, that its repetition is nothing but a recognition, there would be no beginning. The beginning is an unleashing, it unleashes itself, and does so necessarily. Consequently, as Heidegger underlines in his lecture on *The Origin of the Work of Art*, the beginning is always accompanied by the danger of regression. Regression is therefore also only really possible there where the event of beginning happens. Heidegger distinguishes the beginning as the possibility of regression from something primitive and rudimentary:

> How is an origin [*Ursprung*] possible at all? It is only ever possible as a kind of leap [*Sprung*]. That is why the *beginning* of an origin is something immediate and sudden. Only that which is an origin, like art in the sense we have explained, can have a beginning. The immediate character of the beginning does not exclude, but on the contrary precisely includes the fact that the latter has long and quite inconspicuously been preparing itself. As a leap the beginning is always a leaping-*ahead* in which everything that is to come finds itself already overleapt, even if only in a concealed fashion. The beginning already contains the end hidden within itself. But the beginning never possesses the rudimentary character of something 'primitive'. The primitive never has a future because it lacks this free leap, this inner leaping-ahead of itself. The primitive can release nothing from out of itself because it contains only that in which it is itself caught up. The beginning, on the other hand, is never primitive, that is, without an origin, but rather originary: the hiddenness of the

not-yet. The apparently helpless, rude and even sparse character that marks it merely betrays its extraordinary harshness over against the hidden fullness which it bears within. Wherever the beginning comes to leap, it is always accompanied by the semblance of a *regression*.

Why does the beginning produce 'the semblance of a regression'? Is the beginning deceptive in character? In this context 'semblance' cannot mean that the possibility of a regression reveals itself as nothing but an illusory appearance. On the contrary, Heidegger is attempting to emphasise the undecidability inscribed in the beginning, that which suspends all decision and thereby precisely necessitates decision. In the beginning one cannot decide whether the beginning represents a regression or not. The beginning regularly does represent a regression, and does so precisely because it is not exhausted by the latter. The regression only reveals itself as mere appearance at the end, that end which is initially concealed but nonetheless, according to Heidegger, contained already in the beginning. But since the beginning contains the end and must leap over itself – as the beginning of the origin – the evidence for what can only ever show itself at the end remains ineluctably ambiguous and suspended: the beginning is never simply evident at all. It produces the 'semblance of a regression' insofar as it leaps over everything that has already prevailed so far, over everything that has already begun:

> For the beginning cannot simply continue what has so far prevailed along the secure and familiar pathways. What has prevailed so far comes to a standstill and begins to fall apart: it is out of joint. Confusion and decline make themselves felt on all sides. That is a consequence not of the beginning but rather of the growing impotence of what has so far prevailed. The beginning finds its ground much deeper than this, and must therefore descend beneath the established ground. Hence it can long remain ambiguous whether the unavoidable semblance of regression conceals a beginning or a downfall.[49]

If the beginning, which reveals itself immediately in all its ambiguity, announces itself for a longer period, and in a more inconspicuous fashion, than any mere commencement, it also always and essentially encourages the growing impotence by which it finds itself threatened. To appeal to Heidegger and explain the 'semblance of regression' simply as a consequence of the growing impotence of what has so far prevailed, to interpret the beginning as an unendangered and independent instance which reveals the regression as illusory after all, is not to understand what makes the beginning into a ground. To the extent that the ground of a beginning lies deeper than the ground of what has prevailed so far, to the extent that the beginning is indeed a ground and that there is no longer any grounding power at work in what has so far prevailed, the groundlessness of the 'established ground' endangers the originary grounding itself. For the beginning as ground is characterised by a 'leaping-ahead'. Let us assume here that the beginning can be as clearly and definitively distinguished from the primitive − or the rudimentary − as Heidegger himself wishes. Would we not then have to relate the primitive to what has prevailed so far? What the beginning brings to light is precisely the fact that what has so far prevailed lacks a future. It encourages the growth of impotence, not only because its own ground lies in previously unapproached depths, but also and above all because the proper securing of this ground does not immediately result from the insecurity and uncertainty which it exposes and to which it also exposes itself. The beginning brings the primitive to light and produces it as well, since it embodies the very possibility of a regression towards the primitive and its impotence. It is for this reason that the beginning harbours its own ambiguity. From a Heideggerean perspective, one could attempt to counter such a line of argument by claiming that from the moment that what has so far prevailed loses its secure standing and unleashes uncertainty, we can no longer speak of an alternative between the continuation of the familiar or the beginning of something other. The decision to be made concerns only the possibility of a rise and the possibility of a downfall. But if the downfall is not to be a negative rise, then the 'logic' of beginning must ineluctably shatter the distinction between the originary and the primitive, between repetition and mere continuation along the paths of that which has no origin.

Repudiation and celebration of destruction

What further conclusions does this 'logic' allow us to draw? It is precisely the ambiguity of the beginning which makes it possible for Heidegger to interpret National Socialism both as the overcoming of nihilism and as its consummation, and not to contradict himself. In his own subsequent remarks on the Rectoral Address Heidegger writes: 'At the time I saw in the movement that had come to power the possibility for an inner gathering and renewal on the part of the people, a path towards the discovery of its historical and occidental vocation. I believed that the self-renewal of the university might be called upon, along with others, to contribute in an exemplary and decisive manner to this inner gathering of the people.'[50] However one might interpret these remarks, nothing could prevent the reader from regarding them as if dictated by the 'logic' of the beginning. In order to contest Heidegger's right to see the National Socialist Movement as such a beginning, one would first have to challenge and bring the 'logic' of beginning itself into question. Even downfall and devastation can be grasped, in accordance with that very 'logic', as a sign of that which begins and of its contamination.

But the 'logic' of the beginning is by no means merely rooted in the singularity of Heidegger's thought, or in its peculiarities. One cannot think any event whatsoever that would not be subject to that 'logic'. This is perhaps most clearly revealed there where the event not only bears another name, but bears the name of otherness. When Adorno starts from the claim that after Auschwitz all culture is trash, and that one cannot write about Auschwitz without thereby exposing oneself to the danger of regression; when he considers Auschwitz as the event in which the guilt of thought and of the entire process of civilisation finds expression; when he rigorously binds the possibility of philosophy to the incommensurability of that event (the event is always more than merely an expression, an expression of something that has already transpired and necessarily transcends its own preparation, its own anticipation, its own announcement), then he too is obeying the 'logic' of the beginning. In this connection it is irrelevant whether he actually opposes the 'philosophy of origins', whether in fact he speaks of a beginning or not. Nor is the fact that there is no question here of a 'historical–occidental vocation' of any decisive significance. It is a structural necessity and not a formal analogy that is at issue here.

In his essay on Beckett, Adorno describes human conscious-ness after Auschwitz as 'bomb-ravaged', a characterisation which recalls the 'explosion of metaphysical meaning' which is mentioned in the opening section of the text. Heidegger defines a beginning in the realm of art as a kind of thrust or shock: 'Whenever art begins, a thrust enters history, and history first or once again begins; history here does not mean: a sequence of happenings, however important these may be, but rather the *transporting* of a people into its task, which is also the people's settling into its endowment, into that which has been given over to it.'[51] Despite all the differences of terminology and perspective (Adorno reflects upon the effects that an event can exercise upon art, whereas Heidegger is attempting to name the originary character and the beginning of art itself), one could say here that the beginning is always a blow, a shock, a thrust or an explosion. If there is a time when it is impossible to decide whether downfall is being transformed into a rise or a rise is being wrested into a downfall, if there is a moment when rise and downfall might hang in the balance together, if there is a period in which the downfall bears the features of a rise and the rise those of a downfall, then this time, this moment, this period lack a site from which one might reflect upon the event, and impede any such reflection. Rise and downfall find their origin in the originary movement of beginning that Heidegger calls the thrust. The repudiation of destruction and its celebra-tion, a celebration already inscribed in the affirmation of the event, bear witness to the experience of this thrust. Both relate to one another in complementary fashion. When Benjamin, during the early 1930s, affirmed the poverty of human experi-ence initiated with the First World War, identifying it with the chance for a new beginning, when he considered the new revo-lutionary naming of things, which rejected everything that resembled humanity, to be more than a merely 'technical renewal of language' and to mobilise language 'in the service of struggle and labour',[52] when he interpreted this mobilisation as one of the characteristic features of the age, he also revealed that such an affirmation is inevitable, however much a critical discourse would want to warn against its dangers. For the very circumstance that Benjamin experienced the First World War as an event already implies a kind of affirmation. Similarly one could reproach Jünger – whom Benjamin resembles here not merely in gesture and rhetoric but also in the shared idea that labour constitutes the central feature of the age – with directly participating in active nihilism with his own book *The Worker* (1932). But it is impossible to indicate the necessity for a nihilistic interpretation of being, as undertaken by Heidegger in his lectures on Nietzsche, without also revealing the necessity of an affirmation, as befits a project which grew directly from an exemplary experience of 'the material slaughter of the First World War'.[53] *This does not of course mean that the affirmation in question can also be justified or that it must continue to determine discourse.* Heidegger says in the lectures on Nietzsche:

> In these days we ourselves are the witnesses to a mysterious law of history, that a people one day can no longer measure up to the metaphysics which has sprung from their own history, and this precisely in the moment when this metaphysics has transformed itself into the unconditioned. It is now revealed, as Nietzsche already recognised in a metaphysical fashion, that the modern 'machine economy', the machine-like calculation of all acting and planning in its unconditional form demands a new kind of humanity which goes beyond the human being that has previously existed. It is not enough that one simply uses tanks, aeroplanes and electronic media of communication; nor is it enough that one has the people who are qualified to use such things at one's disposal; it is not even enough that man merely commands this technology as if it were something indifferent in itself, beyond utility and damage, construction and destruction, capable of being used for anything whatsoever by anyone whatsoever. It rather requires a kind of humanity that is itself fundamentally appropriate to the unique fundamental essence of modern technology and its metaphysical truth, that is, the kind of humanity that can be entirely commanded by the essence of technology, precisely in order to control and employ the individual technical processes and possibilities in question'.[54]

What is striking about this description is that it is more than merely a description. The overcoming of nihilism can be accomplished only through its completion and consummation. Once again the thinking of the event – of the event of being – calls forth both affirmation and repudiation. It is quite true that nothing seems further from Heidegger's intentions than any act of simple affirmation or simple repudiation. But he is nonetheless incapable of thinking and describing the event without in part exposing this very description to the dynamics of affirmation and repudiation. This is not to be explained by reference to some subjective incapacity or to an insufficiently thorough approach on Heidegger's part. For it results from the 'logic' of the beginning. Affirmation and repudiation are prior, as it were, to the subject who affirms or repudiates something.

Michael Theunissen concludes an examination of the concept of negativity in Adorno with the following remark: 'For Adorno himself is what he once labelled Beckett: a "simplifier of horror" who refuses simplification'.[55] How are we to understand this claim? The author wishes to maintain that Adorno's philosophy, in spite of its own claims, is 'in a certain sense not negativistic enough'. On the one hand, it remains caught up in an 'epistemological optimism' and ties itself 'through its dependence upon metaphysics to pre-negativist models of interpretation', while on the other hand – through a kind of deliberate inconsequence – it 'cancels its claim concerning the untruth of the whole' and thereby fails to avoid 'nihilism in the vulgar sense', as the 'confession of the senselessness of everything'. A thinking that understands itself as the thinking of an event, and names this event, can never be 'negativistic enough': it must necessarily simplify horror. The event programmes its own simplification, just as it always summons up a prior, ungovernable and inseparable pairing of affirmation and repudiation. In this respect the name which the event receives in each case is of secondary significance.

Simplifications: learning from a 'national catastrophe'

The simplification of the event can be traced to the totalising effect of its name, of its proper name ('Auschwitz' or 'Germanien') or of a designation that functions as a name ('the national catastrophe'). Every event that is named, that is, every event recognised as such, is a caesura which transforms both what has been and what is to come. The simplification in question reduces the event to the triggering cause, the culminating point or the paradigmatic case of some development which can be interpreted under a positive or a negative sign.

The reduction to a paradigmatic case of historical development serves perhaps to translate the prior repudiation, and is thus already programmed by the event in this respect. But if it does translate the prior repudiation, it must also be regraded as the translation of the prior affirmation which precedes all repudiation. In the context of this reduction of the event, already accomplished once the event is located within a historical development that it also confirms, the prior affirmation can subsequently assume the form of a distinctive privilege. Karl–Otto Apel claims that 'precisely we Germans could, or should, have learned *something particular* through the experience of our national catastrophe'.[56] How does this particularity, which permits the learning of something so particular and thus a particular learning, present itself to the 'subjective consciousness' (of Apel)?

I am not *primarily* thinking here of the 'Second World War', of a struggle for control of the world, one which resulted in a completely new constellation of world powers: a constellation in which Germany, having been divided in two, now merely played a role as the line of demarcation between the power blocs. Nor am I referring primarily to the feeling that the kind of national sentiment or patriotism that had developed in Europe during the nineteenth and the beginning of the twentieth century was radically called into question by our own experience. (This feeling already disturbed me when in 1940, at the age of 18, I became a military volunteer, along with the rest of my school year; however, it does not yet provide the authentic criterion for an awareness of the truly unparalleled character of what we experienced; it only points us in the appropriate direction.) What prevailed at that time was the initially vague feeling that 'everything was false', namely everything that we had supported, in the same way in which all good patriots generally do and should do. But this already broaches the issue at stake in the formula explicitly discussed at this conference: 'the destruction of moral self-consciousness'. In addition to all this, there also arose – for me at least – the quasi-speculative thought that we had perhaps experienced something that hardly any other generation of combatants had experienced, something that might well harbour a particular insight – an insight that could or should prevent us from simply returning to normality in the same way as all the other participants – the victors – perhaps could and would do so.[57]

There is no cause to doubt the integrity of someone who thus expresses himself in the name of his 'subjective consciousness'. However, the entanglement of biographical and theoretical issues, the reference to experience – or to a certain 'vague feeling' – as a foundation for a 'quasi-speculative thought', the appeal to a concept of experience that already results from a theoretical – or speculative – reflection, all this certainly allows one to regard these observations as more than merely an expression of autobiographical sentiments externally related to reflective thought.

Apel's remarks claim to possess a paradigmatic relevance. How are we to reconcile the assertion that 'national sentiment or patriotism' was radically called into question by the experience of the Second World War with the qualification of the catastrophe as a 'national catastrophe'? In order to support his argument Apel is forced to assume a German identity the possibility of which is not radically affected or called into question. The radicality thus finds its limit in the possibility of a national identity. The catastrophe affects a nation and its self-understanding as a nation. That is why it can be appropriated by the affected nation as a catastrophe peculiar to itself. It is for this reason – and for this reason alone – that the survivors, who continue to participate in a national identity, a national self-consciousness and a national self-understanding, can regard the catastrophe precisely as a lesson for the nation, and thereby attain to a different self-understanding than before. Because the German is able to appropriate the catastrophe as a catastrophe for his nation, he is also in a privileged position to think a 'quasi-speculative thought' (does the qualification here refer to

some defect which attaches to speculation after the catastrophe?): namely the thought that the Germans have had an
experience unavailable to those who have fallen victim to a
certain omission, grounded in the structure of their own historical existence, and who have returned to 'normality', or are at
least already prepared to entrust themselves to 'normality' once
again. Apel does not define the concept of normality. But in
this context he can only mean that a certain ethical insight (the
insight into the only possible ethics, namely discourse ethics)
remains closed to the victors themselves. The victor falls victim
to an illusory victory. The 'national catastrophe', therefore, is
not simply a catastrophe that threatens to destroy one nation
but possesses a paradigmatic status of its own. It is the catastrophe of all catastrophes since those whom it afflicts thereby
secure for themselves a privileged access to the – consensual –
truth, however paradoxical this may sound, however incompatible it may seem with the transcendental-pragmatic attempt to
determine an ultimate ethical foundation. The privileged access
to a truth which is not supposed to be a privilege of anyone
corresponds to the indestructible character of national identity.
Apel's 'subjective intention' may be directed against the exact
opposite of this, but 'objectively' he participates in the (philosophical) nationalism that he rejects. (Perhaps the pathos of his
lecture actually results from this contradiction.) Transcendental
pragmatics, precisely because it still represents a residual philosophy of history, must face the difficulty involved in thinking the
relationship between the universal and the particular. For this
reason, it is possible to regard the (philosophical) nationalism
implied in the argumentation of the transcendental-pragmatic
thinker, as an effect of the difficulty he must face. That Apel's
argumentation cannot succeed without a (philosophical) nationalism is a relevant claim in the context of a residual philosophy
of history.

The 'we' that Apel evokes here without further explanation
and assumes as something self-evident in the given situation,
denotes the Germans in general, those who possess or who are
capable of possessing some consciousness about this 'national
catastrophe'. But the experience which is said to generate the
quasi-speculative thought actually belongs to a particular
'generation of combatants', a generation without parallel

because it has experienced something in a way in which 'hardly' any other generation' has 'ever' experienced it. What does it mean then to be German? To be German means, so one is forced to conclude from Apel's argumentation, to have participated in the war with patriotic conviction in order then, after the war, to have learnt something better, namely that 'everything was false'.

A delaying pseudo-rational reasoning

The 'we' to whom Apel refers names a collective subject or an intersubjectivity which results from the universalisation of a particular experience, one that is paradigmatic in its very particularity: not all Germans actually participated in the war, not all of them participated in it in the same way as Apel. One cannot avoid asking why the cause of the 'national catastrophe' should be sought in the war alone. There is little difference between Apel's approach here and that of Heidegger, who interprets the world war as the catastrophe which is brought on by technological-global domination of nihilism: the war is no longer an expression of 'national sentiment' but a way of prosecuting the 'struggle for world domination'.[58] The monumentalisation of the 'national catastrophe', the explicit acknowledgement of its privileged character, simultaneously represents its (unacknowledged) minimalisation: where the 'transcendentally necessary counter-factual anticipation of the ideal conditions of discourse' is posited as the 'telos of history', 'the time following the First World War' appears as the paradigm case in the context of the continuing crisis in the adolescence of humanity. [The time following the First World War is a time of crisis which fails to accomplish the required foundation of 'moral self-consciousness' because the cathartic effects of the 'national catastrophe' have not yet made themselves felt, and because the insight into the new and imminent ethic is still lacking: namely as a result of that 'historical relativism which was first developed in Germany', and which had led, even before the First World War, and before the 'fateful radicalisation of historicism which can appeal to Heidegger', to the 'paralysing of a potential post-conventional moral consciousness of principles on the part of scholars and intellectuals'.][59] The

reduction of the eventful character of the event (its incorporation into a *concept* of history, into a 'minimal teleology', for
example) permits a certain privileging (just as the identity of
history is left unaffected here, so too the identity of the 'bearers
of history' remains untouched by the power of the event). On
the other hand, it is the privileging itself which opens up the
way for the reduction in question. This of course does not of
itself serve to sanction the kind of position 'which only thinks
in terms of the categories of "happening"'.[60] The fact that the
simplification implied in the event cannot be circumvented does
not legitimate every simplification. Perhaps Apel himself comes
closest to the essence of the event (for the 'national catastrophe'
is indeed 'something unparalleled from the world-historical
perspective') when he mentions the role of a certain 'delaying
pseudo-rational reasoning' which bears witness to the power of
the event. But he fails to clarify the structural necessity of what
he interprets in terms of psychological and epistemological
concepts, of what in its a-rational (not irrational) precedence has
always already contaminated the 'potentially rational moment':

> From the psychological point of view it may well be that a
> secret wish for compensation after the defeat also played a
> role in this [in the 'quasi-speculative thought']. I would cer-
> tainly not like to arouse the impression that this insight, that
> everything was false, simply imposed itself upon me without
> any inner resistance – and that means, without a kind of
> 'delaying pseudo-reasoning' (in Kant's sense) and without
> certain defensive reactions on my part. But this is insufficient
> simply to explain away the potentially rational moment har-
> boured in the aforementioned assumption of something
> unparalleled here. This moment is rather to be unfolded in
> what follows and examined with regard to its claim to valid-
> ity'.

One should not have to underline that it is not a question here
of 'explaining away' anything. At the same time we may be
permitted to express some doubt whether Apel himself does not
proceed in such a fashion when he all too hastily isolates the
'potentially rational moment'. The psychological and epistemological characterisation he offers is perhaps unfortunate because

it allows him to forget the precedence of affirmation and repudiation and designates something posterior to it. The event
disempowers the subject: the agent that affirms and repudiates is
not a subject that could compensate for something or engage in
a pseudo-rational reasoning about it. Adorno and Heidegger
understood more of the power of the event than Apel. No
rationality can recuperate the 'regression', the suspension of the
subject.

Shock

The 'explosion of metaphysical meaning' as registered by
Adorno annihilates the 'unity of aesthetic coherence and meaningfulness'.[61] In his *Aesthetic Theory*, Adorno defines the destruction of this coherence and meaningfulness, of the context it
forms, as shock: 'The shocks inflicted by the most recent works
of art are the explosion of their very appearance' (AT:131;
ET:84). If the 'appearance', that is to say, if the manifestation of
a context formed by coherence and meaningfulness once represented a 'self-evident *a priori*', this *a priori* disintegrates now
with a 'catastrophe through which the essence of appearing is
first completely revealed'. Is it possible to establish a relationship
between the category of 'shock' that Adorno introduces here
and the 'thrust' that Heidegger discusses in *The Origin of the
Work of Art*?

Adorno makes double use of the category of shock. In the
first place he employs it in a negative sense. The shock is the
moment when the alienation or de-familiarisation of the familiar at once enables and suspends the act of recognition. If it is
the principle of montage that underlies this experience, the
surrealist use of shock provides its specific model. Insofar as
surrealism 'exposes the experiences of childhood through its
explosions' – as Adorno remarks in his retrospective essay on
surrealism – it lends a 'familiarity' to alien and estranged images
precisely through shock, a familiarity which translates into the
question 'Where have I seen this before?'[62] An earlier experience
is thus announced through shock as something somehow
already known, although it also evades simple recognition at
the same time. Shock allows something old to befall us as something new, and something new to befall us as something old:

the moment of shock is provoked by a sense of non-simultaneity, the sense of ageing. Only that which has become obsolete, so Adorno tells us, cannot age. Exposed to non-simultaneity – to becoming, to history, to ageing, to death – the subject becomes aware of the ever-same selfsameness of its own non-simultaneity – of its reification, its subjection to nature. But this awareness does not allow it to secure a previously constituted interiority for itself: 'It is a paradoxical thing about modernity that, constantly caught up in the spell of the ever-sameness of mass-production, it possesses a history at all. This paradox estranges it from itself and expresses, in the "images of modernity's childhood", a subjectivity that has also become estranged from itself along with the world. The tension which is discharged as shock in surrealism is the tension between schizophrenia and reification, and precisely not therefore the psychological expression of a living interiority.'[63] The experience of shock, in which we are instantly startled, is the experience of a non-simultaneity which prevents recognition: the subject can no longer recognise itself in its history – in its experience. This appeal to the category of shock is negative for three, essentially interconnected, reasons. (1) Shock betrays the lack of unity on the part of the subject. (2) Since this lack of subjective unity, this estrangement and alienation, can be deciphered historically and socially as reification, the shock itself is subject to history: 'After the European catastrophe [is the distinction between a "national" and a "European" catastrophe relevant here?] the shocks of surrealism have lost their power.'[64] The impotence of surrealist shock, it is true, is not a particular or unique impotence. In *Aesthetic Theory* Adorno passes the same verdict upon the principle of montage itself: 'As a measure deliberately directed against the insinuation of organic unity, the principle of montage was expressly calculated to shock. Now that the shock effect has become blunted, the materials of montage have themselves turned into so much indifferent stuff' (AT:233; ET:155–6). (3) Since alienation and its presentation are historically and socially conditioned, shock can be defined as a negative experience which remains bound to its own other: 'But if surrealism itself strikes us as obsolete today, this is because human beings now already deny themselves that consciousness of denial that was captured in negative form in surrealism.'[65] Whether the connection which the logic of negativity (of shock) establishes between these aspects is a closed and seamless one depends upon whether that which belongs to the world of things is already reified, whether the assimilation to this world is a product or a consequence of reification. If the childhood experiences exposed by surrealism are those of libidinal cathexis, if surrealism assembles 'moments which spark a memory of those objects of the subsidiary drives through which the libido was first awoken', can one simply reduce fetishism to the commodity, or absolutise the insight that the fetishistic fixation of modernity is essentially mediated by the commodity character? Or to put the question more precisely: is there such a relation of dependency between the representation and the represented, is the mediating character of that which lives 'outside of the realm of the aesthetic', so decisive that the category of shock can be employed only in a negative fashion? The answer which Adorno supplies to this question in the essay on surrealism is clear: 'It is certainly *imagines* which are plundered by surrealism, but they are not the invariant and ahistorical ones of the unconscious subject, to which the conventional approach would so much like to neutralise them. They are historical *imagines* in which the innermost character of the subject becomes aware of itself in its outermost manifestation, as the imitation of something that is social and historical. [Why does Adorno speak so directly of "imitation" here, and why does he allude to the problem of mimesis in this connection?]' The logic of negativity (of shock) is a logic of the subject which ultimately recognises itself in its history and its experience, and thus sustains and withstands its inner contradiction.

But one cannot properly rest with this interpretation. For Adorno's *Aesthetic Theory* also contains the elements for a different way of thinking about shock. The 'explosion of appearance' which reveals the 'essence of appearing' is itself a characteristic feature of all art, and not merely of 'the most recent works of art' in which the tension is immediately discharged as shock: 'By virtue of its character as appearance art is already penetrated teleologically by its own negation; the sudden dawning of appearance, its unexpected rising, gives the lie to aesthetic semblance' (AT:132; ET:85). Appearance therefore is not exhausted in the manifestation of an aesthetic coherence and meaningfulness as the *a priori* of art. This manifestation is the semblance of art. The relationship between semblance and appearance which separates the work of art from itself is decisive for its relationship to history, at least to the extent that the coherence and meaningfulness of the aesthetic context are formed as a historical continuity and this is ruptured by the explosion – by shock, by catastrophe. Over against historicism, which would like to gauge the historical in art from its 'location in real history', Adorno insists on the fact that every work, within its own 'monadological core', is already a process of becoming: 'What appears in the work is its inner time, and the explosion of appearance blasts through the continuity of the latter' (AT:132; ET:85). Hence the explosion of appearance is more than merely an inner-aesthetic reflex of the explosion of metaphysical meaning that transpires in the moment of the 'European catastrophe'. If we wished to express Adorno's thought here in a particularly pointed form, we could claim that the essence of art, or more precisely its origin, can be experienced only in the coincidence of a rise and a downfall, only in the shock with which art appears and disappears. The shock is necessary because art as appearance brings forth semblance – there is no appearing without semblance – and in bringing it forth already abandons it to destruction. There is therefore neither pure shock nor pure appearance. The appearance which lacked its suddenness would be no more an appearance than semblance could be semblance without the coherence and meaningfulness of the aesthetic context and the continuity of becoming. The strange does not result from the estrangement or the alienation of the familiar – quite the contrary. The familiar 'as such' is strange and the strange 'as such' is familiar. It is only for this reason that the question: 'Where have I seen this before?' resists all rhetoric and maintains a trembling and suspended answer. Art is never identical with itself, never creates an appearance in which it would return to itself and recognise its own identity: shock permits the experience of that constitutive and irreducible non-simultaneity of art in which it returns to itself only in order to displace itself. Thus the experience of shock is also different from an experience of negativity which rests upon the semblance of appearance. The non-simultaneity is not the history of the subject or of art as subject, but an original interruption of history in the very process of its constitution as a coherent context of meaning. But if non-simultaneity blasts through the logic of negativity (of shock), then it is itself non-simultaneous, as it were, and does not permit a concept of non-simultaneity to be formed.[66] The experience of shock can be read as the experience of an existence which undermines its own definition as subject from the very first. Existence as event – or as beginning – is experienced in shock.

Revolution and revolt

Benjamin too had perceived the coincidence of rise and downfall in the beginning. In his essay on surrealism he interpreted this coincidence as a doubling of political action, of an action fraught with tension and internal ambivalence, of an action that turns against itself. The intoxication and the anarchy of revolt must be placed in the service of the revolution, of its method and its discipline, of its 'constructive' and its 'dictatorial' moment:

> In all its books and undertakings surrealism circles around the problem of winning over the forces of intoxication for the cause of the revolution. It could even describe this as its ownmost task. With regard to this task, it is not enough to recognise, as we do, that an intoxicating element is alive in every revolutionary act. This element is identical with that of anarchy. But to lay the emphasis exclusively upon it would be to neglect the methodical and disciplinary preparation for the revolution in favour of a praxis wavering between a mere exercise and the premature celebration of its success.[67]

The distinction which Benjamin draws between revolt and revolution here is no absolute distinction: revolt continues to live on in the revolution and does not merely model itself upon the former. Revolt must be carried over into a revolution in order to evade the death and downfall to which as anarchy and intoxication it is dedicated. It is only the revolution that can sustain the life of revolt. Revolt thus survives within the revolution. When it remains isolated and left to its essential uncontrollability, it seems to become intoxicated with itself and thereby collapse in the reflected image of its own enthusiasm. But the revolution begins with revolt, begins with anarchy: the problem of its translation and survival would never arise otherwise. The 'intoxicating element' that is 'alive in every revolutionary act' refers us to an act or to a – political – action which announce the coming, or perhaps only the possibility, of a revolution. In intoxication and anarchy the revolution appears ahead of itself and threatens at the same time to suffocate its own beginnings. Revolt is therefore also the other of revolution, not merely a herald which still lacks a – true – consciousness of its task or mission, one which simply anticipates and hence postpones the event. Revolt represents an 'experience of freedom' which dispenses with 'the sclerotic liberal-moral-humanistic ideal of freedom', and is initially accomplished independently of the revolutionary experience – independently of the experience of construction and dictatorship. It is for this reason that both experiences must be 'welded together': this is the very juncture which indicates the place and significance of surrealism. But we harbour a 'false' conception of the 'essence of intoxication', as Benjamin adds, a conception which proves to be 'undialectical' rather than 'illogical': 'Logical and illogical – a sterile opposition. The true opposites, that is the two conceptual terms placed at right angles to one another, are logic and dialectic.'[68] The 'logic' of intoxication produces an aesthetics entangled in prejudices, one which grasps art as a reaction of surprise. Intoxication is connected with a state of permanent surprise, of continuous shock, of uninterrupted assault, while that which has a surprising effect is sought in what is beyond the everyday, as a stereotype of surprise: a 'truly fateful romanticism'. If the translation of the surprising character of revolt over into revolution is to be successfully accomplished, if the power and force of the beginning are not to be forfeited, if that which begins is not to fall short of itself – a danger that is given with the distinction between revolt and revolution – then the dialectic of intoxication must be grasped as its essence, and we must recognise that 'the reader, the thinker, the flâneur, and the one who awaits something are also types of illuminati, just as much as the opium-eater, the dreamer, the intoxicated one'.

This is a declaration of war on humanism and a celebration of construction. In his reflections on 'Experience and Poverty' (1933) Benjamin returns to the essential motifs of the essay on 'Surrealism' (1929). The experience of poverty is that of a generation 'which between 1914–1918 was subjected to one of the most monstrous experiences of world history', one exceeded only by the experience of the generation that participated in the Second World War – if Apel is to be believed: 'A generation which had still gone to school by horse-drawn carriage, now stood beneath the open skies in a landscape where nothing had remained unchanged except the clouds, and there, in the middle, in a force field of destructive torrents and explosions, stood the tiny and vulnerable human body.' Do these profoundly significant changes predispose the human being, which no longer corresponds with the humanistic picture of the world, to a construction which is constitutive for the revolution?

When he speaks of revolution in the essay on surrealism, Benjamin is thinking of the Russian Revolution. Thus he notes: 'In order to assess strategically the front that was opened up by surrealism, one must compare the attitude towards Russia that is expressed by other contemporary literary figures.'[69] Benjamin is referring here to the 'sabotage' that was directed against the Russian Revolution: the 'bourgeois ressentiment', the 'feeling of obligation not to the revolution itself, but to traditional culture'. The problem of tradition and destruction that is posed with the revolution – for revolution presupposes destruction – is reversed in the relationship between revolt and revolution. Here the revolution must resist the destruction that is presupposed in the form of revolt and thus secure itself against the threat of a counter-revolution. Benjamin's own particular 'attitude towards Russia' should not tempt us to deny the parallel with Heidegger's conception of the 'National Socialist revolution'. The common feature which allows us to draw this parallel is obvious: both Heidegger and Benjamin think of the revolution in terms of a commitment to leadership, to will and service, to dictatorship, method and technical organisation. In each case they think of the revolution as a commitment whose necessity is revealed with the dissolution of former bonds and attachments. All of the undeniable differences here can ultimately be traced back to this common feature, this shared perspective which announces the law or the 'logic' of the beginning, the coincidence of rise and downfall in the thrust, in the shock, in the suddenness of a surprise. Any investigation that would emphasise, for example, Benjamin's specifically political-aesthetic interests or rightly direct our attention to the idea of a new 'image and body space', will also have to account for this 'logic' of the beginning and for the counter-turning it involves, for a logic which is not dialectical, though it does not oppose dialectics.

Commemoration

Just as revolution relates to revolt, and tradition to destruction, so too experience [*Erfahrung*] relates to lived sensation [*Erlebnis*]. Benjamin thematises both of these concepts in his writings on Baudelaire. There is no experience without memory: 'In fact experience is a matter of tradition, in collective as well as in private life. It is formed less from individual details strongly fixed in recollection than from accumulated and often unconscious data that flow together in the memory.'[70] Whereas recollection does not, as such, denote the existence of experience, one can retrieve experience from memory. Memory preserves and seals up experience; experience owes its existence to the possibility of accumulating and gathering conscious and unconscious, fixed and fluid data in a kind of vessel or funnel, a pit or a well. It is difficult to define the limits of memory. Its lines of demarcation do not run between the poles of the private and the public, the individual and the collective, the conscious and the unconscious, the voluntary and the involuntary, the recollected and the unrecollected, the subjective and the objective. No individual possesses memory as an individual, no individual can appropriate experience as an individual, but no individual is therefore deprived of memory or banished from experience: 'Where experience in the strictest sense prevails, certain contents of one's individual past are connected in memory with those of the collective past. Cultic practices, together with the ceremonies and festivals associated with them ... repeatedly encouraged the fusion between these two elements or matters of memory. They provoked commemoration at particular times and were devices for commemoration throughout life. In this way volun-

tary and involuntary commemoration come to lose the character of mutual exclusivity'.[71] Memory and experience, which pass
on what has happened and protect it from oblivion, sustain the
tradition: and what do we mean by tradition if not the repetition of what has happened? Such repetition expresses itself in
the cultic ceremony, in the festival, in the calculation of time
which corresponds to the calendar. In the fifteenth thesis on 'the
concept of history', Benjamin writes that the revolution introduces a new manner of calculating the time and does not
simply content itself with destroying the old system: 'The
conscious awareness of exploding the continuum of history is
peculiar to the revolutionary classes in their moment of action.
The Great Revolution introduced a new calendar. The day
with which the calendar begins functions as a historical time-
lapse. And in fact it is the same day which returns continually
in the form of feast days, themselves days of commemoration.
Calendars, therefore, do not count the time in the way that
clocks do. They are monuments to the consciousness of
history.'[72] What then are the most important claims articulated
by this discourse concerning revolution and history, commemoration and caesura, memory and experience? They can be schematically presented as follows.

(1) The first day (of the revolutionary calendar) is the day in
which history is suddenly concentrated (is not every calendar
per definitionem a revolutionary calendar?): the date of the beginning gathers up the past and the future for which it now serves
as an absolute point of reference, gathers the rise and downfall
of revolution and establishes the requisite discipline by articulating itself as in principle repeatable.

(2) Commemoration is made possible by the repetition of the
dated beginning – in this original, originary and gathering date,
in this moment of 'historical time-lapse', the beginning touches,
as it were, itself. It captures and contains itself in one. The repetition is described as a festival – as a day of gathering – which is
always at once an interruption and a consolidation in which rise
and downfall once again coincide. Commemoration is always a
commemoration of the beginning, of rise and downfall, not
merely of the downfall provoked by the explosion of the historical continuum, but of the downfall inscribed in the rise, of the
regression which revolution brings in its wake. Commemora-

tion endangers what it confirms since it can also liberate the 'powers of enthusiasm' which have never entirely submitted to the revolutionary regime and which, from the viewpoint of the revolution, are certainly an expression of 'regression'.

(3) The commemoration of the beginning, in which mourning and joy intersect, does not remember a specific date which has found a place in memory and now belongs to experience, but remembers rather the origin of memory. If we wished to generalise Benjamin's observations, we could claim that the origin of memory can receive different and incompatible names. The names of 'Auschwitz' and 'Germania', for example, supply the absolute date for two philosophical calendars in relation to 'the National Socialist revolution'. As such they already celebrate the named and dated event – this is why ceremonies designed to commemorate the date of the meeting at Wannsee or the '*Reichskristallnacht*' prove to be intolerable and unacceptable. If we wished to avoid such celebrations, we should have to imagine forgetting the date in question. But how would we attempt to interpret such a forgetting? On the one hand, the forgetting of a date signals the definitive translation or transition of revolt into revolution, of downfall into rise. On the other hand, all forgetting opens the way to regression.

(4) Insofar as the cult, the festival, the calendar discloses the domain of experience and tradition to the individual, a domain over which the individual as such – as a private person – has no control, it is possible to master that which has been experienced in a manner that is not wholly contingent. The calendar is a device, an artefact, an institution which dislodges the artificial 'mutual exclusivity' of voluntary and involuntary commemoration, an exclusivity instituted by the power of information technology, by the press. This exclusivity is, for its part, contingent. Whereas – natural – experience includes what is experienced, the information that is its – artificial – counterpart erects limits between inner and outer: 'After Proust it is a matter of contingent chance whether the individual discovers an image of himself, whether he is capable of mastering his own experience. To depend upon chance in this matter is by no means simply something self-evident. The inner concerns of man do not possess this hopelessly private character by nature. They only acquire it once the outer concerns have forfeited the chance of

being assimilated into experience.'[73] The individual abandoned to chance is the product of inurement over against experience, a process in which inclusion is converted into exclusion. But if the calendar itself is not given 'by nature', if it fulfils the function of gathering precisely to the degree that it distinguishes itself from nature as a 'monument to the consciousness of history', its mediation does not remain untouched by chance. Benjamin points out that this consciousness of history after all merely takes the form of a ruin: it is a consciousness that has scarcely left any traces in Europe 'for a hundred years now'.[74]

(5) A monument must be erected. The introduction of the calendar necessarily occurs after the event, at the time of evening: 'The July revolution still witnessed an incident in which this consciousness [of history] attained its proper recognition. On the evening of the first day of struggle it transpired that in many areas of Paris people had begun shooting, at the same time but independently of one another, at the tower-clocks.' However strange this simultaneity may strike us — is it dictated by the beginning concentrated within the date? — it cannot change the non-simultaneity which finds expression in stating a particular time, in stating that the shooting happened 'on the evening of the first day of struggle'. The non-simultaneity of dating which can also be gauged from the difference between revolt and revolution, implies that the beginning remains to come. The commemoration of the beginning behoves a future that is no more at our disposal than the beginning: 'It is well known that the Jews were forbidden to enquire into the future. But the Torah and the practice of prayer do instruct them in the art of commemoration. This is how the spell of the future was broken for them.'[75] The beginning prescribes, as Heidegger observes, its own repetition and thereby dates itself. 'Germania' as name is the (quasi-absolute) date of the beginning, that is, it is the repetition of the beginning or of the Greek inauguration, a repetition yet to be retrieved and therefore still to be repeated, and the repetition of the beginning already retrieved and therefore already repeated by the Greek inauguration. If indeed the name 'Germania' can be deciphered as the name of the naming *one cannot name*, then we must describe the 'logic' of the beginning as a pluralisation, multiplication and dissemination of dates and calendars that can

never be delimited or surveyed, that cannot in its very essence be dated or grasped in calendary terms at all.

(6) Benjamin does not identify the time-reckoning of the (revolutionary) calendar with that of the clock. In order to ground the claim that there is an analogy between Benjamin's discourse and Heidegger's 'logic' of beginning, it is necessary to consider the analysis of 'dateability' which Heidegger provides, for example, in *Being and Time*. Such a procedure, of course, would be meaningful only on condition that we also ask after the place and significance of Heidegger's investigations into fundamental ontology within his thought as a whole. From the perspective of fundamental ontology dateability is grounded in the temporality of Dasein as 'concerned reckoning, preparing and protecting':

> But every 'then' is, *as such*, a 'then when...', every 'once' a 'once, when...', every 'now' a 'now that...'. We describe this apparently obvious relational structure of 'now', 'once' and 'then' as *dateability*. In this context we must completely disregard whether the dating is accomplished factically with reference to a calendary 'date'. Even without such 'dates' the 'now', 'then' and 'once' are more or less determinately dated. And if the specific determination of dating is absent, that does not mean that the structure of dateability is lacking or contingent.[76]

And Heidegger adds later:

> This public dating, in which everyone assigns himself his time, is one which everyone can 'reckon on' simultaneously, and it makes use of a publicly available *measure*. This kind of dating reckons with time in the sense of *measuring time*, which in turn requires an instrument for measuring, namely a clock. And this implies: *along with the temporality of Dasein as thrown, as abandoned to the 'world', as giving itself time, something like a 'clock' is also already dis-covered, that is, something ready to hand which has become accessible to presenting apprehentation in its process of regular recurrence.*[77]

The question to be asked is therefore this: is there a date and a calendar for a beginning, or are calendar and date alike – dateability in general, whether that of the calendar or the clock – merely calculating factors which necessarily distort the character of a beginning?

Experience, lived sensation, reflection

Revolution creates the possibility of a context – of a tradition – which is always also incompatible with revolt – with destruction. It secures the basis and ground for experience. Lived sensation resists revolution because it represents an occasion for an at least virtual interruption of the context of experience as a whole. Benjamin defines lived sensation as a shock registered by consciousness. In this sense there is no experience of shock, but only an immediate 'sensation of shock'.[78] Whenever a shock is sensed – is parried or mastered – the context of experience has potentially become permeable. Lived sensation tears the subject out of this context: 'The only thing that can become an element of *mémoire involontaire* is what has not been "sensibly experienced" [*erlebt*] explicitly and with consciousness, what has not been encountered by the subject as a "lived sensation".' Certainly it is true that the context of experience that belongs to memory includes voluntary and involuntary commemoration, so that we might conclude that although sensation is not indeed a possible 'element of *mémoire involontaire*', it is a possible element of the context of experience. We must reject this conclusion, however, since it ignores the particular character that attaches to lived sensation. For the latter does indeed mark the conscious retention of what has been accepted through the protective shield of consciousness: an incident is sensed which incorporates itself 'immediately into the register of conscious recollection'. The lived sensation restitutes the 'mutual exclusivity' of voluntary and involuntary commemoration. To think this exclusivity is to think lived sensation and precisely not experience:

> The greater the share which the moment of shock has in our individual impressions, the more unremittingly consciousness must be ready to act as a defensive shield against incoming stimuli; the greater the success with which consciousness operates here, the less the impressions are able to enter

experience in the broader sense; and the more they fulfil the concept of merely lived sensation. Perhaps the singular achievement of the defence against shock ultimately lies in this: it assigns a precise temporal position in consciousness to the incident at the cost of the integrity of its content. That would be the ultimate achievement of reflection. It would turn the incident into a matter of lived sensation. If reflection in this sense is suspended, then the pleasurable or (usually) unpleasurable fear would fundamentally arise, that which, according to Freud, sanctions the interruption or suspension of defence against shock in the first place.[79]

The condition of the possibility of experience lies in the reduction of the shock-moment's share in an impression: the aim of the revolution must be to reduce this share to a minimum and, tendentially at least, to uncouple impression and shock. For is it not revolt that represents the strongest resistance to the experience of revolution? What is revolt but a shock which no subject and no consciousness is capable of parrying, a shock which revolution must strive to forget – or repress – if the context of experience is to be re-established? Is it not possible to trace the instability of revolt back to the fact that it fails in the last analysis to concentrate itself as a lived sensation, just as it fails to incorporate itself immediately into experience? Perhaps it is precisely this instability, which throws all who revolt into a state of intoxication, that represents the real danger for the revolution because it perpetuates the dislocation, the rupture, the thrust – all expressions which Benjamin borrows from Gide and Rivière in order to characterise the 'shock-sensation' in Baudelaire. Revolt (a sensation before all lived sensation) and revolution (experience) find their place where consciousness is interrupted or suspended, where it does not intervene or where it has not yet solidified – a consciousness that, as Benjamin emphasises, rather than gathering memory-traces appears instead as a protective shield. The 'interruption or suspension of shock' can represent either a perpetuation of terror (determined by pleasure or aversion) or a (pre-reflective) constitution of the context of experience. In any case the shock is original or originary – and that means: shock belongs to the beginning and marks an existence before all experience and all lived sensation.

Angel of history

In his 'theses on the philosophy of history', Benjamin binds the 'revolutionary chance' of thought to 'a Messianic stilling or halting of events'. The overthrowing movement − the storm unleashed by the interruption of progress − arises precisely from what is petrified and motionless: the storm of progress ceases to drive the 'angel of history' ineluctably 'into the future against which its wings are turned'. Paralysed and entirely isolated, thought is more motile than ever once it quits the domain of universal motion. The 'struggle over an oppressed subjugated past' concentrates itself into a 'revolutionary chance' when the historical object crystallises as a monad before the − 'historical materialist' − thinker. But if history − if the past − as the object of thought is indeed to petrify, thought must be able to move within a 'constellation saturated with tensions' and suddenly, on the basis of this tension, to come to a halt. This coming to a halt imparts a 'shock' to the constellation, whereby thought and its object transform themselves into a monad. The shock is the moment of immobility. For here the angel ceases to be itself. The angel embraces history, reluctantly opens its wings to greet the catastrophe which 'continually heaps up ruins and piles them before its feet'. Unable as it is to move its wings once the storm of progress has filled them and prevented them from closing, the angel that ceases to be itself ceases to harbour the wish to tarry, 'to wake the dead and to put together what has been dashed asunder'. Is this wish not inseparable from the gaze fixed upon the catastrophe? What Benjamin calls the 'revolutionary chance' − the chance of thought − can be traced back to a shock, to a petrification in the moment of highest tension. The historical materialist perceives this chance, he perceives 'the chance of blasting a particular epoch out of the homogeneous course of history; he blasts a particular life out of the epoch, a particular work out of the life's work. This procedure bears fruit in that the life's work is preserved and transcended *in* the work, the epoch preserved and transcended *in* the life's work, the entire course of history preserved and transcended *in* the epoch.'[80] In other words: it suffices to isolate a single fragment in order to bring the unifying homogeneity of history to the point of explosion. The fragment of the past is that second of the future of which Benjamin says that, for the Jewish people, it is the 'narrow gate through which the Messiah' may appear.

But leaping out of the continuum of history already depends upon the past presenting itself to thought as a 'tradition of the oppressed'. The 'revolutionary chance' – unlike that of revolt – is chained to a concept of history. In his eighth thesis on history Benjamin states the following:

> The tradition of the oppressed teaches us that the 'state of emergency' in which we live is not the exception but the rule. We must attain to a conception of history that is in keeping with this insight. Then we shall clearly realise that it is our task to bring about a real state of emergency, and this will improve our position in the struggle against Fascism. One reason why Fascism has a chance is that its opponents confront it in the name of progress as a historical norm. The current amazement that the things we are experiencing are 'still' possible in the twentieth century is *not* philosophical. This amazement is not the beginning of knowledge – unless it is the knowledge that the view of history which gives rise to it is untenable.[81]

Even if the concept of history, which the historical materialist wrests from the tradition, from the context of experience, from the memory of the oppressed, is not the same as the concept of progress and should not be associated with the normative consciousness of the latter, even indeed if it is not a philosophical concept at all, it still constitutes a unity. It will always be possible therefore to interpret the recognition of the present in the scurrying image of the past, and interpret the waiting or the expectations of those 'past generations' which face us contemporaries like the tragic chorus and yearn for their gaze to be returned, in terms of such a unity. It is the unity of revolution, the unity which the revolution essentially requires. The revolution serves to unify history – an observation which does not itself endorse the historicism which Benjamin criticises. One could say that revolution is history and thus choose the briefest, at once the poorest and richest, of all possible formulations. This is by no means incompatible with the interpretation of history as catastrophe. There is a heliotropism of history: 'Just as flowers turn their heads towards the sun, so too what has been strives, by virtue of some hidden heliotropism, to turn itself towards *that* sun which dawns in the skies of history.'[82] On the other hand, the shock always remains something pre-revolutionary which shatters the concept of history. The past which shock transforms into a monad flashes forth in the moment of danger as a – crystalline – image in which past and present are entwined: 'a breath of the air that once touched earlier lives' brushes us not because the world-spirit – as the subject of history – has now passed over to us, but rather because the beginning is ever to come. Any hearing of a voice is capable of provoking a shock for every voice to which we hearken 'returns the echo of silent voices past'. In this shock no world-historical mission is revealed, nothing is revealed at all, nothing comes to pass except a coming, but precisely thereby the 'continuum of history' is blasted open: the marking of an existence before all experience, and all lived sensation, is an opening for the coming of the other.

Political theology

Why does Benjamin, at a quite decisive point, refer to political theology? The 'state of emergency' is the rule. The task is to break this rule and help a 'real state of emergency' to reality or realisation. Is the 'real' state of emergency, which indeed still lacks reality, an exception from the rule of exception, from the exception as rule, is it a state of emergency in a state of emergency, is it another rule which substitutes for the rule of the exception? Would Benjamin ultimately like to relinquish the schema of rule and exception which, so it seems, underlies the paradox of exception as rule? Is he attempting to think a reality without rule and without exception? The first discussion that Benjamin dedicates to the exception as rule is to be found in the theory of sovereignty which he developed in his book *The Origin of German Tragic Drama*. In this book, he alludes to Carl Schmitt's *Political Theology* and writes: 'He who rules is already destined in advance as the holder of dictatorial power in a state of emergency which has been produced by war, revolt or other kinds of catastrophe.'[83] Benjamin makes this remark in reference to the Princely Ruler in the age of the Baroque. The Prince fulfils his function insofar as he excludes the state of emergency. This exclusion, however, is itself based upon the universalisation of the state of emergency: the latter is excluded when there is no state which is not a state of emergency. If the sovereign power, as Schmitt argues, is 'the one who decides concerning the state of emergency', then the paradox of the exception as the rule implies that the decision concerning the state of emergency precedes the distinction between rule and exception to which it nonetheless remains bound. Before one can decide at all, a decision has already occurred: the decision here does not separate the exception from the rule, but rather cripples the process of deciding and distinguishing.

How does Schmitt understand the distinction?

It is only the exceptional case that renders the question concerning the subject of sovereignty, and that is to say, the question concerning sovereignty in general, an actually relevant one. Whether a case of emergency is present cannot be determined with the clarity of subsumptive logic, and nor can we identify the substantive measures to be taken if it really is a question of the extreme case of emergency and its termination. Both the presupposition and the content of competence here are necessarily unlimited in character. In the constitutional-political sense, there is no competence here at all. The constitution can at most merely indicate who is permitted to act in such a case. If this action is not itself subject to any control, if it is not shared out in some fashion, as it is in the practice of constitutional states, between various mutually limiting and counter-balancing sites of authority, then it is quite obvious who is the sovereign. He decides both whether there is an extreme case of emergency and also what is to be done in order to terminate it. He stands outside of the normally binding legal order, and yet continues to belong to it since he is responsible for deciding whether the constitution can be suspended *in toto*. All the tendencies of modern constitutional-political development conspire in this sense to eliminate the sovereign.[84]

If sovereignty owes its actuality to the state of emergency, then it only really exists in the latter: the state of exception gives the rule to sovereignty. Expressed in another way: the principle of sovereignty asserts itself when the state of emergency prevails. But in relation to what can the state of emergency itself be recognised? In relation to what can the principle of sovereignty itself be identified? The answer is unambiguous: in relation to the decision. The introduction of a state of emergency is always the consequence of a decision in which sovereignty is actualised, indeed through which or as which the principle of sovereignty is first constituted. A decision which is only required by a lack of knowledge, which betrays a deficiency within the legal system, one through which, as Schmitt observes, the system is maintained, cannot banish its own blindness by being shared out and transferred to autonomous executors. This remains the case even if no decision was ever made without the desire to complete the knowledge in question, to remedy the deficiency, to control the moment of blindness. In a certain sense the decision is always already that absolute which, according to Adorno, it was 'once intended to serve' (ND:59; ET:49). It is marked by its blindness towards the *logos*: if we attempt to apply the modern criterion of *principium reddendae rationis* here, the decision can only act as a blind and demented form of interruption. That is why any decision can only be grounded to a greater or lesser degree. If we content ourselves with ascribing this recognition of sovereign power at work within the constitutional state simply to an expression of an anti-democratic affect, we can easily forget that the cause of this affect does not lie simply within the psyche of the individual subject or the socio-historical context, but also in the essence of the decision itself. Any attempt to think democracy which overlooks this problem and rationalises the act of decision runs the danger of condemning itself from the very beginning. Schmitt confronts the metaphysics of rationalism with a metaphysics of life:

> A rigorously consistent rationalism would claim that the exception proves nothing, that only the normal state of affairs can constitute the object of scientific interest. The exception merely confuses the unity and order of the rationalist schema ... But no philosophy of concrete life may shrink from the exception and the extreme case; it must rather interest itself in these in the very highest degree. For

such a philosophy the exception can be more important than the rule, not through some romantic irony in favour of the paradoxical, but with the full seriousness of an insight which probes more deeply than the lucid generalisations of the average and repeatable. The exception is more interesting than the standard case. The standard case proves nothing, the exception proves everything; the latter not only confirms the rule, the rule only lives at all by virtue of the exception. In the exception the power of real life breaks through the encrusted mechanism that has ossified through repetition.[85]

'Life' is the name Schmitt bestows upon exception. The state of emergency in which the constitution and the regularity of a rule are suspended points towards a decision which empowers itself through life. Because it must always be decided on each occasion whether an extreme case obtains or not (although the extreme case does not take the form of simply 'obtaining' – for it would only render all decision superfluous if it did), one can never capture the extreme case in conceptual terms, can form no concept that might subsume it under a rule and facilitate recourse to it for the purpose of ultimate clarification. For the decision to be made does not only concern the state of emergency; it is always made *in favour* of the exception if indeed it eludes control by any already guaranteed and pre-established knowledge – by repetition and its mechanism. (That the opposition between life and rationality is employed in this context to justify a certain kind of anti-rationalism is symptomatic but not completely decisive: recognising the a-rational character of a decision does not necessarily involve endorsing a metaphysics of life, which is also a – romantic? – metaphysics of the interesting.) Sovereignty therefore tends to drive the question concerning the exclusion of the state of emergency into the background, to dissipate the difference between the normal and the extreme case, to declare the state of emergency to be the rule. What Benjamin is thus attempting to articulate, when he postulates the introduction of a 'real state of emergency', is perhaps a decision which does not secure itself in or as the subject of itself, but rather opens up the coming of the other.

De-cision

If the one decision were merely to be replaced by another, nothing would really be changed fundamentally – no more would be changed by the substitution than by the renewed introduction of the rule of rule. Rationalist and vitalist metaphysics merely supplement one another. However, the decision itself is already inscribed in the beginning and its 'logic', and cannot be delimited and excluded. In his *Beiträge* Heidegger shows that the origin or beginning is such a de-cision: 'What is here called de-cision [*Ent-scheidung*] moves into the innermost essential midst of being itself and thus has nothing in common with what we mean by making a choice or anything of this kind. De-cision rather means: the very dissension that separates and in separating first allows the event of appropriation to come into play, the event of just this *openness* in dissension as the clearing for the self-concealing and still un-decided, man's belonging to being as the founding of its truth and the appertaining of being to the time of the final god.'[86] The 'time of the final god' is the time of the repetition and retrieval of that beginning 'which reaches out furthest of all'. To the extent that the beginning is an opening (the beginning of which Heidegger speaks here or the revolutionary shattering of history which harbours something beyond all disposal, something revealed by Benjamin's distinction between revolution and revolt or by the Messianic moment in his thought), it proves to be de-cisive in the sense explicated by Heidegger: in the sense of a dissension which creates an opening. The de-cisive constitutes the counter-turning of the beginning, its coming and its forgetting: what is the revolution but the forgetting of the shock that unleashes the intoxication of revolt, an intoxication which does not simply capture and contain the shock in the moment of lived sensation and which therefore is itself a shock in which anaesthesia and the highest attentiveness coincide? As an interruption of knowledge the de-cisive enforces a decision which does not solidify into a subject, just as it does not itself function as a subject. This, of course, is not to deny that when Heidegger calls upon 'Germania' and names naming, he restitutes the decision as subject, as sovereignty; it is not to deny that when Benjamin speaks of the 'struggling', 'oppressed' and 'avenging' class which

is 'the subject of historical knowledge'[87] and which will bring
the work of liberation to an end in the name of generations of
victims', he subjects history to a unity which occludes precisely
the de-cisive. But what is the significance of such an occlusion,
if we remember that Benjamin undertook a very real struggle
against National Socialism and Fascism and conceptualised it as
such? How are we to assess the legitimation of death – of sacrificial death? 'The class forgot ... the meaning of the will to
sacrifice' which is nourished on 'the image of enslaved forebears'.[88] Is the oppressed class the sovereign which decides on
the 'real state of emergency'? This thought is quite compatible
with a certain rationalism expressed in one of the aphorisms
from *One Way Street*:

> For whether the bourgeoisie wins or loses the fight, it remains
> doomed by the inner contradictions that in the course of its
> development will prove deadly. The only question is whether
> its downfall will come through itself or through the proletar-
> iat. The continuance or the end of three thousand years of cul-
> tural development will be *decided* by the answer to this
> question. History knows nothing of the bad infinity conveyed
> in the image of the two wrestlers locked in eternal combat.
> The true politician reckons only in dates. And if the abolition
> of the bourgeoisie is not completed by an almost calculable
> moment in economic and technical development (a moment
> signalled by inflation and poison-gas warfare), all will be lost.
> Before the spark reaches the dynamite, the lighted fuse must
> be cut. The intervention of a politician, the danger to which
> he exposes himself, the speed with which he acts are technical
> – not chivalrous in character.[89]

Technical rationality and decision seem to combine (almost)
seamlessly here, namely in the appointed date of the revolution,
in the institution of the – revolutionary – calendar. Total mobilisation must be taken into the service of the revolution.

The thrust of thatness

Heidegger locates the experience of thrust not in the beginning
in general, but in the beginning of poetic inauguration, in the

beginning of art. In the final version of Heidegger's essay on the work of art the emphasis shifts from the relation between commencement, thrust and history towards that between the thrust and the createdness of the work:

> The emergence of createdness from the work does not mean that the work is to give the impression of having been made by a great artist. The point is not that the created work be certified as the accomplishment of an able individual, and its maker thereby brought to public attention. It is not the 'N.N. fecit' that is to be made known. Rather the simple 'factum est' is to be held forth into the open by the work: namely this, that the unconcealedness of what is has happened here, and first happens precisely as this happening; or, that such a work *is* at all, rather than is not. The thrust that the work as this work is, the unremitting character of this inconspicuous thrust constitutes the steadfastness with which the work reposes within itself. Precisely where the artist and the process and circumstances of the genesis of the work remain unknown, this thrust, the 'that' of createdness, emerges most purely from the work.[90]

The 'that' stands in a relation of gradual opposition to the name: the more illegible the name, the more exposed its bearer. Not only the artist: his work still bears his name, even if it also bears another name or title. What is true of the name of the artist is true in every case of the name of the work of art, unless, of course, the name of the artist remains unknown and the name of the work is known. From the name still to be named (*nomen nominandum*) and the unknown name (*nomen nescio*) no path, only a thrust leads to the mere bearer, the bearer without a name. The unknown name can be a name still to be named, but the bearer in all its exposure, or its 'purity', lacks a name, is indeed no longer even a bearer. The name, which is bound by no arbitrary bond to the benamed since the latter must be named in order that it might appear ('Insofar as language names a being for the first time, such naming first brings the being to the word and to appearance'[91]), simultaneously obscures the being in its thatness. The name is the obscuring of the thatness which emerges through the thrust of the work. But if the relationship between name and benamed, without which there could be no 'drift to the work' and thus no truth either, is not completely external or arbitrary, then the name obscures its own thatness. To the extent that we experience the originary thrust of art in the work, the thrust that belongs to the beginning, to the extent that we experience the createdness of the work and thus the creating itself, the self-extinguishing of the name in the moment of naming allows us to gather that names are, that there are names and that there is not nothing. The rise or dawning happens as decline or downfall. But is not Heidegger simply referring here to the name of the one who created the work? Can one infer anything from this particular name, from this proper name, about the name, about naming in general? Would such an inference not amount to a glorification of the artist? We can respond to these questions as follows: just as the 'that' of createdness disappears in this createdness – the thrust is required to experience it – so too the 'that' of the name, the naming disappears in the name. What is at stake in this context is not a vague analogy: for creating is initially a naming. The propositional structure 'just as ... so too' leads us astray. It would be more appropriate to say that the 'that' of createdness disappears because the name procures the disappearance of naming without which no being would appear.

Thus it is quite true that Heidegger does not locate the experience of thrust in the beginning in general. But is not the beginning always a poetic inauguration, the inauguration of language in the name? The wavering, the indecision as to the link between beginning, language and name, may arise from the fact that in the essay on the work of art Heidegger cites examples from painting, sculpture and music, from Van Gogh, Nikolaus Gerhart and Beethoven. (Heidegger also wavers when he identifies the beginning with the origin, an identification which can already be found in his lecture course on Hölderlin, only then to separate it from the commencement, the occasion and the origin itself: 'Just as every origin has its beginning and every beginning its commencement, so too every commencement has its occasion.'[92]) In the final version of the essay on the work of art, Heidegger leaves no room for doubt: 'All art, insofar as it allows the arrival of the truth of beings as such to happen, is *in its essence poetry*.' On the other hand, Heidegger also recognises the difficulties involved in this formulation: 'If all art is in essence poetry, then the arts of architecture, painting, sculpture and music must be traced back to poesy. That is pure arbitrariness. It certainly is, as long as we assume that those arts are varieties of the art of language and that it is indeed permissible to characterise poesy by using such an easily misinterpretable expression. But poesy is only one mode of the clearing projection of truth, that is, of poetry in the widest sense. Nevertheless, the work of language, the poem in the narrower sense, does possess a privileged position amongst the arts as a whole.'[93] Heidegger is therefore not attempting to proceed in a reductionist manner and treat the arts in general as so many derivative forms of one – particular – art. (If the individual arts were to be derived from one individual art, then that individual art itself would no longer enjoy an individual character of its own like the other forms of art, it would be the essence of art as such, of art in its unity.) Heidegger warns against all such deriving and all such derivations: in a way poesy is already a lower form of poetic composing in the 'narrower sense' since it seems to encourage misinterpretation. If the axiomatic claim that all art is in essence poetry is not a consequence of reductionism – for does not the latter confuse the derived with the original? – then it is because poetry in the 'wider sense' can by no means be identified with language. The distinction between poetry in the narrower sense and in the widest sense helps Heidegger, in the first instance, to dispel the reductionist suspicion. One must therefore ask how the privileged characterisation of poetry 'in the narrower sense' – of language, of the name – can itself be grounded. How can one privilege the inauguration of language in the name without falling into a kind of reductionism? Heidegger writes:

> In order to see this, only the right concept of language is needed. In the usual view of the matter, language is regarded as a kind of communication. It serves for exchanging words and agreeing appointments, and for coming to an understanding in general. But language is not only, and not primarily, an audible or written expression of what is to be communicated. Language not only puts forth in words and statements what is overtly or covertly intended for commu-

nication, but alone brings what is, as something that is, out into the open for the first time. Where there is no language, as in the being of a stone, a plant, an animal, there is also no openness of what is, and consequently no openness either of that which is not, or of the empty.

Once again misunderstandings seem to arise from a conflation of the original and the derived. If we fail to grasp that language deserves a privileged position, then we inevitably reduce it to a derivative significance. Heidegger returns the charge of reductionism to those who raise it in the first place. The privileged position of language for Heidegger is already sufficiently attested by the privileged position of man as the speaking being, as the being that brings beings as beings to appearance in and through language. But from this perspective how can one sustain the distinction between poetry in the wider and poetry in the narrower sense? Is poetry in the wider sense not derived from poetry in the narrower sense? Is poetry as inauguration not always related to language as the naming that opens up beings? 'This naming names forth and appoints a being to its being from its being.' There is no benaming without this naming forth and this appointing, no naming that, in naming, does not name forth and appoint. In poetry in the narrower sense, which is also the essential sense (insofar as it is extended here sense withdraws from the essence, and thus from itself), being names itself in its difference.

The essence of the work of art

As that which belongs to the beginning and as the experience that something is rather than is not, the thrust participates in the essence of language. It is what begins in and as language. There is counter-turning only there where the thrust breaks through all homogeneous measure. The counter-turning of what begins in and as language must be thought as the counter-turning of the name: that the beginning is characterised by an originary forgetting means that the name is the forgetting of naming and remains ever to come, a return which has yet to occur. The benaming of naming (the name 'Germania' as the name of a certain mission and a certain heritage) strives to recuperate this coming, to neutralise this thrust, to enforce the return. In the last analysis 'Germania' hinders the thrust which belongs to the beginning. If the *pseudos* is interpreted by reference to 'the realm of veiling and concealing', as Heidegger argues in his lectures on Parmenides, the thrust uncovers the pseudonym as the essence of the name. The name is its own pseudonym, on the condition that the covering is a showing. But what the thrust shows is not the 'concealed essence of the author and his task as a writer', it is rather the showing itself.[94] What begins in and as language is remembered and forgotten in the thrust through which the createdness of the created thing or the inaugurated of the inauguration (of language) comes forth. Thrust and creating, thrust and inaugurating, thrust and composing, thrust and naming belong together. For the disclosing of beings as such, and therefore the self-naming of being in its difference, happens in language.

> Language itself is poetry according to the essential meaning of the word. Since, however, language is that happening in and through which it becomes possible for a human being to disclose beings as beings, poesy or poetry in the narrow sense is the most originary poetry according to the essential meaning of the word. Language is not poesy because it is primal poetry; rather poesy transpires in language because language preserves the original essence of poetry. Building and shaping, on the other hand, always happen already, and happen only, in the openness of saying and naming ... They are in each case a proper way of poetic composing within the clearing of what is, which has already happened, unnoticed, in language.[95]

Heidegger begins his inquiry into the origin of the work of art with the question concerning the thing, and the thingly character of the work (Adorno sees this as a direct attack upon idealism) and takes the presentation of equipment through a work of art as his point of departure precisely in order to arrive at the thingly character of the thing, the workly character of the work, the thingly character of the workly. But it is by no means accidental that the nature of equipment is actually revealed by a painting, by a 'specific art', a 'realm of art' which, for all its supposed independence, nevertheless presupposes the 'fundamental art', and does so all the more strongly the less we turn our attention to the relation of priority here. Plastic arts (the arts of sculpture and architecture) have their own place in the openness created through the inauguration of language. Thus, in the final pages of the section entitled 'The Thing and the Work', Heidegger says:

> The equipmental character of equipment was uncovered. But how? Not by a description and explanation of a pair of shoes actually present; not by a report about the process of making shoes; and also not by observation of the actual use of shoes occurring here and there; but only by bringing ourselves before Van Gogh's painting. This painting spoke. In the vicinity of the work we suddenly found ourselves somewhere else than we usually tend to be.[96]

The thrust which belongs to the beginning, estranging us from the usual and the habitual, always displaces us over into another place. We find ourselves, therefore, where we are not. Benjamin describes this being outside of oneself or this ecstasy as intoxication. Our attentiveness is heightened in finding ourselves thus dis-placed and prevents the 'hackneyed habitualness of equipment' from asserting itself as 'the only and apparently exclusive type of being belonging to it'. But we are dis-placed elsewhere on the basis of a speaking. The possibility of being outside of oneself, which does not refer to some kind of substantial self-possession or being-at-home with oneself, but merely to an effect of habituation, itself lies in the possibility of exposure to language. Heidegger is capable of considering the painting as he does only because it is already held within the open domain of language and is itself able to speak, even if it is indeed no 'linguistic work of art', no 'work of language'. But if we pursue this line of thought further, would we not have to seek the workly character of the work outside of the work, and in another language?

In contrast to equipment, the character of having been brought forth is inscribed as such within the work. Or more precisely: it stands out from the work precisely as inscription. In order that beings can be disclosed as such, in their very being, the character of having been brought forth and inaugurated must relate to itself as such: 'In the work the createdness has been expressly created in with the creation, so that it expressly stands out from what has thus been brought forth.'[97] Now the equipmental being of equipment does not simply consist in its thatness, any more than the workly being of the work is exhausted in its thatness. It is reliability, according to Heidegger, which constitutes the equipmental character of equipment, and preservation or the 'comportment of tarrying' [*Verhaltenheit des Verweilens*] which constitutes the workly character of the work. But what the habitualness through which something becomes usual and commonplace allows us to forget is also always the character of having been brought forth and inaugurated, that is, the 'that'. Equipment lends itself far more readily to such habituation than the work since the latter reveals the distinctive structure of a being-outside-itself-within-itself, of an interior exteriority as it were. By virtue of this relationship to itself the work does not close in to form a totality, but rather opens itself in the thrust:

> To be sure, 'that' it is fabricated is also a property of all equipment that is available and in use. But this 'that' does not expressly emerge in equipment; it disappears in its usefulness. The more handy a piece of equipment is, the more inconspicuous it remains that, for example, such a hammer is, and the more exclusively equipment thereby keeps to its equipmental character. In general, of everything present to us, we can note that it *is*; but even then it is only noted in order to fall into the oblivion that marks everything commonplace. And what is more commonplace than this, that a being is? In a work, by contrast, this, that it *is* as a work, is just what is unusual. The event of its being created does not simply reverberate through the work; rather the work projects before itself the eventful character that the work is as this work, and has always already done so. The more essentially the work opens itself, the more luminous becomes the uniqueness of the fact that it is rather than is not. The more essentially this thrust comes into the openness, the stranger and more solitary the work becomes. In the bringing forth of the work there lies the offering 'that it be'.[98]

This character of having been brought forth divides into the fabricatedness (of equipment) and the createdness (of the work).

Createdness is distinguished from fabricatedness by virtue of its self-relation, which must be interpreted as an opening and cannot therefore be conflated with a totalising form of self-reflection. What Heidegger describes as thrust is nothing but the self-opening self-relation of the created work which never coincides with itself. This is not so much because its original identity is bifurcated and finds itself drawn into a movement of 'bad infinity', but rather because it has originally – as commencement or event – already overtaken itself. Heidegger is not concerned with the created work as the fruit of the creator, of his skills and abilities. On the contrary, the created work reveals itself the more clearly, the more the name it bears remains illegible. If the work finds its essence in poetry as the naming inauguration of language, then the created work is something inaugurated: 'The essence of art is poetry. The essence of poetry, in turn, is the inaugurating of truth. We understand inaugurating here in a threefold sense: inaugurating as bestowing, inaugurating as grounding, and inaugurating as beginning.'[99] The naming which belongs to the beginning surpasses what is 'ready to hand and disposable' and opens in the thrust the name which already places itself at our disposal as the customary, as something to which we have become habituated.

Preserving and offering

To the three ways of inaugurating which Heidegger enumerates in the essay on the origin of the work of art, there correspond three ways of preserving. 'Preserving' here is not simply a matter of conserving and storing, which would capture and contain the thrust in terms of 'familiarity and connoisseurship' in order to incorporate the work into the 'art business'. Preserving rather lets the work be a work. In other words: it first allows the offering of the 'that it be'. Can we not also interpret the drift or movement of self-relation, which is structurally implied in the work, and through which the latter distinguishes itself both from what is ready to hand and from what is present at hand (the latter is derivative from the ready at hand), as the preserving movement of the work itself? In order to relate to itself, the work must also simultaneously preserve itself in its opening. But in truth there is no simultaneity here: if the refer-

ence to self-relation signifies that inaugurating or naming reveal
themselves as such, that the inaugurated or the name open up
themselves and highlight their own thatness (in his early essay
on language Benjamin identifies divine creation with the giving
of names), then preservation is that suspension, that wavering,
in which inaugurating (bestowing, founding and beginning) has
not yet become an inauguration and naming not yet a name.
The work, which is outside of itself within itself insofar as it
relates to itself, preserves itself in its thrust, in its opening, in its
counter-turning, without thereby safeguarding any substance or
identity to itself. As event, as beginning, the name remains to
come: naming exposes the name (bringing forth is an offering
up) and in the very same movement, the movement of self-relation or preservation, allows it to effect a forgetting of the beginning, and to serve the self-exhibiting art business which
conserves and stores the work of art in a merely museological
sense. The not yet of the name cannot itself be pre- or post- co-
ordinated chronologically as a past or coming present. It comes
to pass as event in the counter-turning as the immemorial and
thus dictates the 'enduring remembrance [*Andenken*] of the inaugurated essence of being' (GRh:214). The that of being is an
immemorial that. But what then is to be remembered, if not
precisely the immemorial? Every name brings us before the task
of such commemoration. That is precisely what Heidegger is
attempting to express when he says, in the lecture on Hölderlin's hymn 'Der Rhein', that a people must commit itself 'ever
anew' to this remembrance. For indeed he understands inauguration as poetic composing, and poetic composing – 'in the
narrower sense' – as a naming which lays the ground for the
existence of a people.

3

Keeping to the Names

The saying of words

It is impossible not to overhear the imperative moment of command in the expression: 'that it be'. Nor does one need to isolate the expression from its context in order to recognise this. The emphasis upon the benaming which happens in authentic poetic composing is an emphasis upon thatness, upon that which brings a being to appearance, and in such a way that we can say precisely *that* it is. The expression 'that it be' is the imperative form which inhabits the process of naming itself, as Heidegger elaborates in *What Is Called Thinking?* Naming is a kind of 'summoning' [*Anbefehlen*]. Of course we must distinguish this 'summoning' from the arbitrary assignment of names. That which is to be named, that which naming summons to appear, is not simply nominated as the name-bearer and then supplied with a name. Between naming and that which is to be named it is impossible to draw a rigid line of demarcation which would permit the external assignment of names. Just as the name and the benamed cannot be thought as two objects which initially stand over against one another, so too the name cannot be thought as an instrument belonging to the subject that confronts an object: the summoning in question here cannot be interpreted as a subjective act.

The name gives rise to the permanent summons that it (the benamed) should appear. The once benamed calls upon itself to appear. That is why one is capable of attending expressly to 'the saying of words'. This 'saying of words' is a saying of names, and one which does not completely reveal its character when subjected to the methods of linguistic science. But Heidegger does not devalue linguistics as the science of language: 'In our attempt to attend to the saying of words we leave the question of the relationship to linguistics an open one. The contributions of the latter could in any case provide an opportunity from which we may receive a suggestive hint.'[100] When we attend to the saying of words as a saying of names, we also attend to this hint. To the extent that linguistics is aware that its claims already presuppose something that is historically given, it can indeed supply such a hint: linguistics provides an opportunity because the historically given, as the object of historiography, 'still remains intrinsically what it is'. Should we understand this attention to the opportunity of a hint in such a way that the meaning invested in a word through a subjective accomplishment might now be liberated from its rigidity and brought to a renewed life?

Originary historical transmission

In his lectures on Hölderlin, Heidegger makes it clear that the poets, the half-gods who are called to inaugurate language – the language of the people – in naming, themselves receive a hint from elsewhere. Heidegger is here pursuing, as he points out himself, the trace of Dionysos in Hölderlin's own poetry: 'Dionysos brings the trace of the vanished gods down to the godless. Bringing the trace – that is, giving and handing on the hints which the gods have given to men, remaining in the intermediate domain, the midst, between the being of men and the being of the gods. It is from out of this intermediation – this being in the manner of half-gods – that Hölderlin grasps the essence and calling of the poet' (GRh:188). What does such 'giving and handing on' consist in? It can only consist in an inaugurating poetry: the poet gives and hands on the hint which he has himself received by fulfilling the task to whose fulfilment he is called. The – divine – hint is the calling of the poet, of the half-god, who belongs wholly neither to the gods nor to mortal men. Before all history the poet grounds an inheritance or transmission through which history first becomes possible at all. The historically 'given' is originally something 'given on'. History and the historically given are only given at all because the 'original origin' is inherited through the hint.

Is Dionysos then the paradigmatic figure of original historical inheritance?

Dionysos is the son of a mortal woman, of Semele, one of the four daughters of Cadmus, King of Thebes. The mother of Dionysos was consumed in the lightning-bolt of his father, Zeus, before she bore the son, and the father shielded him from this conflagration with the cooling shoots of ivy. A testament to the union of god and mortal woman which begat him, Dionysos testifies to the being of both, *is* himself this being in the most original unity. Dionysos is not merely one half-god amongst others, but the pre-eminent half-god. He is the 'yes' of the wildest life, inexhaustible in its urge to beget, and he is the 'no' of the most frightful death through annihilation. He is the bliss of enchanted transport and the dread of hapless horror. He is the one precisely insofar as he is the other, that is, he at once is and, in that he is, is not; and in that he is not, he is. (GRh:189).

Through his begetting – through his doubled being or through the doubling in his being – Dionysos becomes the mediator. As mediator he bears witness because his begetting has generated within himself 'the urge to beget' and the urge to 'annihilation'. The logic of this passage resembles that which Franz Rosenzweig made his own in a quite different context: in *The Star of Redemption* he identifies the Jews as a people who, in contrast with the Christian community of the faithful, testify to their own calling – their election as the chosen people – by immediate appeal to a testifying continuity of generation. Whereas the Christians require the proselytising word to testify to their faith and be heard as such, generation and name alone suffice for Jewish testimony.[101] The rest is silence. The same logic, therefore, serves in one case to define Judaism and in another to define the Greek essence that is literally embodied in Dionysos, the mediator and half-god: 'But for the Greeks being means "presence" – *parousia*. This half-god absents himself in being present, and presents himself in being absent. The image for one who is absent in being present and present in being absent is the mask. This is an exemplary symbol for Dionysos, if understood, that is, in the metaphysical-Greek sense: as the original mutual relatedness of being and non-being (presence and absence)' (GRh:189f.). Dionysos is the embodiment of being as thought by the Greeks and testifies to the latter as such through the

manner of his begetting. Being testifies to itself in the very
shape and figure of the half-god.

How does the testifying of Dionysos relate to the testifying
of man? In the first part of the lecture, Heidegger claims that
man is the 'testifying witness of being' who exists 'by virtue of
language' in the 'midst of the uttermost strife'. Does the figure
of Dionysos point towards that 'essential definition of man as
thought in an original manner' to which Heidegger, in *What
Is Called Thinking?*, traces the 'doctrine of man as person'?
'The idea of apprehending includes within itself, and indeed as
a progressive series: registering, receiving, taking up, taking
through, and that means speaking through ... Insofar man as
the apprehending one apprehends what is, he can be thought
as the *persona*, as the mask of being.'[102] Reverence for the
mask: must we recognise man himself, for whom the mask is
no mere appurtenance or allegorical device but rather an
'exemplary symbol', indeed an essential characteristic, as a half-
god, as a reincarnation of Dionysos? The question which forces
itself upon us here can ultimately be formulated as the question
concerning the relationship between generation, testimony and
language. If Hölderlin is, as Heidegger claims, the poet of the
Germans, and thus the half-god who inaugurates the essence of
the German people in the beginning, then the sense and vocation of 'Germania', the sense and the vocation of the name in
general, depend upon the response of the Germans themselves.
But Hölderlin is the first to think the half-god and thus
requires the thinker too: 'The thinking of the poet – "of the
half-gods now I think" – finds its grounding in the poetic
composing of the thinker' (GRh:286). Is there an institution –
an institutional grounding – for 'poetical and thoughtful
knowing', a university, an educational establishment or centre,
a research foundation for the German people that would be
free from the demands of 'technical organisation'? Heidegger
himself, in the moment that he speaks of grounding, of 'poetical and thoughtful knowing', is presenting a lecture in a
German university. Does not this itself already imply the
necessity for a certain institutionalisation? What is it to institute
a name, a unifying name or a name that is bereft of unity ('If
we wish to name the established gathering of the individual
sciences in accordance with teaching and research a university,

that is now simply a name, not a unifying and obligating spiritual power'[103])?

'The midst of being'

Dionysos is a mediator between the 'gods who have fled' and 'godless men' because he stands in the midst, because he is riven by a yes and a no, because the yes and the no of his essence are themselves riven. The event – the naming, the original inheritance and transmission that inaugurate history and the historical inheriting and transmitting of names – takes place neither in the domain of the gods nor in the domain of man: it finds its site rather in the midst. In his book *The Logic of Sense* Gilles Deleuze draws attention to the fact that the event – which, to be sure, he does not identify with what Heidegger calls a 'midst' – exercises a doubly directed effect, and that no knowledge and no name are capable of fixing it. It therefore proves impossible to conceive of any 'subject' of the event.[104] For Heidegger the midst is not a site of equilibrium. Thus one could argue that the geopolitical description of the midst provided in the *Introduction to Metaphysics* can only be appreciated and understood if the midst is taken as the site of the event: 'Only a historical people is truly a people. But it is only historical when it happens on the ground of the midst of being, when the between is there, when the half-gods, the creative ones, let the happening work as history' (GRh:284). Heidegger delivered his Hölderlin lectures in the winter semester of 1934/5, and the *Introduction to Metaphysics* followed in the next summer semester. In the section of the *Introduction* which Heidegger dedicated to the 'fundamental question of metaphysics' ('Why are there beings at all, and not rather nothing?'), he says that 'Europe lies within the great pincer between Russia on the one side and America on the other'.[105] Heidegger counts the 'flight of the gods' and the 'massification of mankind' amongst the shared symptoms of the 'spiritual decline of the earth' which can be recognised precisely in the metaphysical identity of Russia and America. He speaks first of the situation of Europe and provides a brief description of its 'spiritual decline', one which is not supposed to express 'cultural pessimism', and then turns immediately to the German situation – not the situation of the German nation, but certainly that of the German people: 'We lie within the pincer.' Is it possible to separate people and nation in this geopolitical description or diagnosis? Not Europe: the midst of Europe lies precisely in the midst and consequently within the pincer. The German people is 'the most endangered people' and is thus also the 'metaphysical' people, one that is afflicted like no other – European – people by that 'desperate blinding and bedazzlement' into which Europe has fallen, and which exposes it not merely to the danger of falling under the domination of Russia or America, but equally to that of 'thrusting a dagger into itself' – for it is indeed 'always upon the point of leaping forth to do so'.[106] Is not this leaping a springing from and out of the origin, a dagger-thrust of being, one which cannot be confused with a free act of suicide because even in 'the freest act of suicide' we can never deprive ourselves of being itself (GRh:174)? Is not this intensification of danger (the European blinding and bedazzlement is most dangerous of all in the midst of Europe, in the realm of the German people) grounded in the fact that it is all the greater, the nearer one approaches the midst as the midst of the event? Is it not precisely the flight of the gods and the godless existence of the masses which announce the closeness of the midst? In this case the blinding and bedazzlement would find its origin in the disproportionate blindness of the creative ones themselves, of the half-god, the inaugurator, the poet. For these always have 'one eye too many' (GRh:267). Like Polyphemus, who has one eye too few, they cannot see through 'the winding and twisting ways' and thus fall victim in the end to simple cunning. Their disproportionate blindness calls forth the time of danger – that is, the danger of blinding and bedazzlement:

> This disproportionate blindness is not a lack, but rather the superior riches of a calling. The higher the origin, the less the attempt to retain it is the simple wretchedness of an arbitrary self-will and empty wishing that never gets beyond incomprehension. The higher the origin, the more original, that is, the more expansive and comprehensive is the authentic will. The latter alone can offer resistance, can create in its reluctance [*Widerwille*] the domain for a collision, the space

for a danger, and thus the possibility of assuming what is encountered into the counter-will, but that means, the possibility of suffering a way of being, and thus of fitting oneself in each case for a sending, and thus of being fate. (GRh:207)

It is clear, therefore, that the interpretation of that which constitutes a 'midst' depends upon its benaming: the transition from the structure of the event to the metaphysics of the German people is possible only if the event – if the benaming as the happening of the event – has already received a name – the name 'Germania'. The name of Dionysos is always also another, a different name.

Metaphysical neighbours

The one who remains in the midst is exposed to danger. Immediately before he characterises the German people as the 'metaphysical' and the 'most endangered' one, Heidegger also describes it as the people 'richest in neighbours'. This richness, which arises from this people's intermediate position, stands in conflict with the poverty of Europe – with that diminishment which reduces the number of neighbours to the two great world powers which make up 'a mighty pincer'. Perhaps the danger of spiritual decline is all the greater, the less the danger derives from a richness in neighbours and the more the poverty grows. This richness in neighbours, which belongs to the definition of the 'sharpest pincer pressure' and thus to the metaphysical character of the – German – people, preserves the very people that exposes itself to danger from danger. There are two ways in which it is possible to interpret the polarisation here (which does not consist in the opposition between the great world powers, since Russia and America are both 'the same metaphysically considered; the same hopeless fury of unleashed technology and the groundless organisation of the average human being'): on the one hand as a growing danger which oppresses the midst of the midst, and precisely through its growing confirms the metaphysical character or the ownmost vocation of the midst; and on the other hand, as a lessening danger, as a lessening whose metaphysical character depends upon the richness in neighbours. The metaphysical character of the German people is both protected from and riven by the danger of desperate blinding and bedazzlement.

In this polarised world, whose diminished neighbourliness effects its unsuspected universalisation, can we continue to speak of neighbours at all, of the metaphysical character of a people? A triumph of the will occurs:

> When the remotest corner of the world has been technically conquered and rendered economically exploitable, when any and every incident in any and every place has become instantly accessible at any and every time, when one can 'live through' an act of regicide in France and a symphony concert in Tokyo simultaneously, when time is only rapidity, momentariness and simultaneity, and time as history has vanished from the entire existence of all peoples, when the boxer is regarded as a great man of the people, when the millions assemble at mass meetings, when all this is regarded as a triumph – then, and indeed then, there still arises, like a spectre hovering above such sorcery, such ghostly manifestations, the question: wherefore? – whither? – and what then?[107]

The metaphysical character undergoes a metamorphosis to become a spectre, or the spectre of a question: it has already fallen victim to the sorcery which it yet continues to resist, it hovers above the sorcery and puts it into question, it strays about within it and fails to find a path. Nothing would seem to remain of that interest of reason, which according to Kant finds unified expression in its three questions, except this spectre. Wherefore the sorcery if it merely destroys every possibility of rational knowledge? Whither the exposure to this sorcery if no rational action is conceivable any longer? What happens when the sorcery reaches its peak and there is no rational hope left? Such an experience of impotence still presupposes reason and the interest of reason as an ultimate measure. But the metaphysical character that Heidegger is here endeavouring to think does not indeed measure itself against such reason.

What does it mean for the neighbouring between France and Germany – the names of two peoples – that the universalisation of neighbouring in the age of technology leads to France and

Germany transforming themselves into neighbours of Japan, and thus inflicts upon their neighbouring a blow or a thrust which no longer has anything to do with the difficulties of mutual understanding (unless the unthought essence of mutual understanding, precisely because it is actually misunderstood, contributes to the very disappearance of neighbouring in and through its technological universalisation)? In 1937 Heidegger published a short text called 'Ways of bringing Things out into the Open' in *Alemannenland. Ein Buch von Volkstum und Sendung* ['Land of the Germans. A Book concerning Folkdom and Mission'], the first volume of the yearbook of the city of Freiburg. The first sentence of Heidegger's contribution reads: 'Again and again we come up against astonishment that two neighbouring peoples – the French and the Germans – who have had the most decisive share in the historical-spiritual shaping of the West, find it so difficult to arrive at mutual understanding.'[108] Heidegger himself seems no more surprised at this astonishment than he is by the widespread conviction that such a mutual understanding between the neighbouring peoples is no longer possible anyway, that therefore the 'avoidance of the most extreme conflict is the most that can be attempted'. But in both cases, according to Heidegger, one fails to grasp the essence of mutual understanding and consequently – one must therefore add – the character of the neighbour and one's own people, the character of neighbourhood as such. For if the French and the Germans have had 'the most essential share' in the 'historical-spiritual shaping of the West', then their neighbouring is not purely geographical and historical but rather metaphysical in character. In order to grasp what neighbourhood means one must come to some understanding concerning the relationship of the neighbours in question, and attempt to clarify in advance what constitutes the essence of mutual understanding itself. The essence of mutual understanding rests upon a reciprocal putting oneself into question, indeed upon a putting oneself in *the* question (does the spectre of the question survive the question and the attempt at mutual understanding?). The more questions, the more neighbours. It is rather striking, therefore, that 'neighbourhood' in Heidegger's 'Ways of bringing Things out into the Open' presents itself as a duality. The richness in neighbours, described in the *Introduction to Metaphysics*, is

measured here against qualitative difference – which does not
obtain between the great world powers – and not against quantitative difference: the people that has *one* real, *one* true, *one*
essential neighbour is also the people that is 'richest in neighbours'. Since the Germans and the French represent neighbouring in its metaphysical character (but may we speak of
'representation' here?), since neither can evade the danger of
misinterpreting and misunderstanding the other, of misinterpreting what is their own and misunderstanding mutual understanding itself, they are also already destined to disclose the
essence of mutual understanding, of what is their own, and of
the other – of what is the other's own. Heidegger is perfectly
consistent, therefore, when he repudiates all compromise solutions here – the 'temporary accommodations', the 'occasional
agreements with the careful balancing of binding claims and
fulfilments', for these are all based upon the conviction that the
avoidance of 'the most extreme conflict' must be the ultimate
aim. Heidegger describes the 'genuine understanding of peoples'
by means of a schema that plays a decisive role in the first series
of lectures on Hölderlin, although it was employed there to illuminate the relationship between the Germans and the Greeks.
Are the Germans and the Greeks neighbouring peoples historically? Heidegger writes:

> The genuine understanding of peoples begins and fulfils itself
> with one thing: and that is the thoughtful reflection, accom-
> plished through creative dialogue, concerning what has his-
> torically been given over to them as an endowment and as a
> task. In such reflection the peoples place themselves back into
> what is in each case their own and thus bring themselves to
> stand with magnified clarity and decisiveness. But the
> ownmost dimension of a people is the creative accomplishing
> which is assigned to it, through which it grows over and
> beyond itself into its historical misssion and thereby first
> attains to itself.[109]

In its metaphysical character, neighbouring – as 'genuine self-
understanding' – is not something simply given or present at
hand, but is a movement of appropriating one's own that places
the people into what is given over to it as historical mission. To

put this differently and in a more precise way, neighbouring is
given over with the people as the opening up of what is given
over to them, of what the people must take upon itself if it is to
appropriate what is most its own.

The French and the Germans shape the West historically and
spiritually: they are 'the history-forming Western peoples'. It is
their share in this formative process which first seals their bond,
rather than need or distress. Even in this 'present hour of world
history' the 'fundamental character of their mission' is
prescribed by the West itself. And this is what must now be
rescued:

> Rescuing here does not simply mean the maintenance of
> something still present at hand, but signifies rather the ori-
> ginally renewed creative justification of its past and future
> history. The self-understanding of neighbouring peoples with
> regard to what is most their own means therefore: giving
> ourselves to understand the necessity of this rescuing as in
> each case our own task. The knowledge concerning this
> necessity springs especially from the experience of that dis-
> tress which emerges with the innermost threat to the West,
> and from the power for a transfiguring projection of the
> highest possibilities of Western existence. But because this
> threat to the West could drive towards a complete uprooting
> and universal confusion, the will for renewal which opposes
> it must itself be accompanied in a fundamental way by ulti-
> mate decisions.[110]

The congruence of these reflections with the discourse of the
Introduction to Metaphysics hardly requires emphasis. The
common elements can be summarised as follows: (1) the distress
afflicting the West is a 'spiritual decline of the earth', an
'uprooting'; (2) decline and uprooting mark the urgency of an
inauguration; (3) inauguration presupposes a knowledge
concerning history, a philosophy that can assert itself against
false conceptions. In the *Introduction to Metaphysics*, Heidegger
mentions 'two apparently different interpretations of science'
which are not in truth distinguishable at all: 'science as techni-
cal-practical professional knowledge' and 'science as a cultural
value in itself'. In 'Ways of bringing Things out into the Open',

he attacks the complementary phenomena of overvaluing and undervaluing philosophy: 'Philosophy is overvalued as soon as we expect any immediately useful effects to flow from such thinking. Philosophy is undervalued if its concepts merely "abstractly" reproduce (in a detached and impoverished form) what our experiential dealing with things has already tangibly established.' The common background of thought allows the difference to leap out all the more distinctly here: in contrast to the *Introduction*, the earlier text seems to share out the metaphysical character of the task. It is anchored in a reciprocal recognition which harbours the 'disquiet of mutual putting oneself into the question out of the concern for shared historical tasks'.[111]

Dualism and duality

What then does that which has been transmitted and thus given over to the neighbours as an endowment consist in? The duality involved here corresponds to the duality in the domain of beings itself: 'The two realms of beings which reciprocally overlay and underlay one another are those of nature and history.' Just as beings are divided into the realms of nature and history, so too the metaphysical character of these peoples 'which bring about history' is divided and forms the neighbouring of the Germans and the French: 'The fundamental questioning concerning nature and the truth character of the knowledge of nature intrinsically involves an engagement with the beginnings of French philosophy in the modern age. In the course of Western history, however, it is the poets [an allusion to Hölderlin] and thinkers of the age of German Idealism who have first approached a metaphysical knowledge of the essence of history.'[112] The neighbouring is undeniably marked by an asymmetry that has its origin in the division of the metaphysical character itself and hence tends to transform the duality into a dualism. This asymmetry therefore is not just a finding that results from 'the external observation and discrimination of certain given characteristics of French thought in contrast to German thought'. The asymmetry here deprives the 'neighbouring encounter' of that balance of reciprocity where philosophical self-understanding transpires and its fundamental conditions are 'clearly brought before the inner gaze': here where the Germans have abandoned all opportunistic politics and opened themselves to an 'actual dialogue of creative minds'. For if the 'metaphysical knowledge of the essence of history' is given along with the Germans as their own endowment, then what is supposedly given over to the French and their neighbouring people alike: namely the saving of the West as the inauguration of history – as the inauguration of the realm of history – must be more alien to the essence of the French than to that of the Germans, however great and essential is the French share in the historical-spiritual shaping of the West, however indispensable may be reflection upon the essence of nature. For in the end it is only those who inaugurate history, those who bestow the name (upon it) that can properly accomplish this reflection: 'Can it come as any cause for surprise that, for many years now, the younger forces in France who have recognised the necessity for liberating themselves from the framework of Cartesian philosophy [thereby breaking out of the realm of nature into that of freedom!], have been striving towards an understanding of Hegel, Schelling and Hölderlin?'[113] But given genuine self-understanding, the break-through of the 'younger forces in France' who are intent on saving the West from its decline (Heidegger, who is generally so derogatory about Spengler, although he takes his thinking seriously as a symptom of the 'world hour', here in 'Ways of bringing Things out into the Open', risks reversing the well-known title of Spengler's book) is no more surprising than the fact that the shapers of history encounter great difficulties in understanding one another in the absence of 'genuine self-understanding'. This salvation of neighbourhood, accomplished by recourse to a division within the metaphysical character, ultimately reveals itself as the salvation of the metaphysical character of the German people, or more precisely: as a salvation of their undivided unity. If we consider other texts (like the Hölderlin lectures) and bring those passages concerning the 'Graeco-German mission' before 'the inner gaze', we cannot avoid placing the penultimate section of 'Ways of bringing Things out into the Open' into an overdetermined context:

When we reflect upon the possible greatness and the criteria of Western 'culture', we are instantly reminded of the histor-

ical world of the early Greeks. But we can thereby also easily
forget that the Greeks did not become what they always and
essentially are by remaining confined within their 'space' [in
order to become what one is, to appropriate the 'space' of
one's own, one must apparently be 'a people without space'].
It was only by virtue of the keenest but creative engagement
with what is most alien to it and most difficult for it –
namely the Asiatic [one may think of Japan's role in the
technological universalisation of neighbouring and the role of
fate in the Greek defeat of Asian power] – that this people
grew into the brief spell of its historical uniqueness and
greatness.

The essence of historical existence

The Dionysian affirmation and negation which Dionysos divides
or splits at the very instant of his birth are both unique. To the
degree that the half-god embodies the presence and absence of
being – embodies non-being in its relation to being – one can
interpret his 'yes' and his 'no' as the source of a duplication: the
'yes, yes' and the 'no, no' of 'busied Dasein', which Heidegger
mentions in the Rectoral Address, conceal by duplication that
'openness of the nothing which anxiety alone reveals'.[114] Nothingness itself – the unique no of Dionysos – 'forces forth' the
'fundamental question of metaphysics': 'Why are there beings at
all and not rather nothing?' The uniqueness of Dionysian embodiment can also be recognised in the fact that Hölderlin is not
the only one to name Dionysos. Nonetheless this naming
remains itself unique. It is true that Nietzsche also calls the half-
god by name in 'the last Western interpretation of being that
also prepares something for the future' (GRh:191). But he
thereby misunderstands 'the essence of historical existence', at
least insofar as he opposes the Dionysian and the Apollonian:

> What Hölderlin sees as the essence of historical existence, the
> wrestling intimacy of what is given-with as endowment and
> given-over as task, Nietzsche also rediscovered under the
> terms of the Dionysian and the Apollonian, but not with the
> same purity and simplicity as Hölderlin; for in the meantime
> Nietzsche had been inevitably exposed to that fatality which

is marked by the names of Schopenhauer, Darwin, Wagner, and the so-called *Gründerjahre*, the period of industrialisation and unification in Germany. Not even to mention the greatest fatality, namely what the subsequent and the contemporary Nietzsche interpretation in all its different forms has made of him. (GRh:293f.)

The structure of Heidegger's argument is a curious one. For the rediscovery of the Dionysian which we owe to Nietzsche was distorted not simply by the interpretations associated with the listed names in the quoted passage, but also by the subsequent 'Nietzsche interpretation'. The fatality to which Nietzsche falls victim by no means comes to an end with the thinker's death. Even after his death it hinders him from thinking his rediscovery in its full purity and simplicity.[115] It is as if all 'Nietzsche interpretation' − 'in all its different forms': thus also including the interpretation which claims him for National Socialism − has served only to slay the thinker's thought and thus, allowing him to die once more of the same fatal sickness which haunted him and infected those who followed, to prevent him from dying at all. It is precisely because, in a certain sense, Nietzsche was not blind enough, precisely because his rediscovery of the Dionysian − in its opposition to the Apollonian − bears the marks of blinding and bedazzlement, that his 'interpretation of being', as the last Western interpretation of the same, prepares 'something for the future'. This interpretation points towards the domain of the greatest danger, towards the midst. The 'future' for Heidegger is always synonymous with the repetition of the beginning. However, the 'subsequent and contemporary Nietzsche interpretation' is fatal because it drives the blinding and bedazzlement so far as to cast oblivion upon its source in that original blindness of the creative one which underlies the 'interpretation of being'.

What then, if we follow Hölderlin, does the essence of historical existence consist in? It consists in the transformation of the endowment ('This has been given to the Germans as their endowment: the capacity to grasp things, the establishment and planning of domains, a reckoning and calculating, an ordering to the point of organising') into a task, into the 'free use' of what Hölderlin calls the people's 'national possession' or the

people's 'own'. What has been given to the German people as
their task is the capacity to be 'struck by being', a capacity
given to the Greeks as their endowment. The task of the Greek
people amounted to a 'binding of the unbound in the struggle
for establishing a work', it amounted to a 'seizing' and 'bringing
to a stand'. The transformation of the endowment into a task
must be regarded as the most difficult of all: learning the 'free
use of one's own', which Hölderlin mentions in his letter to
Böhlendorff as cited by Heidegger here, is more difficult than
any other kind of learning and therefore more dangerous. In his
essay on 'The Question of Guilt' Jaspers defines what the
German people possess as their 'own' in the same way as
Heidegger does with his allusion to Hölderlin, with an allusion
which is not simply a paraphrasing repetition: 'We must first
take what has been given as an endowment into pure preservation, but only in order to grasp and seize what has been given
as a task' (GRh:294). The people's 'own', Jaspers says, is not a
fixed piece of property but a task. And does not Adorno's
conception of the untouched forces of that which is German
correspond more closely to the idea of a task than to the idea of
an endowment? We can clearly see that the repetition of the
beginning is the repetition of something unique and a unique
repetition from the fact that endowment and task can turn one
into the other. It is this reversal which first constitutes 'the
Graeco-German mission' and the uniqueness of the name in
which history is gathered: 'It is because what has been given as
an endowment and what has been given as a task is imparted
differently to the Greeks and the Germans that the Germans,
precisely with regard to what is their own, will never surpass
the highest accomplishment of the Greeks. That is the
"paradox" here. Insofar as we fight out the struggle of the
Greeks, although with the fronts reversed, we become not
Greeks, but Germans' (GRh:293). If the German people were
simply to incorporate the Greek heritage, if they were simply
to transform what is the Greeks' own into a constituent element
of themselves in order to feed upon its power, then the repetition would not be a repetition of the unique, would not be a
repetition determined by the beginning. It is only insofar as the
Germans do not surpass 'the highest accomplishment' of the
Greeks that they are capable of accomplishing the history inau-

gurated by the opening up of the Greeks in the name of Germany – in the name 'Germania'.

The legitimising power of the name

How are we to take Heidegger's reduction of the 'production of corpses in the gas-chambers and death camps' to a mere example of the sway of technological domination, if we consider it from the perspective opened up by the distinction between endowment and task? This remark from the lecture on 'Enframing' [*Das Gestell*], delivered in 1949, would appear to confirm a failure: the Germans have not been able after all to transform what was given to them as their endowment (planning, calculating, ordering, organising) into their task, and have mistaken the one for the other. That is why they failed in the face of the endowment and the task alike, why they failed to grasp 'the essence of historical existence'. Such an argument already bestows a certain sense upon the 'production of corpses in the gas-chambers and death camps' by inserting it into the context of a 'mission', as a possibility of failure and defeat. What happened is thus justified because it was first made possible by a 'mission' that is presented as the truth of history. The name 'Germania' as the name of this 'mission' legitimates 'the production of corpses in the gas-chambers and death camps' in the very moment that such a production functions as an example of the greatest danger – the danger which Heidegger at least implicitly already warns against. One might be tempted to take the reference to the technical administration of death as the index of a rupture or discontinuity within Heidegger's thought (where National Socialism is now interpreted solely under the aspect of the planetary domination of human beings through technology). But the distinction between the endowment and the task also marks a continuity which is particularly striking precisely because Heidegger chooses the concepts of calculating, organising and planning to characterise what is given to the Germans as their endowment. It is quite true that this argument depends upon bringing together statements that were made at quite different times. But it should not be overlooked that Heidegger continued even after the Second World War to maintain the idea of a Graeco-German mission in relation to language.

Perhaps the act of naming is sufficient to create the possibility of meaning or sense, and with it that of a justification of the benamed. Does the name exclude the 'perfect senselessness' for which it can stand ('Auschwitz')? In an essay on the social sciences and the study of concentration camps, published in 1950 and translated into German under the title of 'Perfect Senselessness', Hannah Arendt writes that on the one hand 'the extermination policy of the Nazis' made 'almost too much sense' and on the other it failed to make 'any sense whatsoever'. That is precisely why 'the adjective "unprecedented" as applied to totalitarian terror receives its full significance' in this connection.[116] The senselessness depends upon an excess of sense: 'The insanity of such systems clearly does not only lie in its first premise but in their very logicality which proceeds regardless of all facts and regardless of reality which teaches us that whatever we do we can't carry through with absolute perfection.'[117] The first premise which can still function to establish and secure a certain sense, allowing at least for some explanation, retreats behind the 'inflexible logic' which produces the excess of sense: 'Under Himmler's regime "any kind of instruction on an ideological basis" was expressly prohibited.' The concept of ideology proves useless: 'for the ideological supersense, enthroned as it were, over a world of fabricated senselessness explains "everything" and therefore nothing'.[118] The greater the excess of sense and the more difficult the discovery of a criterion that would securely establish and stabilise any sense, the more senseless and thus the more improbable the events: '[The Nazis] were quite convinced that one of the best chances for the success of this enterprise lay in the extreme improbability that anybody in the outside world would believe it to be true.'[119] It is certainly the case that Arendt herself appeals at several points in the essay to a criterion that would securely establish and stabilise sense here, as when, for example, she introduces a friend–foe schema in order to explain the 'intolerance' of the 'revolutionary principle'.[120] But she also goes so far as to transfer the senselessness that results from the excess of sense to the measures subsequently taken to establish sense. Where dying is perpetuated (the camp victim is placed 'into a permanent state of dying' and death is no longer notified) and the 'anxiety in the face of dying' gives way to the 'fear of responsibility' (is not responsibility as the responsibility of a – moral – subject, of a personality, itself a sense-ensuring criterion and thus a disturbing factor for the 'inflexible logic' which produces the excess of sense, a sense which cannot be led back to anything, either to a subject or a person?), it must be considered as a 'senseless' act 'to hang a man for murder who took part in the fabrication of corpses (although of course we hardly have any other course of action). These were crimes which no punishment seems to fit because all punishment is limited by the death penalty.'[121] From the sense-lessness of excessive sense as the principle of destruction Hannah Arendt infers the 'perfect' otherness of the system that is erected upon it.

Stability of sense

The law which has no choice remains ever guilty. If the punishment is so terrible that no guilt any longer corresponds to it, then the condemned one, as Hannah Arendt explains in another text (*The Image of Hell* of 1946), becomes the innocent one: 'The gas chamber was more than anybody could have possibly deserved, and in the face of it the worst criminal was as innocent as the new-born babe.'[122] But perfect innocence, or perfection itself, indicates a guilt that can no more be 'a consequence of human action' than can such an innocence or perfection. On the other hand, the guilt which is brought upon themselves by those who pronounce an incommensurable punishment, also always appears as the sign of an innocence which death itself cannot taint: 'For Göring the death penalty is almost a joke, and he, like all his fellow-defendants at Nuremberg, knows that we can do no more than make him die a little earlier than he would have done anyhow.'[123] It is therefore possible to interpret the observation that 'the Nazis in their attempt to produce a badness beyond vice have established nothing but an innocence beyond virtue' in a double sense: innocence passes over immediately into guilt, guilt passes over immediately into innocence, on the part of the guilty and on the part of the innocent, in the world of the guilty and in the world of the innocent. Where guilt and innocence reciprocally nullify one another, where they no longer serve as a sense-ensuring criterion, as a criterion for the stabilisation of sense, the law which condemns the guilty and absolves the innocent is *a priori* guilty. Doubtless the name can acquire the function of a sense-ensuring criterion, of a criterion which contributes to the stabilisation of sense. Every named event distinguishes itself from other events and thereby already makes sense. If history itself has a name, then every named event is overdetermined by this name. As such, however – as the name of history – the name is senseless: it has too much or too little sense. In the name, as Adorno recognises, we are struck with blindness. Is it possible to separate this blindness of the name, which necessarily emerges once the name is privileged, from the blindness of the inaugurator who always privileges the inaugurated name? Does not the name, in accordance with its essence, threaten the stability of sense? Is the 'world full of fabricated senselessness' not the total immanence of the name?

Given as endowment and given as task

During the period in which he was extensively engaged with Nietzsche (from around 1936), Heidegger returned to the opposition between the Dionysian and the Apollonian, and once again – in a context expressly concerned with the task and calling of the Germans – he placed Nietzsche alongside Hölderlin. This time the emphasis – despite certain qualifications – falls upon what unites the two:

> What Nietzsche of course could not know, despite from his youth being more clearly aware than his contemporaries of who Hölderlin was, is the fact that Hölderlin had already, in deeper and nobler fashion, seen and grasped this opposition [the 'opposition in the existence of the Greeks which Nietzsche described as the 'Apollonian' and the 'Dionysian']. This great recognition is hidden in a letter to Böhlendorff. The letter was written on 4 December 1801, shortly before Hölderlin's departure for France. Hölderlin here opposes, in the essence of the Greeks, the 'holy pathos' and the 'Western *Junonian sobriety* of the gift for representation'. This opposition is not to be regarded simply as a neutral historical observation. It reveals itself rather to the immediate reflection upon the fate and calling of the Germans. We cannot do more than allude to this here, since Hölderlin's own knowl-

edge could only be properly elucidated by an interpretation of his work. It is enough if we can surmise from this allusion that the variously named conflict of the Dionysian and the Apollonian, of holy passion and sober representation, is a hidden stylistic law for the historical calling of the Germans, and which must one day find us ready and prepared to give it shape. This opposition is not a formula with whose help we might attempt to describe 'culture' alone. With this opposition Hölderlin and Nietzsche have erected a question mark before the task given over to the Germans, that of historically discovering their essence.[124]

The shaping and articulation that are demanded by the 'stylistic law' that constitutes the historical calling of the Germans (does not a 'stylistic law' always demand shaping?) is what is given over as the task: it appears in the Nietzsche lectures as if the relationship between endowment and task had been imperceptibly reversed, as if the *shaping* of the conflict between the shapeless and that which shapes would already ascribe priority to the latter. And why? Perhaps because music, or more precisely: the inner affinity between music and the Dionysian, presents a danger to inauguration, to poetic composing, to the name. Heidegger traces the break with Wagner who in the Hölderlin lectures belongs in the realm of 'fatality', to Nietzsche's understanding of what is given as a task, an understanding without which the 'stylistic law' and the historical calling in question would have remained concealed, and without which Nietzsche would never have marked the task as a task. The question mark thus erected, threateningly and invitingly, 'before the task of the Germans', indicates that it is given over precisely as a task, something that must be taken over in uncertainty, in the absence of any knowledge concerning the outcome. Nietzsche, according to Heidegger, has released himself from a spell: 'It was this intoxicated tearing away towards the totality through which the man Wagner and his work drew the young Nietzsche into his spell; yet this was only possible because there was something in Nietzsche himself which responded to this, namely that which Nietzsche called the Dionysian. But because Wagner merely sought after the intensification of the Dionysian and a kind of self-dissolution within the latter, while Nietzsche sought rather to shape and tame the Dionysian, the rift between them was already predestined.'[125] To the extent that the separating and isolating concentration upon the Dionysian, whether produced by its 'intensification' or producing its 'intensification' in the first place, hinders him from approaching the task, that is, from approaching history, Nietzsche also fails to penetrate through to the essence of the Dionysian. For it is only in its relation to what is given as a task that what is given as endowment can itself be recognised. Here, what is given as endowment, is what 'in Nietzsche himself' strengthens the spell of intoxication and exposes him to the 'tearing away' which harbours the 'rift' between Wagner and himself precisely because the man and the work are equally caught up together. The predestined moment 'in Nietzsche himself' and the historical vocation of the Germans pass over into one another: Wagner and Nietzsche are emblems of the Dionysian that unleashes itself and must be tamed. Does not the Dionysian, once unleashed, turn against its own double nature? Does not the doubling of Dionysos, which preserves him from transgression in the very act of transgression, contain the task of shaping and forming? Does the Dionysian in its intensification unleash itself from its double nature and with this from the task of shaping and forming?

The unleashed, rushing and whirling Dionysian moment transforms itself into a compensatory element, into a stimulant – and thus also into a tranquillising narcotic – which distracts from the task that is given over:

That Richard Wagner's enterprise should inevitably fail is not simply grounded in the predominance ascribed to music in relation to the other arts. Rather: that music could assume this priority in the first place was already grounded in the fundamental and increasingly aesthetic attitude to art in general. This is the conception and evaluation of art from out of the mere condition of feeling and the increasing barbarisation of the latter into the simple seething and surging of self-abandoned feeling. On the other hand, this stimulation of intoxicated feeling, this untethering of 'affects', could be regarded as the rescuing of 'life', especially in the face of the growing neutralisation and impoverishment of existence through industry, technology and economics, all in the context of the debilitation and decay of the formative power of knowledge and tradition, not even to mention the absence of any and every great sense of purpose in human existence. Abandonment to the waves of feeling inevitably tried to fill the missing space of a grounded and articulated standing amongst beings, something that poetic composing and thinking alone are capable of creating.[126]

In spite of his intention to produce a *Gesamtkunstwerk* or all-embracing work of art, Wagner actually bestowed on music a primacy which robbed poetry and language of their 'decisive shaping power'. But music can only claim such primacy for itself insofar as art, and consequently the all-embracing work of art as well, remains in thrall to the aesthetic.

The 'philosophical reflection upon the essence of art and the beautiful' already begins, so Heidegger claims, as aesthetics. Heidegger dates this beginning back to the Platonic-Aristotelian age, to the moment when 'great (Greek) art, but also contemporaneous great (Greek) philosophy' was coming to an end. The history of the knowledge of art as the history of aesthetics begins with the distinction between form and matter. This leads to the modern turn or turning-point which places the affective condition of the human being at the centre of attention. And in the end the now independent domain of the Dionysian, that is to say, of music as the 'raging and burning of the senses', takes the place of poetry. The musical-Dionysian opposes itself to the poetic and inaugurative, to the process of shaping in and through the name. In the essay on the origin of the work of art Heidegger defines shape or form [*Gestalt*] as the 'created being of the work' which 'sets out' [*feststellt*] truth. Music and poetry mark the two poles in the structure of the beginning. At this point Heidegger is certainly at the furthest remove from Adorno who sees in music the 'attempt to name the name itself'. Hence, what initially bars Nietzsche's access to 'the essence of historical existence' is the interpretation of the Dionysian in terms of aesthetics, in terms of the metaphysics of art. But even then when he interprets the opposition of the Apollonian and the Dionysian in terms of the will to power – and Heidegger wishes to delineate this (predestined) displacement –

Nietzsche thinks the Dionysian in a metaphysical manner. In his lecture on the figure of Zarathustra, Heidegger leaves us in no doubt about this:

> Metaphysical thought rests upon the difference between that which truly is and that which, in comparison, does not constitute true being. What proves to be decisive for the *essence* of metaphysics, however, does not lie in the fact that the said difference presents itself as the opposition between the sensible and the supersensible, but rather in the fact that this difference, in the sense of a cleaving, remains the primary and sustaining element. And it even continues to persist when the Platonic hierarchy with regard to the sensible and the supersensible is reversed, and the sensible is experienced more essentially and in the further sense that Nietzsche designates by the name of *Dionysos*. For the superabundance, to which the 'great yearning' of Zarathustra is directed, is the inexhaustible constancy of becoming, as which the will to power wills itself in the eternal return of the same.'[127]

The shaping that is beholden to the will to power is bound to one of the names of Dionysos which fails to open up 'the essence of historical existence'.

The names of Dionysos

If we wished to assemble the names of Dionysos in Heidegger's thought, if we wished to call Dionysos by the name he receives from Heidegger, we would have to distinguish – schematically – at least five names.

(1) Dionysos is the name of the half-god in general. He transmits, as Heidegger says along with Hölderlin, the trace or the hint of 'the gods who have fled' to those who have been abandoned by them: to the 'godless ones'. It is because Dionysos, in this case, does not represent simply one name amongst others, that all the other names of the half-god – like the name 'Hölderlin' as the proper name of the poet – relate to him metonymically. In this connection one must not forget that Dionysos, through the manner of his begetting, already testifies to his being a half-god; Hölderlin testifies to it merely

through the inauguration of language which transpires in or as poetry.

(2) Dionysos is the name of the embodiment of being as at once absent and present. For the half-god is the bearer of a symbol which can be said to be the 'emblem' of being. This symbol – the mask – represents the 'original mutual relatedness of being and non-being (presence and absence)'. Thus embodied being is neither divine nor human in essence. It appears bodily in the between.

(3) Dionysos is the name of the half-god who, through the abstract universalisation of his name (the Dionysian) and a later interpretation (Nietzsche opposes the Dionysian to the Apollonian), designates the moment of a historical calling (or a 'stylistic law' of history) which Hölderlin thinks 'more purely' and 'more simply' before Nietzsche. The question which Heidegger is attempting to approach here is the question of what is given as endowment and what is given as task. As 'holy pathos', as the 'capacity to be struck by the power of being', the 'Dionysian' – as Heidegger notes in accordance with Hölderlin – was given to the Greeks as endowment, but is given over to the Germans as task.

(4) Dionysos is the name of the half-god who, in the adjectival form of his name, denotes the aesthetico-musical dimension as the completion of metaphysics – and of art. This act of naming brings with it a reversal of the historical calling: what was once given as endowment is now given over to the German people as task (or so one can infer from Heidegger's interpretation of Wagner). The people's efforts must be directed to a taming and shaping of the Dionysian that has become independent. For the Dionysian as conceived musically, and therefore aesthetically, endangers the unity of inauguration and the name. Heidegger identifies this danger with reference to Wagner's notion of the *Gesamtkunstwerk*, of the all-embracing work of art which presents itself as the 'celebration of the community of a people'.[128] It would be a misunderstanding to regard Heidegger's attack on Wagner simply as a subsidiary counterpart to the engagement with Nietzsche. Is the reason for this attack not to be sought ultimately in the fact that Heidegger himself is centrally concerned with the inauguration of a unity for the German people, and must therefore distance himself

from the sort of unity inaugurated in 'the all-embracing work of art' as the potential ground for a 'celebration of the community of a people'? Like Heidegger, Adorno also stresses that the element of 'intoxication' belonging to the all-embracing work of art constitutes an indispensable '*principium stilisationis*' insofar as it generates the 'delusory appearance of an ideal unity', the 'delusory appearance of absolute closure and presence'.[129] When Heidegger quotes a fragment by Nietzsche directed *against* Wagner and adds: 'The absolute here [in the all-embracing work of art] is now only experienced as the purely indeterminate, as a total dissolution in pure feeling, as a sinking dispersal into nothingness', this can be related directly to Adorno's observation that 'nothingness dwells within the innermost cell of this [Wagnerian] construction of the redemptive process'. In contrast to Horkheimer, we should note that Adorno also shares with Heidegger an antipathy to Schopenhauer who associates redemption with entry into the nothingness of Nirvana. Whereas Heidegger generally contents himself, it is true, with summary judgements in this regard, Adorno goes beyond the gesture of antipathy, as the passages on Schopenhauer in the *Essay on Wagner* and *Negative Dialectics* reveal. But the difference here is also substantive in character. Adorno defends the claim that, in the all-embracing work of art, it is music that is actually subordinated to language, even when the word is unable to assert its priority continually: 'For the sake of the attempted synthesis of all media it is the inner consistency of the most decisive element, namely the music, that is neglected. The pseudo-metamorphosis of music into language, something which had been advancing ineluctably ever since the *stile rappresentativo* and a process to which music owed so much of its own emancipation, reveals its negative moment as soon as it degenerates into a parasitic relationship to language and now merely imitates the movement of linguistic intention.'[130] Does Adorno's claim simply form the counterpart to Heidegger's here, in that it is now music – in Adorno's aesthetic theory – and now poetry – in Heidegger's philosophy of art and language – which is privileged respectively?

(5) Dionysos is the name of the half-god in whose name Nietzsche consecrates the realm of the sensible or the sensuous. Heidegger interprets the sensible here as the constancy of

becoming secured by the will to power as it liberates itself from the resentment of time – of the past which eludes it – and incorporates beings into the circle of the eternal return of the same. Does this doctrine of the will to power and the eternal return of the same simply presuppose a reversal of Platonism, one which fails to disturb the hierarchical schema and is merely brought to completion through the essential extension of the sensible? In the Nietzsche lecture we read the following: 'With the elimination of any distinction between the true and the merely apparent world the downfall of metaphysics begins. "Downfall" however is not cessation or termination, but is rather the end as the ultimate and most extreme accomplishment of the essence. It is only the highest essence that can experience a "downfall".'[131] Heidegger's remarks here are intended to elucidate Nietzsche's proclamation that the apparent world has been eliminated along with the true one. It is of course tempting to transfer Heidegger's dictum that only 'the highest essence' – only the metaphysical essence – experiences a 'downfall' to the calling of the metaphysical people – namely the Germans...

A key figure

In his investigations concerning *The Philosophical Discourse of Modernity* Jürgen Habermas takes the figure of Dionysos as the key figure in his understanding of Heidegger, and indeed in his understanding of a certain modernity in general. It is initially rather striking that Habermas considers the introduction of the half-god, which indicates an intellectual prejudgement on his part, as a hermeneutically legitimate procedure that does not even require any explication as such. He does not therefore refer to a single one of the names which Dionysos receives in Heidegger's thought. In other words, there is not a single quoted passage which might illuminate the choice of Dionysos as a potentially key figure for the interpretation of Heidegger's thought. This is all the more surprising in that Habermas shows no hesitation in ascribing 'the role of Dionysos' to being directly – i.e. without adducing any textual support – and citing a passage in which Heidegger does indeed speak of being and beings, but precisely not of the half-god. It seems as if the obligation to produce conclusive textual evidence were simply superfluous: Heidegger's thought bears the name of Dionysos. But this does not of itself suffice to show that the procedure adopted by Habermas is an intrinsically fruitless one. It is quite conceivable, for example, that a sufficient number of passages to support his claim could subsequently be discovered, or that the introduction of the half-god as a key figure does actually produce a clarifying effect even without appealing directly to the appropriate textual evidence. One must of course emphasise the peculiarity of this procedure, given that Habermas himself accuses Heidegger of claiming some 'privileged access to the truth', of appealing to some 'special kind of knowledge *beyond* self-reflection, and beyond discursive thought in general'.[132] Only a careful analysis of the text is capable of creating any clarity here.

'Dionysian messianism'?

In the fourth part of his lecture course, essentially concerned with Nietzsche's thought as representing a kind of 'turning-point' in philosophy and modernity, Habermas comes to address, for the first time, the supposed relationship between Heidegger's 'thinking of being' and 'the Dionysos myth'. After observing that Heidegger wished to take over the essential themes of Nietzsche's 'Dionysian messianism' (a strange Judaeo-Greek pairing) and avoid 'the aporias of a self-reflexive critique of reason', Habermas continues: 'Heidegger's later philosophy [his thinking after the 'turn'] can be read as an attempt to translate the Dionysian event from the arena of an aesthetically revived mythology into philosophy itself. Heidegger is initially confronted with the task of placing philosophy in the place that was occupied for Nietzsche by art (as the counter-movement to nihilism) in order then to transform philosophical thinking into the arena where the ossification and the renewal of Dionysian powers can take place.'[133] But the relationship between poetry and thought is in truth essentially more complex and far less transparent than the summary exposition of Habermas. This is particularly obvious if we consider Heidegger's first lectures on Hölderlin which immediately precede the period of his engagement with Nietzsche and, just like the later essay on *The Origin of the Work of Art*, accord a pre-eminent position to poetry. It would surely be very difficult to discover a simple formula or common denominator that could serve to grasp the relationship between poetry and thought here, as Habermas attempts to do. And this not only because the various writings in question destroy the supposed unity of the two, but rather, and above all, because the relationship between poetry and thought intrinsically harbours an unusual structure of original supplementarity or supplementary originariness, as we can also appreciate if we give careful attention to Heidegger's remarks concerning Hölderlin's hymns 'Germania' and 'The Rhine'. Habermas appears to proceed strategically on a self-created drawing-board of 'modern' philosophy at his own disposal where the relevant themes are constantly 'transposed', 'transformed' and 'renewed': Dionysos is introduced as a philosophical figure so that being can then assume its 'role'. Thus it is not so surprising to come across the following remark: 'Heidegger, like Hegel, is convinced that art has come to its essential end with the Romantics.'[134] Heidegger's remarks on the end of art by no means reveal the univocal sense that Habermas ascribes to them. Since Habermas does not quote any particular passage, one is forced to infer what he means. There is a passage in Heidegger's lectures on Nietzsche, to which Habermas may be alluding here, that reads: 'In the very historical moment when aesthetics attains to the greatest possible height, breadth and rigour of its development, great art is at an end. The completion of aesthetics shows its greatness in that it expressly recognises and pronounces this end of great art. This last and greatest aesthetic of Western thought is that of Hegel.'[135] If, however, Habermas were to refer to this passage, one would not so much draw his attention to Heidegger's qualified ratification of Hegel here ('Hegel never meant to deny the possibility that individual works of art would later continue to be produced and appreciated'). One would rather emphasise that the end of 'great art', which is the focus of Heidegger's summary remarks on Hegel, refers back to the logic of the 'completion of aesthetics' and not *primarily* to Heidegger's own 'classicistic understanding of art'. If, however, Habermas were to consult the 'Afterword' of the essay on *The Origin of the Work of Art*, where Heidegger also alludes to Hegel's 'claim', he would certainly owe us an interpretation of the following sentences: 'The decision concerning

Hegel's claim has not yet occurred. For behind this claim there
stands the course of Western thinking since the Greeks, a thinking which corresponds to a truth of beings that has already
come to pass.' The 'Afterword' does not contradict the lectures
on Nietzsche. The latter clearly reveal that 'great art' comes to
its end twice, first at the point when aesthetics was first developed in Greek philosophy, and then with the completion of
aesthetic thought in German Idealism. But although 'great
Greek art' still lacks 'a thoughtful conceptual reflection', such a
reflection is by no means – at least in Heidegger's eyes – synonymous with aesthetics.[136] Habermas conflates art with the
aesthetic, fails to explicate the concept of aesthetics that Heidegger is employing, and which differs from the customary
concept of the same, and suggests that Heidegger is proclaiming
the end of art – as or with Hegel – from some metaphysical
'standpoint'. But it is absolutely necessary to grasp the completion of aesthetics and the end of art – which aesthetic philosophical reflection has recognised – against the background of
another beginning of thinking and poetic inauguration which
itself effectively repeats the original beginning (and simultaneously to ask after the 'greatness' in question here: the greatness of the – stormy – beginning, the greatness of art, the
greatness of metaphysics – or of aesthetics).

It may be true that 'a comparison with Walter Benjamin
would reveal how little Heidegger was ever touched by any
genuine experience of avant-garde art'.[137] But such a comparison
would be meaningful only if one seriously engaged, for
example, with the essay on *The Origin of the Work of Art*, and
did not avoid asking whether the 'category' of thrust is really
compatible with any 'classicistic understanding of art'. Might it
not be possible to bring the idea of 'thrust' into a relevant relationship with Benjamin's concept of 'shock'? Habermas does
not raise such questions. He is intent rather on emphasising the
'philosophical' dimension of that 'Dionysos myth' he thinks he
can recognise in Heidegger's thought precisely as its most decisive feature: 'Philosophy must once again take upon itself a task
which it had relinquished to art in the Romantic period –
namely that of creating some equivalent for the unifying power
of religion in order to counter the diremptions of modernity.
Nietzsche had placed his hopes for the overcoming of nihilism

in an aesthetically renewed Dionysos myth. Heidegger projects this Dionysian event upon the screen of a critique of metaphysics which thereby acquires an increased world-historical significance of its own.'[138]

Heidegger's experiences (in the realm of thought) are said, therefore, to revolve around philosophy as the secularised form of religion. In order to justify this interpretation (which he arbitrarily drapes with the imagery of a philosophical cinema), would Habermas not have to consider all those explicit reflections on faith, religion and theology with which Heidegger attempts to secure the independence of philosophy or thinking as such? In this context it is not without significance that in the Nietzsche lectures the 'all-embracing work of art' is not rejected because it represents a 'numerical or purely quantitative unification of the arts' (for such an additive and external unification would hardly live up to the Wagnerian concept anyway), but rather because it would like to constitute the 'celebration of the community of a people', that is, because it attempts to inaugurate a religion – or indeed religion itself.[139] At first sight, therefore, Heidegger's assessment of the all-embracing work of art – the expression of aesthetic art – would seem to confirm the claim that art is no longer capable of capturing within itself the unifying power of religion. But how do matters stand with regard to the significance of poetry and its naming power? Does not Heidegger expressly accuse Wagner, the would-be inaugurator of a religion, of weakening the 'shaping power' of poetry and language by subjugating them to the 'domination of art as music'? Certainly: this weakening is the result – arising from the history of being – of the 'completion of aesthetics'. But it is therefore all the more urgent – in Heidegger's eyes – that we open up the way for a naming inauguration and a nonaesthetic reflection upon the essence of art.

How then are we to understand this expression, 'Dionysian Messianism', with which Habermas attempts to characterise Heidegger's thought of – and after – the turn? Has Heidegger simply contented himself with translating or transferring the Dionysian in Nietzsche's sense (in the sense in which Habermas interprets the Dionysian in Nietzsche's sense, in the sense in which Heidegger interprets the Dionysian in Nietzsche's sense, in the sense in which Habermas, in the sense of Heidegger's interpretation, interprets the Dionysian in Nietzsche's sense) from art over into philosophy? What is the character of the bond which connects 'the critique of metaphysics' with 'the Dionysian event'?

Remembrance: 'empty readiness for subjugation' or 'posture of resistance'

One way of answering these questions is suggested by something Habermas says in connection with the 'concept' of grammatology as developed by Jacques Derrida: 'The memory of the Messianism of Jewish mysticism and the abandoned but well-circumscribed site once occupied by the God of the Old Testament preserves Derrida equally from the political-moral insensitivity and the aesthetic tastelessness of a New Paganism richly spiced with Hölderlin.'[140] What can be inferred from this statement? (1) Heidegger's 'Dionysian Messianism' rests upon a forgetting of the Messianism of Jewish mysticism. Because there is no well-circumscribed site for the God of the Old Testament in 'Dionysian Messianism', Heidegger is forced to pay the price of a political, moral and aesthetic atavism. Habermas clearly supposes that the transition from polytheism to monotheism represents an irreversible intellectual advance, a progress in the realm of spirit which continues to remain decisive for philosophy. The expression 'Dionysian Messianism' can then only be properly understood if we define the Messianic in terms of the Dionysian and not the other way around. That is why, in the last analysis, there is no Graeco-Jewish pairing at issue here. (2) The more the 'memory of the Messianism of Jewish mysticism' fades, the greater the significance of a 'New Paganism' becomes, something that reveals not merely a philosophical but also a 'political-moral' and 'aesthetic' dimension (Habermas mentions Hölderlin: this time the culinary metaphor replaces the cinematographic one; one is tempted to ask what philosophical, political and moral consequences follow from such arbitrary and deceptively vivid formulations). The 'political-moral' and the 'aesthetic' dimension are of particular relevance here because one can follow, like Derrida, the 'pathways' of Heideggerean thought and still be protected – by the Jewish God and the Jewish Messiah – from the threat of 'insensitivity' and 'tastelessness'. It is thus in politics, morality and aesthetics that the consequences that necessarily follow from the 'ontological turn of Dionysian Messianism' – the translation of the Dionysian into philosophy – and from the forgetting of Judaism – the religious over-determination of philosophy – clearly reveal themselves.

It is not merely these remarks on Derrida's relation to Heidegger that indicate how decisive the Jewish tradition is for the choice of perspective which allows Habermas to present Heidegger as a thinker of 'Dionysian Messianism'. By translating the Dionysian into philosophy, Heidegger transforms the Messianism which Habermas ascribes to Nietzsche as predecessor. (Of course Nietzsche is more than simply a predecessor: the protagonists of the philosophical discourse of modernity gather under his 'banner' for the 'final contest'.) The reversal of Platonism calls forth a twisting inversion of Messianism: 'Nietzsche's Messianism which still left room for "assailing salvation" (as it is called in Jewish mysticism), is twisted with Heidegger into an apocalyptic expectation of the catastrophic advent of the new. At the same time, Heidegger borrows the conceptual figure of the absent god from his exemplary Romantic forebears, especially Hölderlin, so as to be able to grasp the end of metaphysics as "completion" and thus as the infallible sign of "another beginning".'[141] This summary can be found in the chapter on Heidegger's 'critique of metaphysics as the undermining of occidental rationalism'. What is the status of the simultaneity that Habermas mentions here? Or to put the question in another way: how Dionysian is 'Nietzsche's Messianism'? Does Habermas simply obscure the Greek heritage – handed down from the Romantics – insofar as he tries to illuminate the Jewish heritage for which in Heidegger – in contrast to Nietzsche and Derrida – there is no 'open space' or 'well-circumscribed site'?

> The half-god Dionysos presented himself to the Romantics and to Nietzsche as the absent god whose 'incalculable remoteness' permitted a godforsaken modernity to understand what energies of social solidarity it had lost in the course of its own progress. The idea of the ontological difference now serves as a bridge between the thought of Dionysos and the

fundamental question of metaphysics. Heidegger separates being, which has always been thought in terms of the being of beings, from beings themselves. For being can only function as the bearer of the Dionysian event if – as the historical horizon within which beings can first come to appearance – becomes autonomous in a certain sense. It is only once being is hypostatised and distinguished from beings that it can take over the role of Dionysos. 'Beings are themselves abandoned by being. The abandonment of beings touches upon beings as a whole, and not only the human kind of being which represents beings as such, in and from whose representing being in its truth withdraws.[142]

What are the different steps of the argument with which Habermas – without once referring to any textual source for this intellectual 'bridge' – introduces the half-god and unveils him as the key figure with which to decipher the meaning of Heidegger's critique of metaphysics? Three steps can be identified. (1) Metaphysics thinks being as the being of beings. (2) With the idea of the ontological difference, Heidegger separates being from beings. (It requires no special acumen to see that Habermas presents the philosophical discourse of modernity as a series of acts – transferring, transforming, perverting, projecting, spicing, gathering, separating ... This 'actionism' is perhaps the most interesting aspect of his account, and that precisely because it is never thematised as such.) (3) Autonomous and hypostasised being is the name which Heidegger bestows upon the half-god Dionysos. (The autonomy of being, according to Habermas, implies heteronomy and replaces memory [*Erinnerung*] with thoughtful 'remembrance' [*Andenken*].)

If this three-step argument is indeed valid, then Habermas can proceed to establish his case that Heidegger identifies the presencing absence and the absenting presence in the essence of Dionysos with the 'original mutual relatedness of being and non-being'. Let us, therefore, examine each step in turn. As for the first step: Heidegger does not claim that metaphysics thinks the being of beings, but that it represents being from the perspective of beings and therefore forgets the ontological difference. As for the second step: one can only separate being from beings if the former has already been represented as a being. As for the third step: autonomous and hypostatised being is not the name which Heidegger bestows on Dionysos, since it is only a being, and not being itself, that can demand autonomy.

What insight does Habermas derive from posing the question of being in the language of beings? It is in withdrawing itself that being disposes itself as fate, as Heidegger never tires of repeating. Being cannot therefore be itself a being that temporarily resides somewhere else and exercises 'positive power' in its absence. The sentences which immediately precede those quoted by Habermas at the end of the passage we have just cited, read as follows: 'The withdrawal, as which being itself presences, does not rob beings of being. However, beings stand in the withdrawal of being itself precisely when they are these beings and nothing but these beings.'[143] The translation of being back into the language of beings, or of metaphysics – and this is precisely what defines the description of Heidegger's thought as 'Dionysian Messianism' – has far-reaching consequences. For in the degree to which Habermas makes no explicit effort to understand the necessity of the ontological difference, in the degree to which he integrates the latter into a philosophical discourse of modernity which has already been identified with 'Dionysian Messianism', Habermas is unable to grasp the difference between object-oriented memory and thoughtful remembrance in anything but a polemical sense. But this difference is decisive for any understanding of the counter-turning of the beginning – the originary opening up of being – and of the name. Habermas claims apodictically: '[Heidegger's] later thought approaches the submissiveness of an empty readiness for subjugation.'[144] The 'emptiness' of this 'readiness for subjugation' is what accounts for the mysteriously 'evocative' character of Heidegger's 'remembrance'. If one has no idea of what one is subjecting oneself to or why one is doing so, if indeed one does not even ultimately know that one is subjecting oneself in the first place, then remembrance is condemned to hopelessness and impotence. It simply becomes a formula for the incessant evocation of the fate of being.[145] Because being cannot simply be translated back into the language of beings – into the language of metaphysics – and because being does not assume 'the role of Dionysos' that Habermas has ascribed to it, remembrance is charged with lacking any relationship to an identifiable object.

Or rather, precisely because being is here translated back into the language of beings, and thus appears remarkably indeterminate in its supposed autonomy, remembrance necessarily appears as purely empty and formulaic. This emptiness irritates Habermas because it hardly forms any stable unity with the previously alleged 'readiness for subjection': 'Certainly, the empty formula of "remembrance" can also be filled in with a quite different attitudinal syndrome, like the anarchistic notion of a subversive posture of resistance or refusal to participate, something which corresponds rather better with the current mood than blind submission to some higher power. But the arbitrariness with which the same pattern of thought can be actualised according to contemporary demands is irritating.'[146]

At the beginning of his lecture on *Dialectic of Enlightenment*, Habermas has absolutely no doubt as to the fact that the overall 'mood' and 'attitude' which governed the authors of the book 'is no longer our own' (that is why we must guard against a 'conflation' that might arise 'in the context of the post-structuralist revival of Nietzsche'). Yet in the middle of the lecture on Heidegger, Habermas confesses his irritation: the contemporary 'historical actualisation' of the idea of 'remembrance' betrays the fact that the 'current mood' is not so incompatible with the kind of critique of reason for which Habermas himself is seeking an alternative. Is it ever possible to say with ultimate certainty that a certain mood is – or is not – 'our mood'? Do not such claims regularly call forth just the opposite claim? That one still depends too much on a mood – is that not all one can say about it?[147] Do they not invariably force us to guard against threatened 'conflations'? If the idea of remembrance – as Habermas supposes – is no less compatible with an 'empty readiness for subjection' than it is with a 'subversive posture of resistance', if it cannot form a stable, that is to say, an identifiable unity with either one or the other, then it invariably transgresses any boundaries that we would impose upon it. Does the 'arbitrariness' of this 'pattern of thought' consist then in such an impossibility? Remembrance is only arbitrary, empty and formulaic for those who would measure it against an object-oriented memory and translate being back into the language of beings. Insofar as it cannot be possessed, insofar as it resists any and every possession, and thus essentially stands closer to a 'posture of resistance'

than to an 'empty readiness for subjection', remembrance testifies perhaps to a certain rigour and openness which by no
means contradict one another: to a rigour which no longer has
anything to do with the helplessness and impotence of arbitrariness, to an openness which is alien to the object-oriented
memory so prone to ideology. Does the irritation which Habermas feels spring from this paradoxical unity of openness and
rigour? Against Habermas it could be argued that with the
name 'Germania', the name which names naming, Heidegger
himself restitutes a kind of object-oriented memory and thereby
constricts the remembrance which is grounded in the counter-
turning of the beginning. The relationship between beginning,
name and remembrance conceals itself from Habermas because
he is too concerned with forcing Heidegger's thought into the
schema of the translation of the Dionysian into philosophy –
into a schema which only facilitates thinking in alternatives: the
philosophical apotheosis of the philosophy of the subject – of
the philosophical discourse of modernity – is precisely what
makes the search for 'another way out' imperative. Nor can
Habermas therefore explain what it is that actually allows for
Heidegger's identification of *Dasein* with the German people. If
there is indeed a 'Dionysian Messianism' – one of the name –
then it finds expression not in remembrance but in an object-
oriented memory.[148]

Meaning, naming, saying

Heidegger seeks after a hint, or at least the 'anticipation of a
hint', in the second part of *What Is Called Thinking?* Thus he
can ask: 'What is named with the words "think", that which is
"thought", a "thought"?' Heidegger wishes to derive a hint
from what is named here. But what is named here is precisely
the naming, the 'originary', the 'originally telling word', the
word which belongs to the beginning and within which the
words 'thinking', that which is 'thought', a 'thought' are gathered. The word of the beginning 'does not signify what is ultimately left over as the standard meaning in the current use of
the word *Gedanke* [a thought]. A thought usually means: an
idea, a representation, a view or an opinion. The originary
[*anfänglich*] word *Gedanc* [the Old English: *thanc*] says this: the

gathered re-minding [*Gedenken*] which itself gathers everything. The word *Gedanc* says something like *Gemüt*: the soul-mood, and "mouot", the heart-mood.'[149] On reading these formulations carefully, we might well conclude that a line of demarcation cleanly separates naming and saying on the one hand and opining on the other: the 'usual meaning' or 'customary opinion' does not attend to the hint, but simply to the 'standard meaning' and is therefore merely an opinion, one which fails to hear the naming and saying word *Gedanc* – the gathering word of gatheredness – within the word *Gedanke*, and thus already recognises it as a word of opinion only. But it would actually be overhasty to draw such a conclusion and thereby simply to inscribe Heidegger into a tradition that extends from Plato's devaluation of 'doxa' through to Hegel's dialectical sublation of 'opining' (of 'meaning' as 'mine'). For the very word *meinen*, 'to mean' or 'to opine', possesses a meaning, as Heidegger emphasises, which inscribes it on the side of 'naming' and 'saying': 'In the originary word *Gedanc* (*thanc*) it is the original essence of memory which holds sway: the gathering of the ceaseless meaning and intending [*Meinen*] of everything that the heart or soul [*Gemüt*] allows to come to presence.'[150] Thinking is in its essence a re-minding which, as memory, keeps to the name. Through naming, saying and meaning, thought keeps to that which calling [*Heissen*] calls, to the naming that allows that which presences to arrive. The counter-turning of thought inscribes forgetting and repetition in this calling – a repetition which cannot be reduced to the 'repetition' of a 'merely repetitive memory' [*Wiedergedächtnis*] since it is the repetition of what is yet to come.

How then does such meaning relate to naming and saying, if it is not to be regarded as their opposite? Heidegger understands this 'meaning' to be 'the inclining [*Zuneigung*] with which the inmost meditation [*Sinnen*] of the heart or the soul turns to everything which comes to presence, an inclining which is not in possession of itself and thus does not necessarily require to be expressly enacted as such'. But does such an understanding not itself suggest a difference that would once again simply remove meaning from naming? For it is through naming that the 'inclining to that which comes to presence' is expressly enacted and takes possession of itself. If, however, that which comes to presence withdraws in the beginning, if naming is originally contaminated by forgetting, if repetition can only restore the power of the name at the cost of benaming naming itself, then all naming also always remains a meaning and is divided within itself, not by an opposition but by a difference. Does not Heidegger draw attention to the meaning in the naming when he locates originary speaking, the speaking which belongs to the beginning, in the essential domain of the 'unspoken' – of language before language, of the name before the name? 'There is need of memory' because naming means and intends, because thinking must thereby keep to the names – to the named and the unnamed. Memory 'in an originary sense by no means signifies the power of recall. The word names the whole disposition – the heart-mood or soul-mood – in the sense of a steadfast and intimate gathering for what speaks essentially to every thoughtful meditation. Memory originally bespeaks something like devotion or the piety of thinking [*An-dacht*]: a gathered and unyielding keeping to ... and not indeed merely to what is past, but equally to what is present, to what may come. What is past, present and to come appear in the unity of their own essential coming *to* presence in each case.' A double movement pervades memory as the gathering of thinking: the 'movement of an essential re-membrance [*An-denken*] of something' and the 'movement of an unrelinquishing and unrelenting retaining'. The more vigorously this movement – which encourages memory to keep to the (meaning and intending) names and to think upon the named and the unnamed – possesses thinking, the more memory attempts to keep its hold upon what has been thought – that of which it is re-minded, that which it commemorates, that which is not merely past but is also to come, the beginning as a task for thinking: 'Out of memory and within memory the soul pours forth a hoard of images, that is, a wealth of sudden sights [*Anblicke*] which themselves catch sight of the soul.'[151] Without the hint, without the sight, there is no language and no memory: and thus no thought.

The soul's hoard of images

The relationship that prevails between thought, memory, the heart, the soul, the image and the sight also calls to mind the relationship that is established through the unifying principle of the transcendental imagination. (The Latin equivalent for heart- or soul-mood [*Gemüt*], according to Heidegger, is *animus* which can be translated in turn as 'soul', although soul in this sense is not to be confused with *anima* and identified with the 'life-prin- ciple' but signifies rather the 'essential presencing of spirit, the spirit of spirit'.[152]) In his book *Kant and the Problem of Metaphy- sics* Heidegger interprets the transcendental imagination as the unity of sensibility and the understanding, hidden in the depths of the soul [*Gemüt*], which allows 'the sighting of the horizon to be formed'. The transcendental power of the imagination 'forms not only the intuitive perceptibility of the horizon, insofar as it "creates" the latter in turning freely towards it, but being formative [*bildend*] in this sense it is also "formative" in a second sense as well, namely in bringing forth something like an "image" [*Bild*] in the first place'.[153] But however far the parallel with Kant might be pursued, it is striking that Heideg- ger, in the context of *What Is Called Thinking?*, defines the soul, which liberates a 'sight' in the movement of retentive gathering, as something which is itself sighted or 'looked at'. It is only as such, only in being so looked at, that the soul can liberate the sight or look of things, can thus pour forth its hoard of images. Could we say with Benjamin that this involves an auratic defi- nition of thinking? If thoughtful re-membrance is auratic in character, then the comparison with the *Critique of Pure Reason* and with Heidegger's book on Kant would seem to encounter a limit. For whereas Benjamin makes the emergence of photogra- phy responsible for the 'decline of aura' and defines aura as the experience of an appearance endowed with the capacity for 'bestowing a look or gaze'[154] – 'this endowment is an original source of poetry' – Heidegger uses photography along with the death-mask and the image of dead eyes as examples for clarify- ing the problem of schematism, the 'art which is hidden in the depths of the human soul': the possibility of the reflected image and the after-image lies in the possibility of the image in general. Benjamin goes on to specify his description of the 'decline of aura' further in terms of a decline of the 'cultic value': for the aura is a phenomenon that possesses a 'cultic character'. It is certainly not the case that the aura is something that is subsequently added on to an appearance and is therefore always capable of being subtracted from it in turn. When we experience an appearance in the emphatic sense, we always have the experience of aura. The definition of aura as 'the unique experience of a remoteness' touches upon the definition of appearance as such: if an appearance is not essentially remote, and consequently unapproachable, if it fails to open our eyes and thus to expect a response, then it cannot be experienced as appearance at all. In the moment of experience it is impossible to fix an investing or endowing subject of experience, or its counterpart, the subject of the 'securing look or gaze' which would escape the 'dreamy abandonment to remoteness'. This is why Benjamin grasps the concept of aura too narrowly when he ascribes the expectation of response solely to one who fully experiences the appearance, who is vouchsafed the experience of aura 'in all its abundance'. Unapproachability is a 'fundamental quality of the cultic image',[155] one which requires a certain collectedness and represents, as Benjamin clearly illustrates with reference to the perception of the work of art, the opposite of that incorporating proximity which is characteristic of distraction: 'Distraction and collectedness stand in a kind of opposition which permits the following formulation: the one who collects himself before the work of art submerges himself within the latter; he actually goes inside the work, as recounted by the legend of the Chinese painter when he beheld his perfectly finished picture. The distracted masses, on the other hand, submerge the work of art within themselves; they overwhelm it with their breaking waves and embrace it in their flood.'[156]

Thoughtful remembrance is not simply auratic in character because collectedness and distraction, cult and the exhibition of the unique are equiprimordial. They are held at once together and apart by the counter-turning of the beginning. Does the priority of the hint or the gaze in Heidegger serve to conceal a certain anthropomorphism, albeit one that is conditioned by language itself? Or is 'the gaze itself inhabited by the expectation of finding a response from that upon which it has bestowed itself'[157] precisely because the soul finds itself already 'sighted' and 'gazed upon', because the inauguration of language already pursues a hint and brings it over to us? Is the thinking which keeps to names re-mindful of this earlier hint? It can keep to names only if more than one name remains.[158]

There is (need)

If the expression 'there is need of memory' is read in its immediate context, it must be understood as follows: 'that which is thought needs memory'. If we detach it from its embeddedness in this context, however, we can perhaps pursue a certain path that is suggested by a remark in the second part of *What Is Called Thinking?* Heidegger translates the beginning of a sentence from Parmenides with the phrase 'there is need' [*es braucht*] and, citing a line of Hölderlin's by way of further elucidation, tarries with this use of the impersonal 'there' and the idea of 'using' and 'needing' that is harboured in the word *brauchen*. Finally, he brings the expression 'there is need', explicitly introduced in the context of his translation of the Greek, into proximity with the expression 'there is' or, literally, 'it gives' [*es gibt*], to which he had accorded express attention in *Being and Time*, the *Letter on Humanism* and the lecture on *Time and Being*. (In *Being and Time* we read: 'The presupposed truth, that is, the 'there is' or 'it gives', with which its being is supposed to be determined, possesses the kind of being, or the ontological significance, of Dasein itself.' In the *Letter on Humanism*: 'But is not said in *Being and Time*, where the "there is" or "it gives" is spoken of, that: "Only as long as Dasein is, is there truth"? Indeed. That means: only as long as the clearing of being comes to pass as event [*sich ereignet*], does being give itself over [*übereignet sich*] to human beings'. In *Time and Being*: 'The giving in "it gives being" reveals itself as the sending and the dispensation of presencing in its epochal transformations.') But is it not possible that misunderstandings may arise from the contextual indeterminacy of the isolated expression 'there is need of memory'? In order to obviate this suspicion, it is necessary to see that there is in truth no question of contextual abstraction here at all. What is the matter of thinking if not this very 'there' which introduces the expression under discussion? What does the remark of Parmenides, as translated by Heidegger, mean other than that the 'there' needs thought: needs 'taking heed of' [*In-die-Acht-Nehmen*] or the thoughtful 're-membrance' of thoughtful memory? If the 'there is' or 'it gives' is supposed to signify that which 'above all gives rise to thinking',[159] if the expression 'there is need' belongs in the proximity of the former, then memory is not just any other object that is used and needed, but is rather what is already named in using and needing the expression 'there is need', a using and a needing which signifies neither a simple utilising nor a simple requiring. The giving is a using and a needing, the using and the needing is a giving. That is why 'there is' and 'there is need' both name thinking – name memory. Both are an ex-propriat-ing event that precisely brings about what is appropriate: Heidegger recognises in giving, in 'the sending of the dispensa-tion of being', an event which 'gives over' and 'gives itself over' and as such lets 'being as presencing' come into its 'own'.[160] This letting also constitutes using and needing: 'What uses and needs lets that what is used and needed come into the ownmost character of its essence and preserves it therein'.[161] What constitutes the essence of this using and needing which hands over – or gives over – what is used and needed into its essence? 'A summoning, a calling is concealed within this using and needing.' Does not the 'there' of using and needing, and of the giving inseparably connected with it, appear now as the original origin or absolute precedence of the name? The name which is not yet a name – 'it' is not yet 'there' or given, and is not yet used or needed – uses and needs itself because, in the absolute precedence which marks its 'there', it 'itself' gives being. Thus in the end the hint of which thought re-minds itself perhaps turns out to be the name which leaps forward and is, ahead of itself, the name in the beginning.

Afterword:
The Reeling Philosopher

There was a philosopher who always liked to hang around wherever children were playing. And if he caught sight of a boy who owned a spinning top, he would immediately get himself ready. Scarcely had the top begun to spin when the philosopher would chase it and try to capture it. It never bothered him that the children shouted and tried to keep him away from their plaything. He was very happy if he could capture the top even as it spun, but only for a moment, whereupon he would throw it to the ground and go away. For he believed that the knowledge of every tiny thing, therefore even of a spinning top for example, would suffice to produce knowledge of the universal. Hence he refused to concern himself with the great problems, since that seemed all very uneconomical. If the tiniest thing were properly known, then everything would be known; and that is why he concerned himself so much with the spinning top. And whenever anyone prepared to spin the top, he entertained the hope that he would be successful this time, and as soon as the top was spinning this hope became a certainty as he rushed breathlessly after it, but once he held the silly wooden thing in his hands he felt suddenly ill, and the cries of the children, which he had not noticed before but now suddenly came piercing upon his ears, drove him away reeling around like a top beneath the blows of a clumsy switch.

Kafka actually relates this story of the philosopher twice, as if it were itself a spinning top and one that thus already called out for repetition. On the second occasion, however, the reader appears to possess a key to the event since the narrator has explained the philosopher – and his behaviour – to us. Giorgio Agamben, who offers an interpretation of this story, recognises the matter of thinking in the spinning top: 'It is as if in speaking we would seize the word: we hold merely in our hands this or that word, which has this or that meaning. We fail to capture in language the word itself, the word that means nothing but the word, nothing but language.'[1] Is there a connection between this failure and the repetition of the story? If we subscribe to the interpretation offered here, then it is surprisingly easy to retell the story from the perspective of Adorno's reflections on the philosophy of language. For what is the significance of the programme of a micrology of thinking if not to show that we must seek the expression of the absolute not in the claim to totality, but rather in the 'materials and categories of immanence'? Is the particular, neglected as it is by the concept in its drive toward the universal, not the name which does not subsume the benamed precisely because it is one with it? Does not the metaphysical experience, as the experience of the name, communicate itself precisely to the child? Does not Adorno warn the philosopher of the illusion that one could ever express the name immediately and hold the absolute within one's hands? If the name could be expressed, it would also be possible to capture through and in speaking the word which signifies language itself. But since we only retain a silly word – a determinate word with a determinate meaning – we must carry on speaking and repeating the word. Nothing guarantees the meaning we ascribe to the word, nothing vouchsafes the deciphering of the story, not even the intervention of the narrator. Like the philosopher continually chasing after the spinning top, we too find ourselves continually hunting for the word. Caught as we are in the tension between concept and name, we cannot simply hurl ourselves directly to the side of the name. Or to express this differently, and in Heidegger's terms: caught in the movement of a beginning which is marked by its own counter-turning, we are unable to bename originary naming itself. Does not Heidegger fall victim to the reeling revel of the philosopher in the very moment that he believes himself to hold more than a silly word in his hands? It is decisive for the understanding of the story that we recognise what it is the philosopher would properly like to grasp here: namely, not the resting object – the silly piece of wood – but the spinning itself, or speaking as such. If he were ever to succeed in uttering the word of the word or in entering fully into the event of language, he would be free of the reeling revel into which we are whirled by language. He would be bereft of the name, bereft of the concept, though not like one who had isolated the concept or the name and incurred guilt in doing so; but rather like one who no longer needs to inaugurate anything. Such thinking would be a thinking without the memory of thought.

Notes

Introduction: Of (From) Germania – After (To) Auschwitz

1 Adorno, GS 11:32. (*Notes to Literature*); ET: Vol. 1, p. 22.
2 The following *philological* objection might be raised at this point. The position that the names of 'Germania' and 'Auschwitz' occupy respectively in the work of Heidegger and Adorno can be determined chronologically; ignoring chronological considerations thus produces the impression that one can indifferently generalise what Heidegger says in the 1930s and Adorno in the 1960s. The following *answer* can be given to this objection. There is no question of denying that there are important chronological gaps and distinctions here which can be investigated philosophically and are philosophically relevant ones, such as the fact that Heidegger's reflections on language had not yet taken their definitive shape by the time of the Hölderlin lectures. Quite the opposite in fact. But these gaps and distinctions should not be regarded as the only decisive criterion of interpretation. For in order to assess Heidegger's continuing commitment to the philosophical primacy of the German language, which did not (as far as we can see) change throughout the subsequent development of his thought after 1935, we must consult the texts that explore the relationship between language, name, poetry, thought and history. The first lecture series on Hölderlin, indeed the experience of Hölderlin's poetry in general, proved to be quite fundamental for Heidegger. Now although we cannot deny that it is only in the late 'Meditations on Metaphysics' that Adorno explicitly speaks of a philosophy *after Auschwitz*, we must reflect seriously upon the follow-

ing remark in *Aesthetic Theory*: 'In the face of actual historical experience, even before Auschwitz, the thought of
ascribing any positive sense to reality was already an affir-
mative lie' (AT:229; ET:152). This sentence has its counterpart in *Negative Dialectics*: 'The Lisbon earthquake sufficed
to cure Voltaire of Leibniz's theodicy, and this surveyable
catastrophe of first nature was insignificant in comparison
with the second catastrophe, a social one, which defies all
human imagining insofar as it created a real hell out of
human evil' (ND:354; ET:361). In the section of the
present work entitled 'Constructing the totality' (see 'Guilt
and Debts', Chapter 3) an attempt is made to explore the
various paradoxes of the chronology.

3   At this point the following objection might be raised from
the perspective of a *critique of ideology*. Any attempt simply
to interpret the names 'Germania' and 'Auschwitz' as
names of an event fails to grasp that the event in Heidegger's thought has a quite different function and place than
in Adorno's. For is it not the case that the inauguration of
history, which Heidegger identifies with the name 'Germania' (or which is to be accomplished through this name), is
grounded in a 'sending or dispensation of being' [*Seins-
geschick*], whereas the historical guilt named by Adorno is
grounded in a 'context of guilt' which assumes a certain
reified independence over against the human agents themselves, but one that can still be seen through in its apparent
independence? The following *answer* can be given to this
objection. What Adorno describes, with recourse to Benjamin, as the 'context of guilt' is produced (if we follow the
argument of *Dialectic of Enlightenment*) through a mimetic
identification with otherness, one that also involves a
certain petrification with regard to the latter: the original
experience of otherness (of nature) does not yet permit the
distinction between a purely 'reflectory mimesis' that
generates reification and an 'organic bonding with otherness'. See the section 'Mimesis' on page 113. On this level,
guilt is something that is *structurally* given: it is true that the
'context of guilt' is not absolute, but it is irreducible. It is
only logical, therefore, that in *Negative Dialectics* Adorno
observes that the guilt he associates with Auschwitz is one

that continually reproduces itself: no subjective act can ever expiate guilt completely; to a certain degree the 'context of guilt' *also* remains something that cannot be seen through. But then an (allegedly) opaque 'sending or dispensation of being' can no longer be opposed to a 'context of guilt' which could (allegedly) be rendered transparent.

4   The problem with many of the more recent studies of Heidegger and Adorno often lies in the fact that they merely emphasise certain partial aspects or generally familiar modes of argument from the perspective of one or other of the two thinkers, without developing any idea of the experiential content of the thinking involved. Thus we have to ask why Adolf Polti's essay 'Ontology as the "Epitome of Negativity"', which concerns itself directly with 'Adorno's interpretation of Heidegger's philosophy', is content simply to repeat the basic outlines of this interpretation before incorporating it into a reconstruction of Adorno's reflections on language that results in a trivial perspectivism. For it is in language – so we read in Polti – that 'the perspectives and intentions of other human beings are given'. Adorno is said to proceed, along with Nietzsche, on the assumption that we cannot 'do justice' to this plurality as long as we 'overburden language with our own opinions and thereby impose upon it a particular perspective with a claim to total truth' (*Martin Heidegger: Innen- und Aussenansichten*, p. 277). Confronted with such an observation, which reduces Adorno's thoughts on language to the uttermost banality, we can only say that it is doubtless well-meaning.

The remarks with which Eliane Escoubas has prefaced her French translation of Adorno's *Jargon of Authenticity*, on the other hand, are particularly illuminating ('Le *polemos* Adorno–Heidegger'). They are free of the kind of ideologically over-determined commentary that results from the formation of schools of thought where this formation determines the debate the way it does in Germany. Escoubas asks whether there is a possible relationship between the *ecstasis* of language in Heidegger and the question of 'constellation' in Adorno (p. 21). The present book also addresses this question explicitly. What Escoubas calls the *ecstasis* of language is thematised here under the title of the 'counter-turning of what begins in and as language' (see Part II: 'Inaugurations'). In his introduction to a selection of Hölderlin's poems and hymns in French translation Lacoue-Labarthe presents the approaches adopted by Heidegger and Adorno in their respective interpretations of Hölderlin and analyses the concept of the 'polemical' in this connection (p. 16). In his thesis *The Sovereignty of Art*, Christoph Menke paves the way for a serious and substantive discussion by focusing on a specific issue, that of 'the thinglike character of the work of art' (p. 159 f.; ET:146f.).

5 H. Mörchen, *Macht und Herrschaft*, p. 8.
6 H. Mörchen, *Adorno und Heidegger*, p. 272.
7 Ibid., p. 273.
8 Adorno, GS, Vol. 11, p. 129. (*Notes to Literature*); ET: Vol. 1, p. 111.
9 Heidegger, *Wegmarken*, p. 26; ET:22f.
10 H. Ott, *Martin Heidegger*, p. 176; ET:183.
11 Mörchen, *Adorno und Heidegger*, p. 274 f.
12 Nothing is changed by the fact that 'Auschwitz' is the name of a 'real' historical event, whereas 'Germania' signifies an 'interpretation' of historical events. The name, or rather the use of the name, forbids us to hypostatise this *initially decisive and undeniable difference*.
13 P. Lacoue-Labarthe, *La fiction du politique*, p. 58; ET:34.
14 In a section of his essay on Beckett, where Adorno opposes the appropriation of the writer for the cause of cultural criticism, we read: 'Even the notion that Beckett depicts the negativity of the age in negative form would easily fit in with the idea that people in the satellite states of Eastern Europe, where the revolution was carried out in a bureaucratic fashion, should now cheerfully devote themselves to reflecting a cheerful era ... The name of the catastrophe is only to be spoken in silence. The catastrophe that has befallen the whole is illuminated in the horrors of the last catastrophe' (GS, Vol. 11, p. 290; ET: *Notes to Literature*, Vol. 1, p. 249). This passage also indicates just how problematic it is to identify Adorno's aesthetic theory with an 'aesthetic of negativity'.
15 Mörchen, *Adorno und Heidegger*, p. 277.

16 K.-O. Apel, 'Die Herausforderung der totalen Vernunftkritik', p. 5.

17 Quite independently of whether the general thesis defended by Menke in his work on the relationship between aesthetic and non-aesthetic experience proves valid – and does not the very experience of the aesthetic as an 'interruptive crisis' deprive art of the autonomy and sovereignty Menke ascribes to it in order to escape a 'purism' which 'anxiously relinquishes any attempt to locate the aesthetic within the differentiated rationality of modernity' (p. 266; ET:254)? – the argument deployed in his specific analysis of Adorno's philosophical siting of the experience of death is relevant to the problem of the name and the event in general. Menke interprets the 'Meditations on Metaphysics' as a 'treatise on the place and the condition of metaphysics in modernity'. These meditations 'are also and at the same time a reflection on the predicament of life and thinking after Auschwitz' (p. 232; ET:219). The author is particularly interested in the general question whether 'the idea of an experience, in the confrontation with which all our discourse plunges into an insuperable crisis, can be explicated in meaningful terms'. He attempts to answer this question by recourse to Adorno's reflections upon the experience of finitude, suffering and death, which themselves largely correspond with Adorno's reflections on the possibility of living and thinking after Auschwitz. The 'experience of death' is insufficient, according to Menke, to secure the 'genealogical grounding of absolute claims', the 'grounding of a negative and unrealisable dialectic'. The principal reason for this insufficiency supposedly consists in the fact that 'any (non-aesthetic) experience of disintegration that is total is not a negation of the achievements of our discourses, but only a loss of relevance for those experiencing them' (p. 234; ET:222). In terms of this distinction between experience and discourse, it is indeed possible for a historical event, one that bears the name 'Auschwitz', for example, to present a problem as far as participation in a discourse is concerned, but it does not affect the functioning of the discourse itself. Here 'Auschwitz' does not mark an 'interruptive crisis', or does so only if we posit the relevance of

this experience as absolute in character. Do such considerations not ultimately raise the question concerning the relationship between history and structure, experience and theory, transcendence and the empirical? Menke appears to overlook the fact that the ideality of discourse itself is relative to the degree that ideality itself cannot be ascribed to the genesis of that ideality. The space of ideality cannot be simply idealised and shielded from the possibility of an experience that can lead to a loss of relevance. Thus Menke does not really clarify exactly what he means by participation in discourse. However unconvincing the idea of a dialectic of enlightenment or the conception of a negative world-spirit might be, they at least imply an awareness of the complexity of all discursive achievements.

Guilt and Debts

1: Fate and Sacrifice

1 W. Benjamin, Vol. II.1, p. 174 (*Fate and Character*); ET:203 (*Selected Writings*, Vol. 1).
2 Ibid., p. 128.
3 Ibid.
4 Ibid., p. 175, (*Fate and Character*); ET:204.
5 Hegel, Vol. 3, p. 496 (*Phenomenology of Spirit*); ET:411.
6 Benjamin, Vol. II.1, p. 139 (*Goethe's Elective Affinities*); ET:308 (*Selected Writings*, Vol. 1).
7 Ibid., p. 359 (*The Origin of German Tragic Drama*); ET:183.
8 Ibid., p. 308; ET:129.
9 Benjamin, Vol. II.1, p. 198 f. ('Critique of Violence'); ET:249 (*Selected Writings*, Vol. 1).
10 M. Cacciari, *Icone della legge*, p. 69.
11 Benjamin, Vol. II.1, p. 199 ('Critique of Violence'); ET:249–50 (*Selected Writings*, Vol. 1).
12 Ibid., p. 175 (*Fate and Character*); ET:204 (*Selected Writings*, Vol. 1).
13 Ibid., p. 176; ET:204–5.
14 Benjamin, Vol. IV.1, p. 141 (*One-Way Street*); ET:482–3 (*Selected Writings*, Vol. 1).
15 Ibid., p. 142; ET:438. Cf. also P. Szondi, *Schriften*, Vol. 2, pp. 287 and 297.

16 Szondi, ibid., p. 289.
17 Benjamin, Vol. II.1, p. 176 (*Fate and Character*); ET:204
    (*Selected Writings*, Vol. 1).
18 Ibid., p. 175 f.; ET:203f.
19 Benjamin, Vol. I.1, p. 295 (*The Origin of German Tragic
    Drama*); ET:116.
20 Benjamin, Vol. II.1, p. 178 (*Fate and Character*); ET:205–6
    (*Selected Writings*, Vol. 1).
21 Ibid., p. 175; ET:206.
22 F. Nietzsche, *Ecce homo*, p. 148; ET:126.
23 Benjamin, Vol. II.1, p. 148 ('On Language as Such and on
    the Language of Man'); ET:65 (*Selected Writings*, Vol. 1).
24 Ibid., p. 150; ET:69.
25 Ibid., p. 153; ET:71.
26 'The world pervaded by Mana, and even the world of
    Indian and Greek myth, are ineluctable and eternally the
    same. All birth is repaid with death, all happiness with
    unhappiness. Men and gods may well attempt, in the time
    that is granted to them, to cast the lot according to another
    measure than that of the blind course of fate, but reality
    still triumphs over them in the end. Even their justice,
    wrested from fatefulness as it is, still bears the features of
    the latter. This justice corresponds to the gaze which
    human beings, primitives as well as Greeks and barbarians,
    caught in a society of wretchedness and oppression, cast
    upon the surrounding world. That is why guilt and expia-
    tion, good fortune and ill, represent the sides of an equa-
    tion as far as mythic and enlightened justice are concerned.
    Justice is submerged in law ... The step from chaos to civi-
    lisation, in which natural relations no longer exert their
    power in an immediate fashion but rather through the
    medium of human consciousness, has changed nothing
    with regard to the principle of sameness. Indeed, human
    beings were forced to pay for this very step by worship-
    ping what actually held them, just like all other creatures,
    in thrall. The fetishes once stood under the law of the
    same. Now sameness itself becomes a fetish. The blindfold
    which covers the eyes of *Justitia* signifies not merely the
    inviolability of law, but also the fact that the latter does
    not originate in freedom' (DdA:32f.; ET:16–17).

27 The more something is subject to law, to the principle of equivalence and thus of reification, the more it is forgotten (for reification, according to Adorno, is a forgetting); the more effortlessly it accommodates itself to the fate which represents the 'reification now magically elevated into the absolute' (Adorno, GS 16:301 [*Quasi una Fantasia*]; ET:56), the less it can simply be absorbed into the 'context of guilt': the 'redemption of things' − and that also means: the redemption of the reified − presupposes the absolutising of guilt. For it is through this redemption that things − the reified − become 'inexchangeable and useless' (Adorno, GS 10.1:286) [*Prisms*]; ET:271.

28 Hegel, Vol. 12, p. 49; ET:34. In the first of his studies on Hegel, Adorno claims that dialectical thinking owes its existence to cunning: 'Hegel introduced the cunning of reason into his philosophy of history to try and explain how objective reason, the actualisation of freedom, is successfully accomplished precisely by means of the blind and irrational passions of historical individuals. This conception betrays something of the experience at the heart of Hegelian thought. The latter is cunning in its entirety. It hopes for victory over the overwhelming violence of the world, something it clearly perceives with no illusions, by turning this violence against itself until it reverts into something quite different' (Adorno, *Drei Studien zu Hegel*, p. 45; ET:42−3). But if Hegel's philosophy cannot simply be reduced to the principle of equivalence, which only anchors every successful demonstration of cunning even more deeply, this is by virtue, as Adorno emphasises in his third study, of a philosophical experience that is always an experience of language, and one whose measure is not to be found in scientific or systematic rationality: 'From the perspective of science or systematic knowledge, something irrational enters, as a moment, into philosophical rationality itself, and it behoves philosophy to absorb this moment, but without thereby abandoning itself to irrationalism. The dialectical method in its entirety is an attempt to master this challenge by liberating thought from the spell of the striking moment and unfolding it as a comprehensive conceptual structure. Philosophical experience cannot

dispense with the appeal to exemplary self-evidence, the kind of evidence that translates into a "this is how it is", against a background of ineliminable vagueness. But it cannot stop here either. If this aspect of self-evidence does not suddenly dawn upon us when confronted with a particularly involved passage from Hegel's logic, if we fail to notice what is emphatically grasped here, even if it is not fully articulated as such, then we shall acquire no more understanding of what is at issue than those who abandon themselves to the vague intoxications of philosophical feeling. The fanatics for clarity may like to extinguish this moment of sudden illumination. Philosophy is supposed to pay, without delay, in cash. Participation in philosophy is estimated, according to the balance sheet, as an investment of labour that must earn its equivalent renumeration. But philosophy resists the principle of equivalence' (Ibid., p. 100; ET:108–9). This moment of sudden and striking illumination, which transcends rationality, first ignites the labour of the concept, connects philosophy with art interpreted as 'apparition' (Cf. AT:128–32; ET:82–5, and A. García Düttmann, *La parole donnée*, pp. 172–9; ET: 85–9).

29 In *Negative Dialectics* we read: 'Utopia would be the non-identity of the subject without sacrifice' (ND:277; ET:281).

30 M. Heidegger, *Vorträge und Aufsätze*, p. 116.

31 F. Nietzsche, *Also sprach Zarathustra*, p. 181; ET:162, and Heidegger, *Nietzsche II*, p. 14; ET: Vol. 3, p. 168.

32 M. Heidegger, *Gelassenheit*, pp. 30 and 58; ET: pp. 59 and 80.

33 M. Heidegger, *Was heißt Denken?*, p. 33; ET:88.

34 M. Heidegger, GA 53, p. 68.

35 Heidegger, *Was heisst Denken?*, p. 44; ET:106.

36 Heidegger, GA 53, p. 68.

37 In the 'Afterword' which Heidegger added in 1943 to his inaugural lecture *What is Metaphysics?*, a passage which Adorno ascribes directly to 'fascistic ideology' in his *Jargon of Authenticity*, we read: 'What is needed is that the truth of being is preserved whatever may happen to human beings and every other being. The sacrifice is the abandonment [*Verschwendung*] of the human essence to the truthful preservation of the truth of being for the sake of beings, an

abandonment which is free of all coercion because it arises from the abyss of freedom itself.' Before deciding whether *this* is a case of 'fascistic ideology', we should consider the following passage from Heidegger's first lecture course on Hölderlin: 'An original community does not first arise with the adoption of a mutual relationship – that only gives rise to society – but community *is* by virtue of the prior bonding of every individual with that which binds and defines *every individual* by elevating the latter. Something must already be manifest which is neither the individual in its being for itself nor the community as such. The comradeship of soldiers at the front is not grounded in the fact that they were forced to come together because other human beings, who were far away, were not at hand, nor in the fact that they first arranged to feel a shared enthusiasm, but rather most deeply and uniquely in the fact that the proximity of death as sacrifice already placed each individual before the same possibility of nothingness, so that this latter became the source of an unconditional mutual belonging to one another. It is precisely death, which every individual human being must die for himself or herself and which individualises every individual with regard to himself or herself in the most extreme manner; it is precisely death and the readiness for this sacrifice that first creates the space of community from which a sense of comradeship arises' (GRh:72f.).

38 Heidegger, GA 54, p. 60.
39 Heidegger, GA 39, p. 126.
40 Heidegger, GA 54, p. 59.
41 Heidegger, *Was heißt Denken?*, p. 85; ET:120.
42 Heidegger, *Nietzsche I*, p. 609 (not included in the English translation of the Nietzsche lectures).
43 Benjamin, Vol. VI, p. 97.
44 Ibid., p. 98.
45 Horkheimer, Vol. 12, p. 281.
46 Adorno, GS 11, p. 37 (*Notes to Literature*); ET: Vol. 1, p. 26.
47 S. Bovenschen, 'Tierische Spekulationen', p. 7.
48 Adorno, GS 11, p. 38 f. (*Notes to Literature*); ET: Vol. 1, p. 27.

49 Ibid., p. 39; ET: 28.
50 Adorno, GS 10.2, p. 637 (*Critical Models*); ET: 159.
51 Adorno, GS 11, p. 474 (*Notes to Literature*); ET: Vol. 2, p. 134.
52 Adorno, *Drei Studien zu Hegel*, p. 128; ET:141.
53 Adorno, GS 11, p. 40 (*Notes to Literature*); ET: Vol. 1, p.29.
54 Ibid., p. 486; ET: Vol. 2, p. 144.
55 Ibid.; ET: Vol. 2, p. 144.
56 Ibid., p. 468; ET: Vol. 2, p. 127.
57 Horkheimer, Vol. 12, p. 498.
58 Adorno, GS 10.1, p. 453.
59 Adorno, GS 16, p. 650. In an analysis of Schönberg's 'sacred fragment' *Moses und Aaron*, Adorno also addresses the relationship between music and the ban on images: 'Music is the imageless art and was thus exempted from this prohibition. That is surely the key for unlocking the relationship between Judaism and music. But on the historical levels of *musica ficta, stile rappresentativo*, an essentially expressive art employed to present to the senses something other than itself, music was still entangled in the image character of all European art. The ever-increasing unity characteristic of the arts, arising from the process of rationalisation and the increasing control over the material, also preserved them, at the same time, as a kind of protective zone for that mythical dimension which was as ostracised by rationalisation as it was by the ban on images. Music learned to imitate' (GS 16, p. 458 [*Quasi una Fantasia*]; ET:230).
60 S. Freud, *Der Mann Moses und die monotheistische Religion*, p. 579 f.; ET:331.
61 In *Aesthetic Theory* the 'rescuing of the past' through art is identical with the memory of suffering: 'If, once better days had come, art were to forget the suffering whose expression it is, the suffering that gives substance to form, one would have to wish for it to disappear altogether ... But what then would art be, as historiography, as the writing of history, were it to shake off the memory of accumulated suffering?' (AT:386f.; ET:261). That poetry can no longer be written after Auschwitz means that now every poem represents a forgetting. What are the conse-

quences of this circumstance – relevant as it is not merely from the perspective of literary genre – for 'art as such' and for the writing of history in general?

62 Horkheimer, Vol. 12, p. 501.

63 *Vierzig Jahre Flaschenpost*, p. 9. The question concerning *Geste* and *Gestus,* gesture and voice, inevitably presents itself at this point. Just before observing that the 'recalling [*Eingedenken*] of nature in the subject' brings Adorno into a 'shocking proximity' to Heidegger's 'remembrance of being', Habermas writes as follows in his *Theory of Communicative Action*: 'Philosophical thought deliberately regresses, in the shadow of a philosophy that has outlived itself and becomes a mere gesture' (Vol. I, p. 516; ET:385). This remark is explicitly directed at Adorno's thinking – at *Negative Dialectics* which Habermas regards as a kind of 'penitential exercise'. The objection would seem to find subsequent corroboration in the letter to Horkheimer. But the concept of regression here rather suggests that Habermas understands the idea of gesture in an essentially restrictive sense. He narrows the idea down – where 'philosophical thought' is concerned – to its exclusively narrowing aspect. In a conversation concerning the 'voice [*Gestus*] of theory', Axel Honneth also adopts this assessment of gesture. He explicitly distinguishes the 'form of the gesture' from 'thought' and relegates it to the domain of art and aesthetics: 'When thought assumes the form of gesture as an ungrounded and decisionistic solution for its own difficulties, this immediately provokes the question as to how such gestural expressions are to be engaged with in a theoretically appropriate fashion. Gestural expressions properly require aesthetic criteria of judgement; but within the field of the sciences aesthetic criteria alone are insufficient to help us judge the validity claims raised by theories' (Honneth/Seitter, 'Ein Gespräch über den Gestus der Theorie', p. 18). To the degree, therefore, that Adorno's thought approaches the gestural dimension, it would seem to relinquish any theoretical validity claim and thus elude a 'theoretically appropriate' discussion. If we measure such thinking against the claims of theory, it proves unable to live up to them. Thinking as gesture is theoretically a case

of regression. It is immediately obvious that the approach of Honneth and Habermas cannot actually take us very far here: once it has already been decided what theory is and what it is not, there is not much more to be done than undertake the appropriate classifications. In this way we learn nothing of any interest from either Habermas or Honneth about the character of voice [*Gestus*] and gesture at all. If gesture is indeed nothing but an 'ungrounded and decisionistic solution' for difficulties, if it simply reduces to the decisionistic act of a subject that entangles itself in its own intellectual aporias because of a falsely chosen approach, there is clearly no point in wasting any further words on the issue.

Most of Adorno's own remarks concerning gesture are to be found in his discussions of aesthetic questions. Must we consider this fact as an involuntary proof in support of the incompatibility which separates a gesture from – philosophical – thinking? One of the chapters in Adorno's *Essay on Wagner* bears the programmatic title 'Voice' [*Gestus*]. Here Adorno interprets the gestural as a 'social impulse': 'Wagner's music is conceived in terms of the gestures [*Gestik*] of striking and beating and is governed by this whole notion. It is in this gestural dimension that Wagner's social impulses are translated into musico-technical ones. If the composer of this period was already estranged lyrically from his audience, then Wagner's music only tends to disguise this estrangement by incorporating the public into the work as an element of its "effect"' (GS 13, p. 28; ET:30–1). To the extent that the gestural moment is interpreted primarily as a 'social impulse', it is recognisable musically only by reference to the 'deficiencies of the technical-compositional articulation' of the work. In Wagner these deficiencies derive from the fact that 'the musical logic, which is everywhere assumed by the material of his age, is softened up and replaced by a sort of gesticulation, rather in the way that agitators substitute linguistic gestures for the discursive exposition of their thoughts' (GS 13, p. 32; ET:34). It is true that music in general remains bound up with the gestural dimension, which it 'preserves within itself', but it has also led 'in the West to a spiritualisation of gesture as expression'. In contrast to gesture, which cannot be developed but can merely be 'repeated and intensified', expression presents us with the 'unrepeatable'. The unrepeatable is therefore a memory of the repeatable which constantly threatens to fall victim to the latter. This is what happens in Wagner: his music attempts 'to reconcile gesture's incapacity for development with the unrepeatable character of expression by allowing the gesture to revoke itself. Revoke itself and also time' (GS 13, p. 37; ET:40). The invariance of Wagner's music, a feature 'which denies all history by recourse to a nature without language', does not contravene the gestural principle of abstract repetition: expression disappears into the gesture that revokes itself.

Adorno never explicitly distinguishes between voice and gesture. Is the voice a kind of objectification of gesture? In *Aesthetic Theory*, Adorno relates it to the moment when something begins: 'Works of art are promises by virtue of their negativity, even to the point of total negation, just as the inflexion [*Gestus*] with which a story would once begin, or the very first sound struck from a sithar, promised something never heard or never seen before, even if it were the most fearful thing imaginable' (AT:204; ET:135). In this connection cf. A. García Düttmann, *La parole donnée* (p. 213 f.; ET 108f.). The voice can, as in Wagner, be determined by repetition, since Wagner's music is governed by gesture; but – whenever something begins – it can also signify the unrepeatable.

Adorno unfolds his thoughts concerning voice and gesture with model reference to works of art. But is it not possible to generalise these thoughts? Do they not also hold for a domain, a dimension, that is, which proves to be inseparable from language? Is this dimension not itself more original than any possible distinction between philosophy and art? Language is inaugurated with every act of beginning although it also simultaneously thwarts the latter: just as the name finds itself already caught up in the movement of language which divides it but does not, however, exhaust it. Through the movement of language, through the labour of the concept, thinking too must approach the name and thereby become a voice or an inflexion. It is not accidental that Adorno speaks of the 'gestures drawn from concepts'. Yet the more thinking becomes a voice or an inflexion, the greater the danger of remaining caught in empty and naked generality, in abstract repetition, in the 'linguistic gestures of the agitator'. This is perhaps what Habermas and Honneth are concerned about. However, both proceed as if one could simply avoid that danger, as if philosophical experience were possible in its absence.

2: Dialectics and the Ban on Images

64 Adorno, GS 10.2, p. 604 (*Critical Models*); ET:131–2.
65 Hegel, Vol. 17, p. 82 f.; ET: Vol. II, p. 208f.
66 Ibid., p. 87; ET: Vol. II, p. 214.
67 Ibid., p. 83; ET: Vol. II, p. 209.
68 Hegel, Vol. 1, p. 297 (*Early Theological Writings*); ET:204–5.
69 Ibid., p. 283; ET:191.
70 Ibid., p. 283 f.; ET:191–2.
71 J. Derrida, *Glas*, p. 58 f.; ET:48.
72 Hegel, Vol. 1, p. 363; ET:247.
73 Ibid., p. 364; ET:248.
74 Ibid., p. 367 f.; ET:250–1.
75 Ibid., p. 369; ET:252–3.
76 Adorno, GS 11, p. 177 (*Notes to Literature*); ET: Vol. 1, p. 153.
77 J. Habermas, *Der philosophische Diskurs der Moderne*, p. 157; ET:130.
78 J. Habermas, *Moralbewusstsein und kommunikatives Handeln*, p. 110; ET:100–101.
79 K.-O. Apel, *Diskurs und Verantwortung*, p. 448.
80 The fact that Adorno employs the concept of negativity points perhaps to a substantialisation of negative dialectics that reveals its dependency upon speculative or systematic dialectics. Werner Hamacher has drawn attention to the function that the non-identical thereby assumes: 'Yet if that other dialectic, to which the systematic dialectic is subjected, presents itself for Adorno as that of the "non-identical" itself, whose "content" still "remains" separated from its "concept", then Adorno substantializes its negativ-

ity. Insofar as he declares the unintelligible and unpresentable element, that which is untrue according to the law of the system, to be the truth of the non-identical, Adorno places the relationship between these competing dialectics under the power of the ontological, and perpetuates *modo negativo* its domination. It belongs to the dialectic of this critique of Hegel, that what it critically destroys is resurrected once again within the critique itself. It is not the 'non-identical itself' and its truth which is at issue here, but the self-repelling movement through which the system of negativity is first constituted – but in such a way that, contrary to its own claims, nothing substantial, no truth, can be left firmly standing, can be interpreted as a criterion of critical judgement either for or against the system' (Werner Hamacher, *pleroma – zu Genesis und Struktur einer dialektischen Hermeneutik bei Hegel*, p. 288 f.; ET:258).

3: Constellation and De-constitution

81 Adorno, *Philosophische Terminologie I*, p. 87.
82 Ibid., p. 26.
83 Adorno, *Jargon der Eigentlichkeit*, p. 10; ET:7.
84 Adorno, GS 10.2, p. 577 (*Critical Models*); ET:108.
85 Adorno, GS 4, p. 218 (*Minima Moralia*); ET:192.
86 Adorno, GS 10.2, p. 577 (*Critical Models*); ET:108.
87 Benjamin, Vol. II.1, p. 149 ('On Language as Such and on the Language of Man'); ET:66 f. (*Selected Writings*, Vol. 1).
88 Adorno, GS 10.1, p. 248 (*Prisms*); ET: 238.
89 Cf. García Düttmann, *La parole donnée*, p. 154 f.; ET: 74f.
90 Adorno, *Drei Studien zu Hegel*, p. 112; ET:123.
91 Ibid., p. 98; ET:106.
92 Ibid., p. 94; ET:101–2.
93 Adorno, GS 1, p. 338.
94 Benjamin, Vol. I.1, p. 216 (*The Origin of German Tragic Drama*); ET:36 (*Selected Writings*, Vol. 1).
95 Adorno, GS 1, p. 341.
96 Ibid., p. 369.
97 Adorno, *Drei Studien zu Hegel*, p. 100; ET:109.
98 Adorno, GS 1, p. 334 f.
99 Adorno, GS 17, p. 40.

100 Ibid., p. 29.

101 Adorno, GS 1, p. 335.

102 C. Schittek, *Flog ein Vogel federlos*, p. 28.

103 Ibid., p. 30.

104 Heidegger, *Nietzsche I*, p. 571; ET: Vol. 3, p. 85.

105 Adorno, GS 1, p. 338.

106 But the enlightened spirit must also speak too much because enlightenment always already entails the enlightenment concerning enlightenment itself. Herbert Schnädelbach has clearly indicated the difficulties that arise necessarily here. First of all he defines enlightenment as a self-directed 'enlightenment concerning oneself' and then explicates the aporetic implications of the concept of enlightenment: 'We can only speak of enlightenment there where enlightenment concerning enlightenment itself is not excluded: in this sense, too, enlightenment is reflexive. It cannot want to distance itself from those processes of self-knowledge and self-transformation which it may well desire to provoke and disseminate. The attempt to distance itself in this way can only succeed at the cost of establishing a new dogmatism, one in which any further enlightenment concerning itself may well appear to it as nothing but an expression of counter-enlightenment. Anyone who has investigated the history of the Enlightenment soon discovers just how difficult it is to draw a clear line of demarcation between the enlightenment of enlightenment and the movement of counter-enlightenment. As long as the counter-enlightenment engages in argument at all, it has already engaged with enlightenment, and this may well be the dilemma of every argumentatively committed counter-enlightenment position. But this also means that enlightenment cannot simply exclude the latter from itself without violating its own principles' (H. Schnädelbach, 'Über historistische Aufklärung', p. 25).

107 Even the *ratio* through which the subject secures its domination over nature (and that also means: over mimesis) is supposed to depend originally upon mimetic behaviour, and not merely indeed as cunning. It thereby threatens itself: 'The *ratio* which represses mimesis is not merely its opposite. Ratio is itself mimesis: the mimesis which assimilates itself to

what is dead. The subjective spirit which dissolves the animistic perception of nature only succeeds in mastering despiritualised nature by imitating its rigidity and despiritualising itself' (DdA:75f.; ET:57). This is indeed how 'imitation enters into the service of domination', but this imitation does not itself depend on the subject that dominates nature.

108 Adorno, GS 13, p. 22 f.; ET:24–5.

109 Adorno, GS 6, p. 530 f.

110 In one of the notebooks that preserved thoughts intended for subsequent incorporation into *Negative Dialectics*, Adorno speaks of a certain 'pre-judgment in favour of idealism': 'All philosophy, by virtue of its very procedure, makes a pre-judgment in favour of idealism. For philosophy is forced to operate with concepts, it cannot glue materials or non-conceptual stuff into its texts … But this already ensures that priority is ascribed to concepts, as the *material* of philosophy. Even matter is an abstraction' (GS 5, p. 531). Thinking as de-constitution at once ratifies and suspends this philosophical pre-judgment. But is not the abstraction that Adorno recognises and objects to in conceptual thought implicit in language itself, in the unity and simplicity of the word? Does not the unified and simple word necessarily relate abstractly to the concrete unity and simplicity of the signified? Such a conception remains caught up within the logic of abstraction that Adorno wishes to disrupt. Jacques Derrida discusses this in connection with Heidegger's question concerning the meaning of being: 'Heidegger reminds us constantly that the meaning of being is neither the word "being" nor the concept of being. But since this meaning is nothing outside of language and the language of words, it is tied, if not to a particular word or to a particular system of language (*concesso non dato*), at least to the possibility of the word in general. And to the possibility of its irreducible simplicity. One could thus think that it remains only to choose between two possibilities. (1) Does a modern linguistics, a science of signification breaking the unity of the word and breaking with its alleged irreducibility, still have anything to do with "language"? Heidegger would probably doubt it. (2) Conversely, is not all that is profoundly meditated as

the thought or the question of being enclosed within an old linguistics of the word which one practices here unknowingly? Unknowingly because such a linguistics, whether spontaneous or systematic, has always had to share the presuppositions of metaphysics. The two operate on the same grounds. It goes without saying that the options cannot be so simple' (J. Derrida, *De la Grammatologie*, p. 39 f.; ET:21).

111 Adorno, GS 10.2, p. 555 (*Critical Models*); ET:89.

112 Ibid., p. 674; ET:191.

113 Any investigation into the question of 'dreams' in Adorno's thought would certainly have to consider the following remarks in one of his letters to Ernst Bloch: 'A great deal of what I wrote in my youth possesses the character of a dream-like anticipation, and it is only dating from a certain moment of shock, which probably coincides with the emergence of Hitler's Reich, that I can really comprehend what it was I was doing then' (GS 1, 384).

114 Benjamin, Vol. II.1, p. 215; ET:732 (*Selected Writings*, Vol. 2).

115 Adorno, GS 10.2, p. 598 (*Critical Models*); ET: 126.

116 Adorno, GS 4, p. 252; ET:220–21.

117 In his reflections on the 'unnameable', Jean-Marie Lustiger has attempted to salvage a theological approach by distinguishing between the 'unnameable' and the 'unsayable': 'What happened there in Auschwitz, in a place that was nowhere, in those years, when time seemed perpetually to be suspended outside of human history, is properly "unnameable", is the realm of the nameless, is Hell. God on the other hand is the unsayable; man cannot name him unless God names himself to man, unless God reveals his name to him. God bestows upon man the grace and joy of the divine names.' What the cardinal ultimately under-estimates here is precisely that the name 'Auschwitz' (the 'unnameable') touches directly upon naming, and thus also upon the naming of the revealed name, indeed upon revelation as revelation of the name. The distinction between the 'unnameable' and the 'unsayable' cannot therefore be sustained. (Cf. A. García Düttmann, *La parole donnée*, p. 187 f.; ET:94f.

118 It is difficult to subscribe to Habermas's interpretation of the concept of guilt. Habermas relegates the incommensurability of guilt with regard to the individual subject to the sphere of intersubjectivity and thereby endorses a position of 'inexorable immanence'. He presupposes a commensurability in principle which is obviously incompatible with the concept of guilt, unless the latter signifies nothing more than an ultimately regulated and already self-obviating 'fall' from the ideal communicative community of agents which is historically anticipated. It is striking that Habermas chooses the phenomenon of something that can never be made good again as an example of the 'unintended product of entanglement': 'The pseudo-natural dynamic character of impaired communicative life-contexts, unlike the "immemorial" character of being or the "happening" of power, still retains something of a *guiltily self-incurred* destiny – even if we can only speak of guilt in an intersubjective sense, namely as an unintended product of entanglement, and one which communicative agents, despite their individual accountability, must ascribe to collective social responsibility. It is not accidental that acts of suicide amongst those close to us produce a shattering effect which momentarily permits even the most hard-hearted to imagine something of the *ineluctable communality* of such a fate' (*Der philosophische Diskurs der Moderne*, p. 368; ET:316). Is the idea of an 'inexorable immanence' (ibid.) really compatible with the concepts of guilt and fate in any but a purely mythical sense?

119 K. Jaspers, 'Die Schuldfrage', p. 170.
120 Ibid., p. 185.
121 Ibid., p. 177.
122 Ibid., p. 183.
123 Ibid., p. 184.
124 Ibid., p. 185.
125 Ibid., p. 128.
126 Ibid., p. 177.
127 Ibid., p. 137.
128 Ibid., p. 178.
129 Ibid., p. 160.
130 I. Kant, *Der Streit der Fakultäten*, p. 357 (A142); ET:151.

131 Jaspers, 'Die Schuldfrage', p. 159.

132 Ibid., p. 173.

133 H. Ott, *Martin Heidegger*, p. 34; ET:28.

134 Heidegger, *Einführung in die Metaphysik*, p. 29; ET:41.
Jacques Derrida has pursued the question of 'spirit' in
Heidegger's work. In relation to the passage where Heidegger speaks of a loss or 'deprivation of spiritual power
[*Entmachtung*]', Derrida writes: '*Entmachtung* dooms spirit to
impotence, robs it of its strength and the nerve of its
authority ... : what does this mean as far as force is
concerned? That spirit *is* a force and *is not* a force, that it
has and has not power. If it were a force in itself, it would
not lose force, there would be no *Entmachtung*. But if it
were not this force or power, the *Entmachtung* would not
affect it essentially, it would not be *of spirit*. So one can say
neither the one nor the other, one must say both, which
doubles up each of the concepts: world, force, spirit. The
structure of each of these concepts is marked by the relation to its double: a relation of haunting' (J. Derrida, *De
l'esprit. Heidegger et la question*; ET:61–2).

135 Adorno, GS 9.2, p. 319.

136 The moment a true national consciousness is distinguished
from a false one, all that is required in order to speak on
behalf of a 'healthy national sentiment' is an interpretation
which identifies health with truth. In the study of 1961
entitled 'Opinion Delusion Society', Adorno claims that
the attempt to separate a 'healthy national feeling' from a
'pathological nationalism' is 'as ideological as the belief in
normal opinions which are opposed to purely pathogenic
ones' – for the tendency to psychological 'over-valuation'
of a national sentiment is already rooted in what is itself
'supposedly healthy' (GS.10.2, p. 589; ET:118 [*Critical
Models*]). He thus implicitly repudiates the kind of philosophical nationalism which the study on guilt and defensiveness still partially reflected.

137 Adorno, GS 10.2, p. 691; ET:205 (*Critical Models*).

138 Ibid., p. 691 f.; ET:206.

139 Ibid., p. 692; ET:206.

140 S. Freud, *Massenpsychologie und Ich-Analyse*, p. 113; ET: 68.

141 Adorno, GS 10.2, p. 695 (*Critical Models*); ET:208.

142 Ibid., p. 701 ET:213. How then does German relate to other languages? Adorno made an attempt to translate some of Verlaine's poems into German, as well as composing a series of variations on French folk songs. One of the aphorisms in *Minima Moralia* is entitled 'On parle français': 'How intimately sexuality and language are intertwined can be seen by reading pornography in a foreign language. When de Sade is read in the original no dictionary is required. The most recondite expressions for the indecent, knowledge of which no school, no parental home, no literary experience transmits, are understood instinctively, just as in childhood the most tangential utterances and observations concerning the sexual crystallise into a true representation. It is as if the imprisoned passions, called by their name in such expressions, burst through the ramparts of blind language as through those of their own repression and forced their way irresistibly into the innermost cell of meaning, which resembles them' (MM:53; ET:48). The French which the German reader experiences as a foreign language, as the language of another country, of another culture, of another nation, is as close to Adorno in its foreignness as only the experiences of one's own childhood can be. Such propinquity, which is based not upon the subject's conscious and waking command of the language, but rather on the confidence of the sleep-walker, is not accomplished through intelligibility as such – through the understanding of subsequently endowed meaning, through the use of a dictionary.

   A brief excursus: Adorno included the essay 'What is German?' in the volume of his writings entitled *Catchwords*. The volume is itself a kind of '*dictionnaire*', albeit one that is not oriented, in accordance with its governing idea, towards identity and continuity, intelligibility or conceptual unity: 'The title 'Catchwords' alludes to the encyclopedic form that, unsystematically, discontinuously, presents what the unity of experience crystallizes into a constellation. [But what kind of 'unity' is in question here?] On the principle of a small volume with somewhat arbitrarily selected catchwords, it would thus be possible to imagine a new *Dictionnaire philosophique*. And the polemical associations, strongly suggested by this title, would be more than welcome to the author' (GS 10.2, p. 598 [*Critical Models*]; ET:126). The catchword 'German' is indeed an exemplary one. It is a catchword in a book that can be read as a sketch for a new *Dictionnaire philosophique*, and thus a catchword amongst catchwords. But in German the 'catchword' is a *Stichwort*, literally a 'cutting', 'penetrating' or 'pointed' word, because it accomplishes exactly what the German expression implies: it turns its cutting edge upon the reader who asks whether 'German' reflects a fantasy, produced by wishful thinking, or who regards it as something self-evident and thus understands the question as a direct challenge. This cutting word spurs the reader on and provokes a welcome polemic. But the cutting word of 'German' also turns its edge upon itself: it is not a word that could simply be included like any other in such a dictionary, and the reader necessarily finds it placed within imaginary quotation marks, suspended as it were. Instead of answering the question 'What is German?', Adorno transforms its significance. As if the word would cut itself. Finally, it is also appropriate to speak of a *Stichwort* in this literal sense because the book in which it belongs takes a French dictionary, Voltaire's *Dictionnaire philosophique*, as its model. In the preface to the Varberg edition of his work, Voltaire writes: 'Ce livre n'exige pas une lecture suivie; mais à quelque endroit qu'on l'ouvre, on trouve de quoi réfléchir. Les livres les plus utiles sont ceux dont les lecteurs font eux-mêmes la moitié; ils étendent les pensées dont on leur présente le germe' ['This book does not demand to be read in a continuous fashion; for at any point that it is opened, one can find something to reflect upon. The most useful books are those where the readers themselves constitute half the share; for they unfold the thoughts from the germ that has been offered to them']. *End of excursus.*

The words that procure propinquity are meaningful even before meaning has been bestowed on them. This blindness lets the reader see because it is the blind words which have the power to call things by their names. Without the power of the blind words, the passions would never discover the meaning which resembles them. Is it this resemblance which transforms words into names? What Adorno reveals with this model of the entwinement of sexuality and language – the entwinement of both *in a foreign language* – strongly suggests that the foreign language is the language of difference, or, in Adorno's terms, the language of the non-identical, a language that is not identical, is not exhausted in its pure intelligibility, a language that by virtue of its foreignness is more familiar to us than our own, a language in which the non-conceptual element (the mimetic, the somatic, the name) asserts itself against the accomplishments of all conceptual identification. (But is there not a determinate identity of meaning even in the foreign word?) The German reader, not entirely in command of French and yet closer to it than any Frenchman, becomes a child again: such propinquity, such closeness, can only be experienced by one who is capable of understanding the language of childhood.

The experience Adorno describes here implies a metaphysics of childhood. One of the principal themes of the essay 'What is German?' is precisely the arduous conceptual attempt to recapture the phenomenon of childhood and to speak its language. Was Adorno not impelled to abandon his American exile because he could no longer endure the distance that separated him from the site of childhood, the distance that the English language itself imposed upon him? 'I simply wanted to return to where I had spent my childhood, where everything specific to me was imparted to the very core. Perhaps I sensed that whatever one accomplishes in life reflects little more than the attempt to regain childhood' (GS 10.2, p. 696 f. [*Critial Models*]; ET:210).

Immediately before the aphorism 'On parle français', itself the sedimentation of the experience of a foreign language, we come across the aphorism 'English spoken':
'In my childhood, some elderly English ladies with whom my parents kept up relations often gave me books as presents: richly illustrated works for the young, also a small green bible bound in morocco leather. All were in the language of the donors: whether I could read it none of them paused to reflect. The peculiar inaccessibility of the

books, with their glaring pictures, titles and vignettes, and their indecipherable text, filled me with the belief that in general objects of this kind were not books at all, but advertisements, perhaps for machines like those my uncle produced in his London factory. Since I came to live in Anglo-Saxon countries and to understand English, this awareness has not been dispelled but strengthened. There is a song by Brahms, to a poem by Heyse, with the lines: *O Herzeleid, du Ewigkeit! / Selbander nur ist Seligkeit*. In the most widely used American edition this is rendered as: 'O misery, eternity / But two in one were ecstasy'. The archaic, passionate nouns of the original have been turned into catchwords for a hit song, designed to boost it. Illuminated in the neon-light switched on by these words, culture displays its character as advertising' (MM:52; ET:47). Once again it is experiences of reading, procured precisely by foreign books, which constitute the heart of the aphorism. But the evaluation of English here by no means coincides with that of French. A foreign language is not merely a foreign language, and can be more foreign than a foreign language that inaugurates a relationship of propinquity in its very foreignness. For the child here English is a language of misunderstanding. Since he cannot decipher it, since the language remains closed to him, he takes the illustrated pages for advertisements, rather than the pages of a legible book. One might think that we are dealing merely with the mind of a child here, one which is still unclear about the nature of legibility, and that English simply stands in for any foreign language as such. But this – trivial – interpretation is ruled out by the following remark: 'Since I came to live in Anglo-Saxon countries and to understand English, this awareness has not been dispelled but strengthened.' Thus the relationship to language that is foreign does *not* depend upon understanding, upon the learnability of the foreign language, upon the ability to translate the foreign words. A foreign language can remain, even for someone now in command of it, a foreign language, a language of remoteness without closeness, a language of misunderstanding. English is a language hostile to children: the child does not understand it, the adult who reads an English text is unable to transform himself back into a child.

Adorno never wrote an English book that really deserves the title. As an exile in England and then America he was forced to formulate sentences in English, but when he did so, he spoke a different language from that chosen for his German books. One seems to be faced with a double choice of language that can be traced back to a linguistic necessity: in English one can only write books that are actually preliminary studies for the book that the philosopher has to write in German. Thus it is hardly surprising if Adorno, who co-authored with Horkheimer the philosophical fragments of *Dialectic of Enlightenment* in the language of his childhood, saw fit to introduce the English translation of *Prisms* with a justificatory foreword. In this foreword he raises the question whether his collection of essays can be translated at all – not because Samuel Weber, the translator, might fail in the task, but because the English language itself resists such a translation. The text to be translated exposes itself in a particularly high degree to the danger of exercising a misleading effect, the danger of being falsified. The author must lend his express support, must warn the English-speaking reader to read the translated text as non-translated, and perhaps as a text that cannot be translated into English, as an untranslatable text. The foreword itself is based upon an original manuscript written in German. The English language stands in need of German, of books in German: 'Although the author is delighted that for the first time one of his German books is now to appear in English – in a very meticulous and thoughtful translation – he is none the less fully aware of the difficulties which confront such texts in the English-speaking world. That he is no stranger to the Anglo-Saxon norms of thought and presentation has been demonstrated, the author believes, in his English-language writings: his contributions to *The Authoritarian Personality*, his essays on music sociology for the Princeton Radio Research Project, and subsequent studies such as "How to Look at Television", or "The Stars Down to Earth". [Some of the contributions gathered together in *Prisms* had been written under the – linguistic – conditions of exile and already been published in an English version prior to the appearance of the English translation of the collection as a whole.] These norms are essential to him as a control, lest he reject common sense without first having mastered it; it is only by use of its own categories, that common sense can be transcended. This, however, must remain the author's aim as long as he considers matters of fact to be not mere fact, unreflected and thing-like, but rather processes of infinite mediation, never to be taken literally. [The *Stichwort* of Adorno's *Dictionnaire* here turns its cutting edge upon the literalness of common sense.] He cannot accept the usual mode of thought which is content to register facts and prepare them for subsequent classification. His essential effort is to illuminate the realm of facticity – without which there can be no true knowledge – with reflections of a different type, one which diverges radically from the generally accepted canon of scientific validity. To justify this procedure it would have been best to restate the considerations now gathered in *Negative Dialectics*' (GS 10.2, p. 803 f. [*Critical Models*]; ET:7). English appears as the language of linguistic infantilism and of control: it classifies and serves to control the one who would oppose control, ensuring that he too can classify, he too can exercise control. The English language rouses and awakens consciousness, although the latter must also simultaneously liberate itself from this very language. In contrast to French, English possesses a merely instrumental function. In the very moment that he would expel the English language as a foreign body, the philosopher is forced to incorporate the same into himself. If the – untranslatable – German language functions as a privileged medium of translation, can it transform the foreign language into itself, can it thereby immunise itself against the foreign body? Does German, as a philosophical language, possess the power to assert itself in and through a foreign language, to rouse the foreign into life, or to instrumentalise the latter for its own purposes? Does German call things by their own names?

143 Adorno interprets the concept of autonomy as signifying 'the individual's responsibility for himself or herself' and

lays claim to it: 'I was aware that there was also something
regressive about the autonomy which I defended as the
author's unconditional right to his own work in its integral
shape over against the highly rationalised socio-economic
evaluation of spiritual products.' Can we detach this
concept of autonomy from the double movement Adorno
describes? On the one hand it remains quite true that 'the
exchange relation, the extension of the commodity-charac-
ter into every sphere, including that of the spirit – what is
popularly dubbed commercialisation – had not, in the late
eighteenth and the nineteenth century, gone as far in
Germany as it had done in the advanced capitalist countries. That at least lent a certain power of resistance to the
sphere of intellectual and cultural production. This sphere
understood itself as a reality in its own right, and not as an
object of exchange. It found its model not in the enterpris-
ing individual acting in accordance with the laws of the
market, but rather in the official who fulfils his duties
towards the established authorities; this is something that
has often been remarked in relation to Kant ... The great
German conceptual projects, through which autonomy,
action undertaken solely for its own sake, was so exorbi-
tantly glorified, were also [on the other hand] quite
prepared to deify the state. The criticisms mounted on the
part of the Western European countries have always, and
equally one-sidedly, emphasised this aspect. The priority
assumed by the collective interest over against private
advantage was coupled with the bellicose political potential
of a war of aggression. The impulse towards infinite
dominion accompanied the infinitude of the Idea itself, the
one did not exist without the other. History has here
revealed itself, up until now, as a context of guilt in which
the highest productive forces, the ultimate manifestations
of the spirit are caught up in collusion with the worst.
Even the thought of action solely for its own sake, given
its remorseless and intrinsic lack of attention to the other, is
not entirely alien to inhumanity. The latter reveals itself in
a certain crowing and all-embracing aggressiveness on the
part of the greatest of spiritual products, namely in their
will to domination' (GS 10.2, p. 693–5 [*Critical Models*];

ET:207–8). In the section of *Negative Dialectics* that is dedicated to Kant's thought, Adorno returns to the theme of these concluding remarks, radicalises them even further and grasps autonomy as the subject's relationship to its constitutive otherness: 'We can only make a judgement concerning this decisive aspect of the ego, its autonomy and independence, by considering its relationship with its own otherness, with the non-ego. Whether autonomy exists or not depends upon what contradicts it, upon its antagonist, upon the object that grants or denies autonomy to the subject; detached from this autonomy is a fiction' (ND:222; ET:223). What then is the connection between a 'simulated national consciousness' ('Guilt and Defensiveness'), the 'fictive lack' of 'national self-confidence' ('What is German?'), and the fiction of autonomy (*Negative Dialectics*)? How is the fictitious character of Germanness entangled with its truth? Adorno's historical and socio-economic analysis is by no means intended to relativise the question of truth: for if the speculative thought is itself thought in the German language, then the conditions under which German has developed necessarily acquire a status essentially different from that which belongs to a merely contingent historical process.

144 Adorno, *GS* 10.2, p. 695 [*Critical Models*]; ET:208.

145 Since Adorno is unable to find an unambiguous answer to the question, he prefers to ask what significance German possesses *for him*. What was it that led him, an exiled Jew, one who was 'driven out with contempt and abuse', to return after all? It would be over-hasty to assume that Adorno is thereby reducing the entire question to simply biographical terms. For then one would also have to appeal to German as a kind of essential quantity: as an essence that secures its own subsistence – its own stock, as it were – independently of the particular fate of individuals.

The reflections contained in the autobiographically coloured pages of the essay 'What is German?' coalesce into a contradiction which is not explicitly named as such. The philosopher who owes his life to a foreign country – perhaps even to *the* foreign country – cannot permit himself, if he would survive as philosopher, to speak the language of that country. He may not speak it without failing to speak it. But the language he feels compelled to speak is the language of his potential murderers, the language of those whose mode of behaviour also possesses a linguistic dimension to it. The survivor, as Jean-François Lyotard has emphasised, has been chosen by the forces of evil in order to bear witness and tell what has happened – at least this is how things must appear to him in the face of almost universal destruction (cf. J.-F. Lyotard, 'Le survivant', p. 268; ET:155.). He has been chosen to continue speaking the language which he has both preserved and betrayed, the very language which harbours, as Adorno claims, the evil, and the absolute horror: the 'spirit' which itself reverts to 'absolute horror' is one of those words, is indeed *the* word, which constitutes the metaphysical character – the 'expressive power' – of the German language.

What are the reasons which lead Adorno to explain and to justify his return to Germany? First of all he attacks the standard German cliché about America: 'However illusory the instrumentally-oriented sense of life may be, however much it closes its eyes to the ever-increasing contradictions and insists that everything is for the best just so long as it works, just as illusory is that faith in spiritual culture which, in its ideal of self-sufficient purity, renounces the realisation of its inner content and abandons reality to power and the blindness which accompanies this power' (GS 10.2, p. 697 [*Critical Models*]; ET:210). In spite of the ubiquitous presence of the exchange principle, Adorno emphasises that American life is also marked by 'sympathy, compassion, a feeling for the lot of the more disadvantaged'. His decision to return to Germany, therefore, is not dictated by the usual German aversion that is coupled with an arrogantly contemptuous attitude to that country. As Adorno observes in *Aesthetic Theory*: 'The alternative between: "What do I get out of it?" or: "To be German means doing something for its own sake", is detestable.' (AT:460; ET:310). It is a certain fidelity to the past, to childhood, that motivates Adorno to leave the land of exile. For this fidelity requires that 'one would rather strive to change things there where one feels truly competent in one's own experience, where one knows how to make distinctions, above all how to understand people properly, than renounce what one is for the sake of accommodating oneself to a different milieu' (GS 10.2, p. 696 [*Critical Models*]; ET:210). But how is the survivor to understand those who drove him out, who denied his right to live, who are responsible for the annihilation of his people? It is striking that Adorno does not attack the name of one people in the name of an other. He speaks about 'what was perpetrated by Germans upon millions of innocent people' and refuses to identify National Socialism with 'the Germans as a people'. Understanding remains essentially bound up with language. Language is that 'objective something' which, over and beyond 'subjective need', impels him to return: 'Not only because one can never, in a newly acquired language, capture what one means to say as precisely, and with all the nuances and attendant rhythm of the thought process, as one can in one's own language. But rather because the German language clearly possesses a particular affinity to philosophy, and especially to its speculative moment ... Historically the German language has, through a process that would really call one day for proper analysis, become capable of expressing something in the phenomena which is not exhausted in their positivity and givenness, not exhausted in their being simply so' (GS 10.2, p. 699 f. [*Critical Models*]; ET:212 f.). Like the linguistic experience of childhood, that of the speculative is a kind of 'unregulated and unregimented experience' that does not content itself with simply classifying the given, thereby resisting the empiricist and positivist traditions of the 'West'. Hence Adorno's return is determined by the speculative moment of the German language, by the excess which reveals the possibility of 'absolute horror' along with that of genuine knowledge. The enlightened spirit returns home as a guardian of language: 'He who returns, and has lost all naivety in relation to what is his own, must combine the most intimate relationship with his own language with a tireless vigilance in the face of the lies that it may encourage' (GS 10.2, p. 701 [*Critical Models*]; ET:213).

It is only from this perspective that we can really understand the function played by foreign or loan words in Adorno's language. Precisely because he recognises the 'double-bind' of German, the guardian of this language cannot accept the idea of a supposedly 'organic character to language' (GS 11, p. 642 [*Notes to Literature*]; ET: Vol. 2, p. 288.). Adorno does not resettle in Germany as the guardian of a de-racinated language. In *Negative Dialectics* he writes: 'The category of the root, of the origin itself, is dominatory in character, a confirmation of who is first in line because he was there first, of the autochthonous over against the immigrant, of the settled over against the nomadic' (ND:158; ET:155). Foreign words can thus furnish 'cells of resistance against nationalism' (GS 11, p. 218 [*Notes to Literature*]; ET: Vol. 1, p. 186). and liberate us from the 'compulsions of identity' (GS 11, p. 26 [*Notes to Literature*]; ET: Vol. 1, p. 17). They resemble the name most closely of all: 'The true words, the fragments of truth, are not the half-forgotten and mythically evocative primordial words of origin. They are the words that have been expressly found and used, the artificial – in short the fabricated words; just as God, according to the narrative in Genesis, did not reveal the names of things to mankind, unless they were disclosed in the moment they were humanly named: in the very act of naming. But every newly established loan word of foreign origin profanely celebrates, in the moment of its appearance, the true and immemorial historical naming once again' (GS 11, p. 643 [*Notes to Literature*]; ET: Vol. 2, p.288–9). To the degree that the 'double-bind' of the German language already divides every one of its words, it also programmes the use of the artificial word, of the foreign word: this – profane – celebration comes to pass, therefore, in German.

146 Adorno, GS 11, p. 286 [*Notes to Literature*]; ET: Vol. 1, p.245–6.
147 Adorno, *Zur Metakritik der Erkenntnistheorie*, p. 33 f.; ET: 26.
148 G. Agamben, *Idea della Prosa*, p. 91; ET:111.
149 'A being radically devoid of any representational identity,

would be absolutely irrelevant to the State' (G. Agamben, *La comunità che viene*, p. 59; ET:86).

PART II: *Inaugurations*

1: *Counter-Turning of the Beginning*

1 M. Heidegger, *Die Selbstbehauptung der deutschen Universität*, p. 13; ET:473.
2 Ibid., p. 11; ET:471.
3 P. Lacoue-Labarthe, *L'imitation des modernes*, p. 169.
4 Ott, *Martin Heidegger*, p. 161 f.; ET:165f.
5 Benjamin, Vol. II.2, p. 433; ET: 805 (*Selected Writings*, Vol. 2); cf.F. Kafka, *The Complete Short Stories*, p. 404.
6 Benjamin, Vol. II.3, p. 1253.
7 Heidegger, *Die Selbstbehauptung der deutschen Universität*, p. 19; ET:480.
8 M. Heidegger, *Denkerfahrungen*, p. 10.
9 Benjamin, Vol. IV.1, p. 419 f.
10 Benjamin, Vol. VI, p. 116 f.
11 Heidegger, *Sein und Zeit*, p. 165; ET:208.
12 Ibid., pp. 28 and 32; ET:51 and 55.
13 Heidegger, *Nietzsche II*, p. 479 (not included in the English translation of the Nietzsche lectures).
14 Heidegger, GA 52, p. 13.
15 In his essay 'Heidegger's Exegeses of Hölderlin's Poetry' Paul de Man, without expressly examining the problem of naming as such, has nonetheless already emphasised the significance of naming if only through the frequency with which it is mentioned. De Man expounds Heidegger's train of thought and engages critically with it: 'Hölderlin states the presence of Being, his word is Being present ...; the metaphysicians, on the other hand ... can never *name* it' (p. 250); 'That which they [the metaphysicians] *name* as the essential is nothing more than Being disguised' (ibid.); 'The poet will no longer *name* the deceitful mask that Being presents to the metaphysician, but its authentic face' (p. 251); 'The poet founds the immediate presence of Being by *naming* it' (p. 252); 'One understands why Heidegger is in need of a witness, of someone of whom he can say that he

has *named* the immediate presence of Being' (ibid.); 'But here is someone – Hölderlin – who tells us that he has seen it, and that, moreover, he can speak of it, *name* it' (p. 253); 'But Heidegger begins to distort the meaning when he continues by showing the poet as *naming* the presence of the present' (p. 256 f.); 'It is not because he has seen Being that the poet is, therefore, capable of *naming* it; his word prays for the parousia, it does not establish it...' (p. 258).

16 In the lecture course on Hölderlin's hymn 'Der Ister', which Heidegger presented in the summer semester of 1944, we read: 'Naming is the name for poetic saying'; but the 'poetic saying' consists precisely in saying something that 'has not yet been said before'.

17 Heidegger, GA 52, p. 14.

18 Heidegger, *Was heißt Denken?*, p. 58; ET:34.

19 Adorno, *Jargon der Eigentlichkeit*, p. 139; ET:xxi.

20 Ibid., p. 14; ET:12.

21 H. Marcuse, *One-Dimensional Man*, p. 95.

22 Ibid.

23 If we consider one of the arguments of *Dialectic of Enlightenment* at this point, we can say that it is precisely this 'formalism' which brings functionalised and operationalised language into the domain that Marcuse defines as that of the indistinguishable. It thereby tends to become that language of 'mythical names' whose 'formalism' (DdA:79; ET:60) – or whose 'rigidity' – secures and breaks the spell of 'omnipotence' (DdA:57; ET:39). Ritual itself, on the basis of its intrinsic formalism, is what sustains within civilisation the memory of the 'mimetic practice of sacrifice' (DdA:210; ET:186) and simultaneously cancels the 'assimilation to nature': 'The Jews appeared to succeed in accomplishing what Christianity had struggled in vain to do: the disempowering of magic by means of its own power, which now turns against itself as worship. They succeeded not so much in extirpating this assimilation to nature as in sublating it within the purified duties of ritual. They thereby preserved for it the reconciling memory without falling back through symbolism into mythology. That is why advanced civilisation regards them as both retrogressive and all too progressive, as both similar and dissimilar,

as both clever and stupid' (DdA:211; ET:186). (The criticism of the concept of symbol implied in this passage, a criticism which Adorno shares with Benjamin and which accompanies a positive re-evaluation of the allegorical, only becomes intelligible once it is brought into connection with the ban on images.) Jewish ritual is certainly no longer a 'bloody ritual', but it remains a ritual nonetheless and cannot therefore simply wash away the trace of blood for all its purity. From this perspective how should we understand Adorno's accusation that Heidegger is performing a 'ritual of naming' (an expression that could almost be described as a pleonasm)? Mere naming which necessarily implies a certain 'formalism' (of the sign) is both nearest to the worship of images and most faithful to the ban on images.

24 Benjamin, Vol. I.2, p. 455 (first version).
25 Ibid., p. 456.
26 Heidegger, *Sein und Zeit*, p. 410; ET:463.
27 Ibid., p. 390 f.; ET:442–3.
28 Ibid., p. 385; ET:437.
29 Ibid., p. 384; ET:436.
30 J. Habermas, *Der philosophische Diskurs der Moderne*, p. 188; ET:158–9.
31 How we read Heidegger's famous dictum *Nur noch ein Gott kann uns retten* ['Only a god can save us yet'] depends upon whether naming is named or not. Named naming allows only *one* interpretation, *a* specific one, namely that which emphasises the *ein* ['a']. But if naming cannot be named, we must read the remark as if there were indeed always an additional god and emphasise the *noch* ['yet']: 'Only yet another god can save us'. In a different context Thomas Pepper has suggested precisely this line of interpretation.
32 J.-C. Milner, *Le matériel et l'oubli*, p. 72.
33 Ibid., p. 74.
34 Heidegger, *Die Selbstbehauptung der deutschen Universität*, p. 15; ET:476.
35 Heidegger, *Vorträge und Aufsätze*, pp. 89–90.
36 Heidegger, *Einführung in die Metaphysik*, p. 6; ET:9.
37 Ibid., p. 39; ET:53–4.
38 Ibid., p. 62; ET:85.

39 Ibid.; ET:86.
40 Ibid., p. 131; ET:182–3.
41 Ibid., p. 38; ET:52.
42 Ibid.
43 Ibid., p. 29: ET:41.
44 Ibid., p. 29 f.; ET:41f.
45 Ibid., p. 145 f.; ET:204f. The thinking of 'repetition' and 'retrieval' [*Wieder-holung*] as a thinking of the beginning is a thinking of singularity, of the once and only: 'Only what is unique can be repeated and thus retrieved. Only what is unique bears within it the ground of the necessity that a return be made to it, that its being-a-beginning be taken over. Repetition and retrieval here do not signify the foolish superficiality and impossibility of the recurrence of the self-*same*. For the beginning can never be grasped as the self-same because it is something that reaches out in advance, and thus in each case always over-reaches differently that which it has begun, determining its own re-peti-tion accordingly' (Heidegger, *Beiträge zur Philosophie*, p. 55; ET:39). The more therefore the retrieving repetition requires itself a retrieving repetition (in the sense of a thinking of the beginning, a thinking that does not name naming), the more urgent it becomes to conceive of the link between name and uniqueness.
46 Heidegger, *Vorträge und Aufsätze*, p. 79.
47 Heidegger, *Einführung in die Metaphysik,* p. 119; ET:165–6.
48 Heidegger, *Zur Sache des Denkens*, p. 53 f.

2: Rise and Downfall

49 Heidegger, *Vom Ursprung des Kunstwerks*, pp. 44 and 46; ET:76.
50 Heidegger, *Die Selbstbehauptung der deutschen Universität*, p. 23; ET:483.
51 Heidegger, *Vom Ursprung des Kunstwerks*, p. 46; ET:77.
52 Benjamin, Vol. II.1, p. 217 (*Experience and Poverty*); ET: 733 (*Selected Writing*, Vol. 2).
53 Heidegger, 'Zur Seinsfrage', p. 10; ET:295 (*Pathmarks*).
54 Heidegger, *Nietzsche II*, p. 165 f.; ET: Vol. 4, 116–17.
55 M. Theunissen, *Negativität bei Adorno*, p. 61.

56 K.-O. Apel, *Diskurs und Verantwortung*, p. 373.

57 Ibid., p. 374.

58 This is not to say that Apel and Heidegger also share the same analysis, but merely that they both regard the (Second) World War as an exemplary experience of a catastrophe that directly affects the 'national sentiment'. Ernst Jünger, for whose nationalism plenty of evidence is available, leaves no doubt, in his book *Der Arbeiter*, that in the technicised world that shapes the modern worker National Socialism – and socialism in general – is a restricted and restricting principle. Freedom as it is understood by nationalism and socialism remains abstract and possesses any justification it has only as a 'mobilising factor': 'The freedom which the two principles of nationalism and socialism are capable of creating is not substantial in nature; it is a presupposition, a mobilising factor, but not an aim. This circumstance suggests that the bourgeois concept of freedom is somehow at work here, that these are struggles in which the individual and the mass are still principal participants' (E. Jünger, *Der Arbeiter*, p. 249) – but not the worker who is neither an individual nor to be counted among the mass. Nationalism and socialism come to grief through themselves, according to Jünger, because 'any power whatever makes use of their rules of the game'. That is why the 'attack which is directed within nations against the classes and estates, against the masses and against individuals, is also directed against the nations themselves, insofar as they are constituted according to "bourgeois" or "French" models. [What is the import and scope of this distinction? Is there another kind of nationalism?] The closure which planned labour bestows upon the space in which it operates, transforming it into a kind of fortress, and the intensification of nationalism itself, must be grasped as an attempt to effect a concentration whose energies transcend the needs of the nation' (Ibid., p. 291). Nationalism is therefore the element of an economy which it cannot control.

59 Apel, *Diskurs und Verantwortung*, p. 474.

60 Apel, 'Sinnkonstitution und Geltungsrechtfertigung', p. 167.

61 Adorno, GS 11, p. 282 (*Notes to Literature*); ET: Vol. 1, p. 242.

62 Ibid., p. 103; ET: Vol. 1, p. 88.

63 Ibid., p. 103 f.; ET:88.

64 Ibid., p. 102; ET:87.

65 Ibid., p. 105; ET:90.

66 A non-simultaneity in which non-simultaneity is so inscribed that it cannot ever be transformed into simultaneity can only be experienced 'in the simultaneity of that which is and is not different; each moment or element of this simultaneity can stand entirely by itself even though it still stands in opposition to the other moment or element'. Cf. García Düttmann, 'Über die Gleichzeitigkeit', p. 85.

67 Benjamin, Vol. II.1, p. 307 (*Surrealism*); ET: 215–15 (*Selected Writing*, Vol. 2).

68 Benjamin, Vol. II.3, p. 1037.

69 Ibid., p. 1035.

70 Benjamin, Vol. I.2, p. 608; ET:110 (*Charles Baudelaire*).

71 Ibid., p. 611; ET:113.

72 Ibid., p. 701 f.; 263–4 (*Illuminations*).

73 Ibid., p. 610; ET:112 (*Charles Baudelaire*).

74 Ibid., p. 702; ET:264 (*Illuminations*).

75 Ibid., p. 704; ET:266.

76 Heidegger, *Sein und Zeit*, p. 407; ET:459.

77 Ibid., p. 413; ET:466.

78 Benjamin, Vol. I.2 (*Some Motifs in Baudelaire*), p. 614; ET:116 (*Charles Baudelaire*).

79 Ibid., p. 615; ET:117.

80 Ibid., p. 703 ('On the Concept of History'); ET:264–5 (*Illuminations*).

81 Ibid., p. 697; ET:259.

82 Ibid., p. 694 f.; ET:256 f.

83 Benjamin, Vol. I.1, p. 245 f.; ET:65 f.

84 C. Schmitt, *Politische Theologie*, p. 12; ET:6–7.

85 Ibid., p. 21 f.; ET:14–15.

86 Heidegger, GA 65, p. 88 (*Beiträge*); ET:61.

87 Benjamin, Vol. I.2, p. 700; ET:264 (*Illuminations*).

88 There is just such an image in *Negative Dialectics*: 'But, as in the sculptures of Barlach or the writings of Kafka, mankind

still keeps dragging itself along, an endless procession of bent figures chained to one another, who can no longer raise their heads from beneath the burden of the existing state of things' (ND:338; ET:345). And in a note here Adorno expressly refers us to Benjamin's 'Theses on the Philosophy of History'.

89 Vol. IV.1, p. 122; ET:469–70 (*Selected Writings*, Vol. 1).
90 Heidegger, *Der Ursprung des Kunstwerks*, p. 65 f.; ET:65.
91 Ibid., p. 75; ET:73.
92 Heidegger, *Vom Ursprung des Kunstwerks*, p. 48.
93 Heidegger, *Der Ursprung des Kunstwerks*, p. 74 f.; ET: 73.
94 Heidegger, GA 54, p. 53 (*Parmenides*); ET:30.
95 Heidegger, *Der Ursprung des Kunstwerks*, p. 76; ET: 74.
96 Ibid., p. 29; ET:35.
97 Ibid., p. 65; ET:65.
98 Ibid., p. 66; ET:65–6.
99 Ibid., p. 77; ET:75.

3: Keeping to the Names

100 Heidegger, *Was heißt Denken?*, p. 91; ET:138.
101 García Düttmann, *La parole donnée*, p. 29 f.; ET:10f.
102 Heidegger, *Was heisst Denken?*, p. 27 f.; ET:61–2.
103 Heidegger, *Einführung in die Metaphysik*, p. 37; ET:51.
104 G. Deleuze, *Logique de sens*, p. 11 f.; ET: p. 3 and 8.
105 In his essay 'The Collapse in the East in 1944/5 as a Problem of National German History and European History', the historian Andreas Hillgruber describes the 'catastrophe' in these terms: 'If one wishes to grasp this event in its full totality and depth, one must look right back into the middle of the nineteenth century. Bismark's attempt, made possible by the constellation of forces established through the Crimean War, to shape the destiny of Europe for the first time from the centre, after centuries of alternating dominance on the part of the more outlying powers in St Petersburg, Paris and London, had finally, after all the successes and defeats, all the unparalleled triumphs and the unprecedented crimes, resulted in catastrophe ... The new outlying powers, the Soviet Union and the USA, now made the middle of Europe into a

central focus of operations in the geo-political struggle which began immediately after their victory' (Hillgruber, *Zweierlei Untergang*, p. 73 f.). This passage reads like a paraphrase of Heidegger's observations. But does Heidegger identify the 'middle' with Prussia?

106 Heidegger, *Einführung in die Metaphysik*, p. 28; ET:41.

107 Ibid., p. 28 f.; ET:41 f.

108 Heidegger, *Denkerfahrungen*, p. 15.

109 Ibid., p. 15 f.

110 Ibid., p. 16.

111 Ibid., p. 17.

112 Ibid., p. 19.

113 Ibid., p. 19 f.

114 Heidegger, *Wegmarken*, ('What is Metaphysics?') p. 116; ET:93 (*Pathmarks*).

115 Nietzsche falls victim to the double character that marks the nineteenth century: 'Between 1850 and 1860 a remarkable interpenetration takes place: once again an authentic and well-preserved tradition, a tradition which originates in the great age of the German movement, becomes entangled with a creeping barrenness and rootlessness of existence. This entanglement comes completely to light in the *Gründerjahre*, the period of great social and economic expansion during the 1870s. One will never understand this most ambiguous of centuries simply by describing its segments one after another. The nineteenth century must rather be defined and determined as it were from two opposite sides at once, from the last third of the eighteenth century and the first third of the twentieth century' (Heidegger, *Nietzsche I*, p. 102; ET: (Vol. 1) 85).

116 H. Arendt, 'Social Science Techniques and the Study of Concentration Camps', in *Jewish Social Studies* 12 (1950), p. 50.

117 Ibid.

118 Ibid., pp. 61 and 62. When Adorno argues – without restricting himself to National Socialism – that 'ideology' and 'reality' are already converging upon one another, and thus coinciding in the sense that 'reality' is being transformed into the 'ideology' of itself, he is also diagnosing the implausibility of a certain concept of ideology to which

Hannah Arendt points in the context of her essay. The 'completely fabricated senselessness' signals the coincidence of 'reality' and 'ideology'. In his 'Contribution to the Theory of Ideology' (1954), Adorno writes: 'It would merely require a slight exertion of the spirit in order to cast off that semblance of things that is at once omnipotent and utterly impotent' (GS 8, p. 477). This remark alludes to the idea of the Messianic Kingdom in which everything would be only slightly changed and thereby changed utterly – an idea which we already find in Sholem, Benjamin and Bloch.

119 Ibid., p. 54.
120 Ibid., p. 56. 'The less enemies Nazism encountered within Germany and the more friends it gained abroad, the more intolerant and the more extremist became the "revolutionary principle".' At this point Hannah Arendt refers to a remark by the State Secretary of the Ministry of Internal Affairs, Wilhelm Stuckert. It would not be particularly instructive to regard the statement in question as an anachronistic expression of the friend–foe schema. Perhaps one could rather say with Carl Schmitt that the precise identification of the friend and the foe (not everyone is an enemy) allows a radical application of the 'revolutionary principle' and thus intensifies the effectiveness of political action. The problem that is posed here is therefore precisely that of identifying politically and of identifying the political. To address the problem in this context would require a discussion of the letter in which Hannah Arendt replied to Gershom Sholem in 1963. Sholem had responded critically to Arendt's book on Eichmann: 'There is in the Jewish language something quite indefinable and utterly concrete that the Jews call *Ahabath Israel*, or love for the Jews. There is no trace of this in you, my dear Hannah, just as with so many other intellectuals from the German left. The kind of argument you are engaged with here would require, if I might put it this way, the most old-fashioned kind of substantive and thorough investigation, especially where such profound emotions are inevitably in play and are provoked by this case involving as it does the murder of a third of our people – and I do indeed regard you as one

who belongs to our people and as nothing else.' Hannah
Arendt responds to this reproach of Sholem's as follows:
'In the first place, I have never in my life "loved" any
particular people or collective, neither the German, nor the
French, nor the American, nor indeed the working class or
anything else of the kind. In fact I love only my friends
and am quite incapable of any other kind of love. In the
second place, this love for the Jews, since I am myself
Jewish, would be suspect to me. I do not love myself, and
nor do I love what, I know, does indeed somehow belong
to my substance' (in: Hannah Arendt, *The Jew as Pariah*,
pp. 241–42 and 246–7).

121 Ibid., p. 29 f.; ET:63–4.
122 H. Arendt, 'The Image of Hell', in *Essays in Understanding*,
    p. 198.
123 Ibid., p. 200.
124 Heidegger, *Nietzsche I*, pp. 123–4; ET: (Vol. 1) 103–4.
125 Ibid.: Heidegger, p. 105; ET:88.
126 Ibid.
127 Heidegger, *Vorträge und Aufsätze*, pp. 122–3.
128 Heidegger, *Nietzsche I*, p. 102; ET: (Vol. 1) 85–6.
129 Adorno, GS 13, pp. 100 and 105 (*Essay on Wagner*);
    ET:104–5 and 110.
130 Ibid., p. 98; ET:103.
131 Heidegger, *Nietzsche I*, p. 631; ET: (Vol. 3) 135.
132 Habermas, *Der philosophische Diskurs der Moderne*, p. 163;
    ET:136.
133 Ibid.: Habermas, p. 121; ET:97–8.
134 Ibid.: Habermas, p. 122; ET:98.
135 Heidegger, *Nietzsche I*, p. 100; ET: (Vol. 1) 84.
136 Ibid.: Heidegger, p. 95; ET: (Vol. 1) 80.
137 Thus Heidegger says in the lecture he delivered in Athens
    in 1967, 'The Source of Art and the Vocation of Think-
    ing': 'Is there still today, after two and a half thousand
    years, an art which stands under anything like the same
    claim as the art of Hellas once stood? And if not, then
    from what realm emerges the claim to which modern art
    in all its domains does respond? Its works no longer arise
    from the defining borders and limits of a world as consti-
    tuted by a people or a nation. They belong to the univers-

ality of a single world civilisation. The general characteristics and structures of this world are projected and governed by scientific technicity' (Heidegger, *Denkerfahrungen*, p. 140). We can ignore whether Heidegger's remarks are diagnostically accurate in this connection. He himself would seem to be clinging here to a specific notion of art – to poetry as the inauguration of a people. Modern art and modern technology, modern art as determined by modern technicity, impede our access to the inaugurative essence of poetry – as an essence which belongs to a 'people' or 'nation'. Before he asks after the claim under which modern art is supposed to stand, Heidegger introduces a line of Hölderlin's. Hence Lacoue-Labarthe, who cites the passage in his book *La fiction du politique*, can claim that Heidegger 'never ceased to bind the possibility of history (of historicity) to the possibility of a people or the people; and this also signifies, as is well known, that he never ceased to link historicity with the possibility of an art (of a *poetry*), of a language, of a myth (of a *saying*, that is, of a relationship to the gods)' (Lacoue-Labarthe, *La fiction du politique*, p. 168; ET:114). Against Habermas, who simply sees a global subordination of art to philosophy in Heidegger's thought – something that is supposed to connect Heidegger with Hegel and oppose him to Nietzsche – we could appeal to an argument which Lacoue-Labarthe mounts against Alain Badiou in another context. For in his *Manifeste pour la philosophie*, Badiou objects that Heidegger effectively abandons philosophy to poetry: 'That is why there can be only a single fundamental critique of Heidegger: the age of the poets has reached its end, and it is also necessary to unpick [*désuturer*] the thread which binds philosophy with its poetic constitution' (A. Badiou, *Manifeste pour la philosophie*, p. 55; ET: 74). But to Lacoue-Labarthe Heidegger's idea of poetry as inauguration is a subordination of poetry to mythos. Heidegger is still guided by the thought of a kind of religious inauguration, and that is precisely why he is so bitterly opposed to the (false) founder of a new religion – to Wagner. It is not the philosopher who is the 'inaugurator of a new mythology', as Habermas thinks, but rather the poet.

138 Habermas, *Der philosophische Diskurs der Moderne*, p. 123; ET:98.

139 Heidegger, *Nietzsche I*, p. 102; ET: (Vol. 1) 85–6.

140 Habermas, *Der philosophische Diskurs der Moderne*, p. 197; ET:167.

141 Ibid., p. 161 f.; ET:134–5.

142 Ibid., p. 162; ET:135. But how could the abandonment of and by being ever affect what has, *per definitionem*, no understanding of being?

143 Heidegger, *Nietzsche II*, p. 355; ET: (Vol. 4) 215. In his book *Réduction et Donation*, Jean-Luc Marion draws attention to a strange and quite uncharacteristic passage in Heidegger which stands in remarkable contradiction to those in which being is understood as the being of beings. The proposition 'it belongs to the truth of being that being never comes to presence [*west*] without beings, that a being never is without being' – as it reads in the 'Afterword', added in 1943, to the inaugural lecture *What is Metaphysics?* – appears in the fourth edition of the work as follows: 'it belongs to the truth of being that being does indeed come to presence without beings, but that a being never is without being' (*Wegmarken*, p. 304; ET:233). Marion's careful analysis of the 'phenomenon of being' shows precisely that what is at issue here is no arbitrary or ideological 'separation of being', as one would have to argue if one were to adopt a Habermasian perspective, but rather the fulfilment and completion of phenomenology.

144 Habermas, *Der philosophische Diskurs der Moderne*, p. 168; ET:141.

145 Ibid.: Habermas, p. 168; ET:141.

146 Ibid.: Habermas, p. 168 f.; ET:140ff.

147 'We are still all too beholden to a mood, we are all too obedient to it. The weariness of mood marks the end of definition and determination. It is not only that mood bestows a particular character upon our determinations; it is not only that our determinations are oriented in accordance with a mood. Rather mood itself incites us to determine others and other things (which by no means excludes indeterminacy)' (García Düttmann, 'Das Wesen der Stimmung', p. 115).

148 In the *Philosophical Discourse of Modernity*, the key term 'anamnestic solidarity' denotes a specific conception of the memory of thought. Habermas is attempting with this term to develop Benjamin's 'Theses on the Philosophy of History'. In this connection he appeals to a study by H. Peukert who interprets Benjamin's thought as an 'impressive and ambitious attempt' to combine theology and historical materialism. Peukert, following Ch. Lenhardt here, identifies the notion of 'anamnestic solidarity' as the 'shared deep structure' which makes this combination possible. It is supposed to define a solidarity which is essentially 'preserved through a kind of "mindfulness" or "thoughtful recalling", through the remembering of the dead, of the beaten and defeated' (H. Peukert, *Wissenschaftstheorie, Handlungstheorie, Fundamentale Theologie*, p. 307 f.). The question concerning such solidarity, according to Peukert, ultimately amounts to the 'question concerning a reality which also makes this solidarity possible in the face of the destruction of the other in death' (p. 355).

Now in his *Preliminary and Supplementary Studies for the Theory of Communicative Action* Habermas already discusses 'the aporia of anamnistic solidarity' to which Peukert refers: 'But how can one remember the definitive and irrevocable abandonment of the victims of the very historical process to which we owe our existence, and remain happy, and find an identity?' Habermas writes: 'If we refuse to restrict the universality of the unlimited communicative community of agents to our contemporaries, but also contra-factually include past generations in the circle of those without whose potential agreement the claim to justice cannot be redeemed, this may satisfy the *logic* of practical discourse. But the posthumously recuperated agreement of the victims remains abstract because such an ethics, which can at best only drown out the cries of the past, lacks the power of *reconciliation*. A blemish or stain still clings to the idea of a justice which has been won at the expense of the injustice inflicted upon earlier generations. This stain cannot be cleansed, it can only be forgotten; but this very forgetting would inevitably leave traces of what has been thus repressed. The intrinsic contradiction in the idea of total justice, by virtue of a universalism that is irredeemable in principle, cannot be dissolved. This is where Benjamin's reflections begin: those who come afterwards can only make up for the contradiction harboured by the very idea of total justice by supplementing the abstract but irredeemable concept of universality with the anamnestic power of a remembering that transcends the concepts of morality itself. This remembrance is realised in the compassionate solidarity with the despair of those who have been hurt and injured in the past, of those who have experienced precisely what cannot be made good. "Compassion" in this respect, namely compassion with the suffering afflicted upon the moral and physical integrity of past generations, represents an ultimate "limit concept" for discourse ethics, in much the same way that "nature in itself" represents a limit concept for the transcendental-pragmatic theory of knowledge. Anamnestic solidarity is a postulate that follows necessarily from the universalistic perspective of discourse ethics, but the very relationship which is established through compassion lies beyond all moral–practical insights' (J. Habermas, *Vorstudien und Ergänzungen zur Theorie des kommunikativen Handelns*, p. 516 f.). Habermas pursues precisely the same line of thought in *The Philosophical Discourse of Modernity* and presents it explicitly as an interpretation of Benjamin: 'What Benjamin has in mind is the supremely profane insight that ethical universalism also has to take seriously the injustice that has already happened and that is seemingly irreversible; that there exists a solidarity of those born later with those who have preceded them, with all those whose bodily or personal integrity has been violated at the hands of other human beings; and that this solidarity can only be engendered and made effective by remembrance. Here the liberating power of memory is supposed not to foster a dissolution of the power of the past over the present, as it was from Hegel down to Freud, but to contribute to the dissolution of a guilt on the part of the present with respect to the past ... It is no longer only future generations, but past generations as well, that have a claim on the weak messianic power of the present. The anamnestic redemption of an injustice, which cannot of course be undone but can at least be virtually reconciled through remembrance, ties up the present with the communicative context of a universal historical solidarity. This anamnesis constitutes the decentering counterpoise to the dangerous concentration of responsibility that modern time-consciousness, oriented exclusively towards the future, has laid on the shoulders of a problematic present that has, as it were, been tied into a knot' (Habermas, *Der philosophische Diskurs der Moderne*, p. 25 f.: ET:14–16).

Anyone who compares the two texts here cited at length may initially note a certain wavering in the argument. This wavering arises from the fact that in the *Preliminary and Supplementary Studies* Habermas defines past injustice as that which 'cannot be made good' (does this condemn reconciliation to an incapacity to transcend a purely virtual status?), whereas in *The Philosophical Discourse of Modernity* (where we are also told that past injustice cannot be undone) he suddenly talks about a 'seemingly irreversible' injustice. This wavering is by no means insignificant. The possibility of realising the unlimited communicative community of agents (and this is the aim of discourse ethics) ultimately depends upon the transformation of 'what cannot be made good' into a 'seemingly irreversible' injustice. The passage from *The Philosophical Discourse of Modernity* also contains a flaw in the argument. It can be identified there where Habermas claims that 'anamnestic solidarity' offers a defence against a certain danger. For the 'dangerous concentration of responsibility', which is said to arise from a time-consciousness that is directed exclusively towards the future, is by no means diminished through the act of anamnestic solidarity. Quite the contrary. The responsibility then weighs more heavily, and the danger then grows stronger. That is why 'anamnestic solidarity' is no mere 'supplement' that can provide us with support in confronting the dangers of universalism – for from the perspective of history the universalistic consciousness is itself oriented towards the future.

If we now consider the two passages as an interpretation of Benjamin, we cannot fail to be struck by the fact that this central concept of compassion does not actually figure in Benjamin's 'Theses' (although the concept of hate certainly does: 'The working class soon learnt to forget both its hatred and its spirit of sacrifice. For both are nourished by the image of enslaved ancestors rather than that of liberated grandchildren' – Benjamin, 'Theses on the Philosophy of History'; ET:262). Of course, the fact that Benjamin does not employ the concept of compassion does not allow us to conclude that the concept is inappropriate here. Indeed it raises a general question of interpretation. But Benjamin certainly grasps the idea of a '*weak* Messianic power' more radically than Habermas does, since it appears here in connection with that of happiness and only becomes relevant insofar as happiness and the past are themselves incompatible with the experience of transience itself, of death. Happiness and the past continue to await redemption, as Peukert recognises. 'The kind of happiness that could awake envy in us', so Benjamin writes, 'exists only in the air we have breathed, amongst people we could have spoken to, women who could have given themselves to us. In other words, our idea of happiness is inalienably bound up with the image of redemption. The same applies to our view of the past, which is the concern of history. The past bears along with it a secret index by which it is referred to redemption. Are we not also touched by a breath of the air which earlier human beings have breathed? Do not the voices, to which we hearken now, bear an echo of those who are long since silent? Do not the women whose favour we seek have sisters who they no longer know? If this is so, then there is also a secret understanding between past generations and the present one. Our coming was expected on earth. Like every generation that preceded us, we have been endowed with a *weak* Messianic power, a power to which the past has a claim. That claim cannot be settled cheaply. This is what historical materialists are aware of' (Benjamin, Vol. I.1, p. 693: (incomplete) ET:256). Remembrance is bound up with a kind of 'mystical causality'. This is how Habermas, in an essay on Benjamin which introduces a distinction between a rescuing critique and a critique that provokes an awareness of things, denominates the transmission of what is given as endowment, or the endowing giving as transmission. But such 'remembrance', in which 'past time' is experienced and which alone can 'break the spell' of the future, is not restricted to the memory of past injustice and acquires its meaning from redemption, from the coming of the Messiah. Habermas abstracts from this. It is because the 'unlimited communicative community of agents' ultimately designates a purely finite immanence that Habermas is forced to relinquish the idea of an overcoming of death and is to secularise the idea of the last judgement. Insofar as he defines memory as the 'anamnestic making good of past injustice' and understands injustice as the violation of 'bodily or personal integrity at the hands of other human beings', he *a priori* excludes from the 'unlimited communicative community of agents' precisely those who have *committed* the injustice. (But who is to identify the latter in each individual case, who is capable of pronouncing judgement upon them, of summoning them to appear before the court in the first place?) The *unlimited* communicative community of agents that is to be (virtually?) established through 'anamnestic solidarity' rests upon the exclusion of what irrevocably eludes the process of communication; or, expressed in another way: the inauguration, the actualisation of the *unlimited* communicative community of agents can never, for structural reasons, succeed. It must always reckon with an additional limit, one it cannot erase because it is the condition of the community's own possibility. 'Anamnestic solidarity' perpetuates the guilt. Discourse ethics reproduces, in fatal fashion, the logic of those who have committed the injustice. For we live, as Jean-Luc Nancy has said, with *all* of the dead: 'this is precisely what the murderer attempts in vain to deny' (J.-L. Nancy, *L'expérience de la liberté*, p. 213; ET:169.).

149 Heidegger, *Was heißt Denken?*, p. 92; ET:139–40.
150 Ibid., p. 93; ET:141.
151 Ibid., p. 92; ET:140.
152 Ibid., p. 96; ET:149.
153 Heidegger, *Kant und das Problem der Metaphysik*, p. 87; ET:61.

154 Benjamin, Vol. I.2 (*Some Motifs in Baudelaire*), p. 647; ET:148 (*Charles Baudelaire*).

155 Ibid.

156 Ibid., p. 465 ('The Work of Art in the Age of Mechanical Reproduction', first version).

157 Ibid., p. 646; ET:147 (*Charles Baudelaire*).

158 In the lecture course *What Is Called Thinking?*, Heidegger says: 'Our words are not isolated lexical words, and, unlike the latter, do not resemble vessels or buckets from which we might draw a given content. Words are the springs where saying burrows, springs which are ever to be discovered and opened up afresh, which are easily buried but whose waters are also unexpectedly abundant. Without returning again and again to the springs the buckets and vessels would remain empty or their content stale' (Heidegger, *Was heißt Denken?*, p. 89: ET:130). If thought as memory is a keeping to..., if what holds sway in 'original memory' is that thanking and re-minding memory which 'thinks what it has thought over *into* what is still to be thought', if what is to be thought calls forth thinking and the thinking that goes to the springs is itself a calling, a calling by name which keeps to what is called and in so keeping strives to conceive the calling, then the name for its part – but do name and thought simply stand over against one another? – is itself a memory of calling. Thinking as such must keep to the names, and do so precisely by 'going to the springs'. And how could it do this without the hint it has already been given?

The thinker who 'goes to the springs' proves to be a poet: 'At the outlying border of the poetic land – or as this border itself? – lies the source, the spring from which the greying Norn, the ancient goddess of fate, draws forth the names. With these she gives the poet those words which, reliable and sure of himself, he awaits as the presentation of what he takes beings to be' (Heidegger, *Unterwegs zur Sprache*, p. 225). But is 'the saying of thought in distinction from the word of poetry' not also 'imageless'? (See Heidegger's 'Winke' in *Denkerfahrungen*, p. 33.)

159 Heidegger, *Was heißt Denken?*, p. 116; ET:189.

160 Heidegger, *Zur Sache des Denkens*, p. 20.
161 Heidegger, *Was heißt Denken?*, p. 119; ET:95–6.

Afterword: The Reeling Philosopher

1   G. Agamben, 'Le Muse IV', p. 73.

Bibliography

Entries are arranged alphabetically by author's surname and, within those by any one author, alphabetically by title (inclusive of definite or indefinite article), other than that any entry for an author's collected works appears first.

Adorno, Theodor W., *Gesammelte Schriften* (hereafter *GS*), 20 vols (Frankfurt am Main Suhrkamp, 1972 ff.).

—, *Ästhetische Theorie (GS* 7). Eng.-lang. edn: *Aesthetic Theory*, Robert Hullot-Kentor (London: The Athlone Press, 1997).

—, *Dialektik der Aufklärung (GS* 3). Eng.-lang. edn: *Dialectic of Enlightenment*, John Cumming (New York: Seabury Press, 1972).

—, *Drei Studien zu Hegel* (Frankfurt am Main: Suhrkamp, 1974). Eng.-lang. edn: *Hegel: Three Studies*, Shierry Weber Nicholsen (Cambridge, MA: MIT Press, 1993).

—, *Jargon der Eigentlichkeit* (Frankfurt am Main: Suhrkamp, 1974). Eng.-lang. edn: *The Jargon of Authenticity*, Knut Tarnowski and Frederic Will (London: Routledge, 1973).

—, *Minima Moralia (GS* 4). Eng.-lang. edn: *Minima Moralia*, E. F. N. Jephcott (London: New Left Books, 1974).

—, *Negative Dialektik* (Frankfurt am Main: Suhrkamp, 1975). Eng.-lang. edn: *Negative Dialectics*, E.B. Ashton (London: Routledge, 1973).

—, *Noten zur Literatur (GS* 11). Eng.-lang. edn: *Notes to Literature*, 2 vols, Shierry Weber Nicholsen (New York: Columbia University Press, 1991–2).

—, *Philosophische Terminologie*, 2 vols (Frankfurt am Main: Suhrkamp, 1973/4).

—, *Prismen (GS* 10:1). Eng.-lang. edn: *Prisms*, Samuel and Shierry Weber (Cambridge, MA: MIT Press, 1981).

—, *Quasi una Fantasia* (GS 16). Eng.-lang. edn: R. Livingstone (London: Verso, 1992).

—, *Stichworte* (*GS* 10:2). Eng.-lang. edn: *Critical Models. Interventions and Catchwords*, H. W. Pickford (New York: Columbia University Press, 1998).

—, *Versuch über Wagner* (*GS* 13). Eng.-lang. edn: *In Search of Wagner*, Rodney Livingstone (London: Verso, 1992).

—, *Zur Metakritik der Erkenntnistheorie* (Frankfurt am Main Suhrkamp, 1972. Eng.-lang. edn: *Against Epistemology*, Willis Domingo (Oxford: Blackwell, 1982).

Agamben, G., *La comunità che viene* (Milan: Einaudi, 1990). Eng.-lang. edn: *The Coming Community*, Michael Hardt (Minneapolis: University of Minnesota Press, 1993).

—, 'Le Muse IV', in *Il gallo silvestre*, Vol. I (Siena: 1989).

—, *The Idea of Prose*, M. Sullivan and S. Whitsith (Albany: State University of New York Press, 1995).

Apel, K.-O., 'Die Herausforderung der totalen Vernunftkritik', in *Concordia. Internationale Zeitschrift für Philosophie*, Vol. 11 (Frankfurt am Main 1987).

—, *Diskurs und Verantwortung* (Frankfurt am Main: Suhrkamp, 1988).

—, 'Sinnkonstitution und Geltungsrechtfertigung', in *Forum für Philosophie*, Bad Homburg, *Martin Heidegger: Innen- und Aussenansichten* (Frankfurt am Main: Suhrkamp, 1989).

Arendt, H., *The Jew as Pariah: Jewish Identity and Politics in the Modern Age*, ed. R. H. Feldman (New York: Grove Press, 1978).

—, 'Social Science Techniques and the Study of Concentration Camps', in *Jewish Social Studies* 12 (1950).

—, 'The Image of Hell', in Hannah Arendt, *Essays in Understanding* (New York: Harcourt, Brace & Co., 1994).

Badiou, A., *Manifeste pour la philosophie* (Paris: 1989). Eng.-lang. edn: *Manifesto for Philosophy*, N. Madarasz (Albany: State University of New York Press, 1999).

Benjamin, W., *Gesammelte Schriften*, 7 Vols (Frankfurt am Main: Suhrkamp, 1972 ff.).

—, *Illuminations. Essays and Reflections*, Harry Zohn (London: Jonathan Cape, 1970).

—, *One Way Street and Other Writings*, Edmund Jephcott and Kingsley Shorter (London: Verso, 1979).

—, *Selected Writings*, Vol. 1: 1913–1926, ed. Marcus Bullock and Michael W. Jennings (Cambridge, MA: Harvard University Press, 1996).

—, *Selected Writings*, Vol. 2: 1927–1934, ed. Michael W. Jennings, Howard Eiland and Gary Smith (Cambridge, MA: Harvard University Press, 1999).

—, *Charles Baudelaire*, Harry Zohn (London: Verso, 1997).

—, *The Origin of German Tragic Drama*, John Osborne (London: Verso, 1977).

—, 'Theses on the Philosophy of History', in *Illuminations. Essays and Reflections* (1970), pp. 255–66.

Bovenschen, S., 'Tierische Spekulationen', in *Neue Rundschau*, Vol. I (Frankfurt am Main 1983).

Cacciari, M., *Icone della legge* (Milan: Adelphi, 1985).

Deleuze, G., *Logique du sens* (Paris: Minuit, 1969). Eng.-lang. edn: *The Logic of Sense*, M. Lester/C. Stivale (London: The Athlone Press, 1990).

Derrida, J., *De la grammatologie* (Paris: Minuit, 1967). Eng.-lang. edn: *Of Grammatology*, Gayatri Chakravorty Spivak (Baltimore, MD and London: Johns Hopkins University Press, 1974).

—, *De l'esprit: Heidegger et la Question* (Paris: Galilée, 1987). Eng.-lang. edn: *Of Spirit: Heidegger and the Question*, Geoffrey Bennington and Rachel Bowlby (Chicago: University of Chicago Press, 1990).

—, *Glas* (Paris: Galilée, 1974). Eng.-lang. edn: *Glas*, J. P. Leavey and Richard Rand (Lincoln, NB: University of Nebraska Press, 1987).

Escoubas, E., 'Le *polemos* Adorno–Heidegger', in Theodor W. Adorno, *Jargon de l'authenticité* (Paris: Payot, 1989).

Freud, S., *Der Mann Moses and die monotheistische Religion*, in *Studienausgabe*, Vol. IX (Frankfurt am Main: Fischer, 1974). Eng.-lang. edn: *The Origins of Religion : Totem and Taboo, Moses and Monotheism and Other Works*, the Pelican Freud Library, Vol.,13 (Harmondsworth: Penguin Books, 1985).

—, *Massenpsychologie und Ich-Analyse*, in *Studienausgabe*, Vol. IX (Frankfurt am Main: Fischer, 1974). Eng.-lang. edn: *Group Psychology and the Analysis of the Ego*, ed. and trans. James Strachey (New York: Bantam Books, 1960).

García Düttmann, A., 'Das Wesen der Stimmung', in *Neue Rundschau*, 2 (Frankfurt am Main: Fischer, 1989).

—, *La parole donnée. Mémoire et promesse* (Paris: Galilée, 1989). Eng.-lang. edn: *The Gift of Language* (London: The Athlone Press, 2000).

—, 'Über die Ungleichzeitigkeit. Zu Italo Calvino', in *Neue Rundschau*, No 2 (Frankfurt am Main: Fischer, 1988).

Habermas, J., *Der philosophische Diskurs der Moderne* (Frankfurt am Main: Suhrkamp, 1985). Eng.-lang. edn: *The Philosophical Discourse of Modernity. Twelve Lectures*, Frederick G. Lawrence (Cambridge: Polity Press, 1987).

—, *Moralbewusstsein und kommunikatives Handeln* (Frankfurt am Main: Sukrkamp, 1983). Eng.-lang. edn: *Moral Consciousness and Communicative Action*, Christian Lenhardt and Shierry Weber Nicholsen (Cambridge: Polity Press, 1990).

—, *Theorie des kommunikativen Handelns*, 2 Vols (Frankfurt am Main: Sukrkamp, 1981). Eng.-lang. edn: *The Theory of Communicative Action*, Thomas McCarthy, 2 vols (Boston, MA: Beacon Press, 1984).

—, *Vorstudien und Ergänzungen zur Theorie des kommunikativen Handelns* (Frankfurt am Main: Sukrkamp, 1984).

Hamacher, W., *Pleroma. Zu Genesis and Struktur einer dialektischen Hermeneutik bei Hegel* (Frankfurt am Main, Berlin and Vienna: Ullstein, 1978). Eng.-lang. edn: *Pleroma – Reading in Hegel*, Simon Jarvis and Nicholas Walker (London: The Athlone Press, 1998).

Hegel, G. W. F., *Frühe Schriften* (Theorie-Werkausgabe [hereafter TWA], Vol. 1, Frankfurt am Main: Sukrkamp, 1970). Partial Eng.-lang. edn: *Hegel. Early Theological Writings*, T. M. Knox (Philadelphia: University of Pennsylvania Press, 1971).

—, *Vorlesungen über die Philosophie der Religion* (TWA: 16–17). Eng.-lang. edn: *Lectures on the Philosophy of Religion*, 3 vols, E. B. Speirs and J. B. Sanderson (London: Kegan Paul, 1895).

—, *Phänomenologie des Geistes* (TWA, Vol. 3). E. Tr.: *Phenomenology of Spirit*, A.V. Miller (Oxford: Oxford University Press, 1977).

Heidegger, Martin, *Beiträge zur Philosophie. Gesamtausgabe* (hereafter GA), Vol. 65 (Frankfurt am Main: Klostermann, 1989).

Eng.-lang. edn: *Contributions to Philosophy: From Enowning*, Parvis Emad and Kenneth Maly (Bloomington: Indiana University Press, 1999).

——, *Denkerfahrungen* (Frankfurt am Main: Klostermann, 1983).

——, *Die Selbstbehauptung der deutschen Universität* (Frankfurt/M.: Klostermann, 1983). Eng.-lang. edn *The Self-Assertion of the German University*, Karsten Harries, in *Review of Metaphysics* 38 (1985): 467–502. Further translations in *Martin Heidegger and National Socialism: Questions and Answers*, ed. G. Neske and E. Kettering, tr. L. Harries (New York: Pentagon House, 1990) and: R. Wolin, *The Heidegger Controversy. A Critical Reader* (Cambridge, MA: MIT Press, 1993).

——, *Der Ursprung des Kunstwerks* (Stuttgart: Reclam, 1982). Eng.-lang. edn: *The Origin of the Work of Art*, in the collection, *Poetry, Language, Thought*, Albert Hofstadter (New York: Harper & Row, 1971).

——, *Einführung in die Metaphysik* (Tübingen: Max Niemeyer, 1976). Eng.-lang. edn: *Introduction to Metaphysics*, G. Fried and Richard Polt (New Haven, CT: Yale University Press, 2000).

——, *Gelassenheit* (Pfullingen: Neske, 1959). Eng.-lang. edn: *Discourse on Thinking*, J. M. Anderson and E. H. Freund (New York: Harper & Row, 1966).

——, *Hölderlins Hymne 'Andenken'*. GA Vol. 52 (Frankfurt/M.: Klostermann, 1982).

——, *Hölderlins Hymne 'Der Ister'*. GA Vol. 53 (Frankfurt/M.: Klostermann, 1984). Eng.-lang. edn: *Hölderlin's Hymn 'The Ister'*, W. McNiell and J. Davis (Bloomington: Indiana University Press, 1996).

——, *Hölderlins Hymnen 'Germanien' und 'Der Rhein'*. GA Vol. 39 (Frankfurt/M.: Klostermann, 1980).

——, *Kant und das Problem der Metaphysik* (Frankfurt am Main: Klosterman, 1973). Eng.-lang. edn: *Kant and the Problem of Meta-physics*, R. Taft (Bloomington: Indiana University Press, 1996).

——, *Nietzsche*, 2 Vols (Pfullingen: Neske, 1961). Eng.-lang. edn: *Nietzsche*: Vol. 1: *The Will to Power as Art*, D. F. Krell (London: Routlege and Kegan Paul, 1981); Vol. 2, *The Eternal Recurrence of the Same*, D. F. Krell (San Francisco: Harper & Row, 1984); Vol. 3, *The Will to Power as Knowl-*

edge and as Metaphysics, J. Stambaugh, D. F. Krell, and F. A., Capuzzi (San Francisco: Harper & Row, 1987); Vol. 4, *Nihilism*, F. A. Capuzzi (San Francisco: Harper & Row, 1982). *The End of Philosophy*, J. Stambaugh (New York: Harper & Row, 1973) contains a translation of pp. 399–490 of Vol. 2 of Heidegger's text.

——, *Parmenides*. GA Vol. 54 (Frankfurt am Main: Klostermann, 1982). Eng.-lang. edn: *Parmenides*, R. Rojcewicz and A. Schwur (Bloomington: Indiana University Press, 1992).

——, *Sein and Zeit* (Tübingen: Max Niemeyer, 1979). Eng.-lang. edn: *Being and Time*, J. Maquarrie and E. Robinson (Oxford: Blackwell, 1962) and: *Being and Time*, J. Stambaugh (Albany: State University of New York Press, 1996).

——, *Unterwegs zur Sprache* (Pfullingen: Neske, 1959). Eng.-lang. edn: *On the Way to Language*, P. D. Hertz and J. Stambaugh (New York: Harper & Row, 1971).

——, *Vom Ursprung des Kunstwerks*. Bilingual edition, German/French, ed. E. Martineau (Authentica: 1987).

——, *Vorträge and Aufsätze* (Pfullingen: Neske, 1954).

——, *Was heißt Denken?* (Tübingen: Max Niemeyer, 1971). Eng.-lang. edn: *What Is Called Thinking?*, F. D. Wieck and J. G. Gray (New York: Harper & Row, 1972).

——, *Wegmarken* (Frankfurt am Main: Klostermann, 1978). Eng.-lang. edn: *Pathmarks*, W. McNeill (Cambridge: Cambridge University Press, 1998).

——, *Zur Sache des Denkens* (Tübingen: Max Niemeyer, 1976).

——, *Zur Seinsfrage* (Frankfurt am Main: Klostermann, 1977).

Hillgruber, A., *Zweierlei Untergang* (Berlin: Siedler, 1986).

Honneth, A., 'Ein Gespräch über den Gestus der Theorie' (with Walter Seitter), in *Spuren*, February/March 1989, Hamburg.

Horkheimer, M., *Gesammelte Schriften* (Frankfurt am Main: Fischer, 1985 ff.).

Jaspers, K., 'Die Schuldfrage', in *Erneuerung der Universität* (Heidelberg: Lambert Schneider, 1986).

Jünger, E., *Der Arbeiter* (Stuttgart: Klett Cotta, 1982).

Kafka, F., *Die Erzählungen* (Frankfurt am Main: Fisher, 1970).

——, *The Complete Short Stories*, ed. N. Glatzer (London: Minerva, 1992).

Kant, I., 'Der Streit der Fakultäten', in *Werke in zwölf Vorlesungen* (Theorie-Werkausgabe), Vol. XI (Frankfurt am Main:

Suhrkamp, 1968). Eng.-lang. edn: The Conflict of the Faculties, M. J. Gregor (New York: Abaris Books, 1979).

Lacoue-Labarthe, Ph., *L'imitation des Modernes* (Paris: Galilée, 1986).

——, *La fiction die politique* (Paris: 1988). Eng.-lang. edn: *Heidegger, Art and Politics: The Fiction of the Political*, Chris Turner (Oxford: Blackwell, 1990).

——, 'Introduction', in Friedrich Hölderlin, *Hymnes, élégies et autres poèmes* (Paris: Garnier Flammarion, 1983).

Lustiger, J.-M., 'Das Unbenennbare', in *Frankfurter Allgemeine Zeitung* (6.9.1989).

Lyotard, J.-F., 'Le survivant', in *Hannah Arendt. Ontologie et politique* (Paris: Editious Osiris, 1989). E. Tr. in: J.-F. L., *Toward the Postmodern*, R. Harvey/M. S. Roberts (NJ: Humanities Press International, 1993).

de Man, P., 'Heidegger's Exegeses of Hölderlin', in P. de Man, *Blindness and Insight* (Minneapolis: University of Minnesota Press, 1983).

Marcuse, H., *One Dimensional Man* (London: Routledge & Kegan Paul, 1964).

Marion, J.-L., *Réduction et Donation* (Paris: PUF, 1989).

Menke, Ch., *Die Souveränität der Kunst* (Frankfurt am Main: Suhrkamp, 1988). Eng.-lang. edn: *The Sovereignty of Art. Aesthetic Negativity in Adorno and Derrida*, N. Solomon (Cambridge, MA: MIT Press, 1998).

Milner, J.-C., 'Le matériel de l'oubli', in *Usages de l'oubli* (Paris: Seuil, 1988).

Mörchen, H., *Macht und Herrschaft im Denken von Adorno und Heidegger* (Stuttgart: Klett Cotta, 1980).

——, *Adorno und Heidegger. Untersuchung einer philosophischen Kommunikationsverweigerung* (Stuttgart: Klett Cotta, 1981).

Nancy, J.-L., *L'expérience de la liberté* (Paris: Galilée, 1988). Eng.-lang. edn: *The Experience of Freedom*, B. McDonald (Stanford: Stanford University Press, 1993).

Nietzsche, Fr., *Also sprach Zarathustra*, in *Kritische Studienausgabe*, ed. von Colli/Montinari, Vol. 4 (Munich, Berlin, New York: Walter de Gruyter, 1988). Eng.-lang. edn: *Thus Spoke Zarathustra*, R. J. Hollingdale (Harmondsworth: Penguin Books, 1969).

——, *Ecce homo*, in Werke, ed. Schlechta, Vol. 3 (Frankfurt am

Main, Berlin, Vienna: Ullstein, 1983). Eng.-lang. edn: *Ecce homo*, R. J. Hollingdale (Harmondsworth: Penguin Books, 1979).

Ott, H., *Martin Heidegger* (Frankfurt am Main: Campus, 1988). Eng.-lang. edn: *Heidegger. A Political Life*, A. Blunden (New York: Basic Books, 1993).

Peukert, H., *Wissenschaftstheorie, Handlungstheorie, Fundamentale Theologie* (Frankfurt am Main: Suhrkamp, 1978).

Polti, A., 'Ontologie als "Inbegriff von Negativität". Zu Adornos Intepretation der Philosophie Heideggers', in *Forum für Philosophie*, Bad Homburg, *Martin Heidegger: Innen- und Aussenansichten* see above.

Reijen, W. von and Schmid-Noerr, G. (eds.), *Vierzig Jahre Flaschenpost: 'Dialektik der Aufklärung' 1947–1987* (Frankfurt am Main: Fischer, 1987).

Schittek, C., *Flog ein Vogel federlos* (Munich: Hauser, 1989).

Schmidt, A., 'Begriff des Materialismus bei Adorno', in L. von Friedeburg (ed.), *Adorno-Konferenz 1983* (Frankfurt am Main: Suhrkamp, 1983).

Schmitt, C., *Politische Theologie* (Berlin: Duncker und Humblot, 1985). Eng.-lang. edn: *Political Theology*, George Schwab (Cambridge, MA: MIT Press, 1985).

Schnädelbach, H., 'Über historistische Aufklärung', in H. Schnädelbach, *Vernunft und Geschichte* (Frankfurt am Main: Suhrkamp, 1987).

Szondi, P., *Schriften*, Vol. 2 (Frankfurt am Main: Suhrkamp, 1978).

Theunissen, M., 'Negativität bei Adorno', in L. v. Friedeburg (ed.), *Adorno-Konferenz 1983* see above.

Index